WORLDS OF THE EAST INDIA COMPANY Volume 21

MARITIME MISADVENTURES IN EARLY MODERN SOUTHEAST ASIA

Frontispiece. Malacca in 1821. *De Rivier, de Kerk, en de woning des Gouverneurs te Malakka* by C. F. Stavenisse de Bruin, 1821.

MARITIME MISADVENTURES IN EARLY MODERN SOUTHEAST ASIA

STORMS, PIRATES, ACCIDENTS AND WAR

W. G. Miller and Ann G. Smith

THE BOYDELL PRESS

First published 2025
The Boydell Press, Woodbridge

ISBN 978 1 83765 286 0

The Boydell Press is an imprint of Boydell & Brewer Ltd
PO Box 9, Woodbridge, Suffolk IP12 3DF, UK
and of Boydell & Brewer Inc.
668 Mt Hope Avenue, Rochester, NY 14620-2731, USA
website: www.boydellandbrewer.com

Our Authorised Representative for product safety in the EU is Easy Access
System Europe – Mustamäe tee 50, 10621 Tallinn, Estonia,
gpsr.requests@easproject.com

A catalogue record for this book is available
from the British Library

CONTENTS

ILLUSTRATIONS

PREFACE

In an age when shipping was the sole means of transport between continents and where commanders consequently enjoyed a high status in society, any records that extend our knowledge of the way in which this industry operated are worth examining.

The present work has three purposes. First, it provides a means of access to the marine records known as 'Protests' concerning the activities of private mariners operating in the crucial years of the late eighteenth and early nineteenth centuries in Southeast Asia. These testimonies are buried within the collection known as the Malacca *Prothocol Books*, part of the administrative records covering the period 1786–1825 at Malacca and now held in the British Library. The records were originally set up by the Dutch and continued to be maintained by Dutch officials during the period of British rule. It is hoped that by exposing them here their contents will be made more accessible for future research.

Second, in addition to providing details of the recorded ships, and the masters and crews of these mainly British, Danish and Portuguese 'country traders' as they were called, this study describes and analyses the dangers that the mariners faced and the tactics they used to overcome the ever-present perils.

Third, the Protests reflect contemporary life, demonstrating how a collection of manuscripts while focused on particularities can open a pathway to a broader perspective on society and events. The work therefore also presents a discussion of the variety of contexts in which the country traders had to operate. The decades covered were ones of intense political rivalry between the British, French, Dutch and Portuguese in the Asian arena, particularly during the French Revolutionary and Napoleonic wars. Furthermore, it was a period of active expansion of scientific, maritime and geographic knowledge as well as improvement in navigational techniques, particularly among the British. The time was also one that saw considerable growth in trade, particularly between India and China, and the extension of European influence and dominance in Asian countries.

Country traders played a significant role in all those developments. This work will hopefully contribute to our understanding of why, how and to what extent they did so.

ACKNOWLEDGEMENTS

We are most grateful to James River Taylor for technical help and for drawing the maps. Saleta Perez Vila provided indispensable assistance in translating the Portuguese language Protests. Debbie O'Donoghue undertook most professionally the difficult proofreading of an early draft.

Annabel Gallop, Andrew Smith, Radin Fernando, Robert Cribb, Geoff Wade, Craig Reynolds and Anthony Reid all provided suggestions and assistance regarding our projected work. Others who read our draft made useful comments. We wish to thank them all. Staff of the National Library of Australia, Australian National University Library, the British Library and Aberdeen University Library provided professional assistance for which we are grateful. We are also grateful to those institutions that gave permission to reproduce illustrations in which they hold copyright.

The authors wish to acknowledge that they alone remain responsible for any errors or failings.

ABBREVIATIONS

AJCP	Australian Joint Copying Project, NLA
ANU	Australian National University
BACSA	British Association for Cemeteries in South Asia
BISEA	British Institute in South-East Asia
BL	British Library
EIC	English East India Company
E.R.	English Reports
Fn	footnote
HMS	His Majesty's Ship
IIAS	International Institute for Asian Studies
ISEAS	Institute of Southeast Asian Studies, Singapore
JMBRAS	Journal of the Malaysian Branch, Royal Asiatic Society
JSBRAS	Journal of the Straits Branch, Royal Asiatic Society
lat.	Latitude
long.	Longitude
NLA	National Library of Australia
n.p.	no pagination
N.S.	Nossa Senhora (Our Lady)
n.s.	new series
VOC	Vereenigde Oost-Indische Compagnie (United Dutch East India Company)

GLOSSARY

Bumpkin, boomkin	short spar at bow of vessel
Cabin scuttle	a utensil to hold coal but may also mean porthole
Cartel	an arrangement allowing exchange of prisoners or permitting communication between warring parties
Catharpin	short rope or iron clamp that helped tie the shrouds
Dammar, damar	a resin from a coniferous tree
Datuk	head person, chief
Dunnage	material stored between cargo to prevent chafing
Gallera , galley	Portuguese three-masted vessel
Gunnel, gunwale	upper edge of ship's side
Gunny sack	sack made from jute
Kincobs	Indian dress material
Konstabel	gunner
Lascar	Indian sailor
Munshi	teacher
Naik, naig	non-commissioned officer of a Sepoy regiment
Nakhoda	Malay sea captain
Pical, picul, pikul	a weight, traditionally as much as a man can carry on a shoulder pole. About 60 kg
Prahu, (prow, perahu)	native boat
Seacunny	quartermaster
Sepoy	Indian soldier serving in British army
Serang, syrang	native head of a lascar crew

NOTES

In quotations, the original spelling has been retained.

The spelling of places as used by the English at the time has been retained (for example, Malacca). Alternate forms of the name, including modern usage, are given in brackets when the word first occurs in the text (for example, Melaka).

We use 'Malacca Strait' and 'Singapore Strait' rather than 'Malacca Straits' and 'Singapore Straits', except in quotations, where we retain the original wording.

Where a word is followed by (?) it means the word or phrase is unclear in the original record.

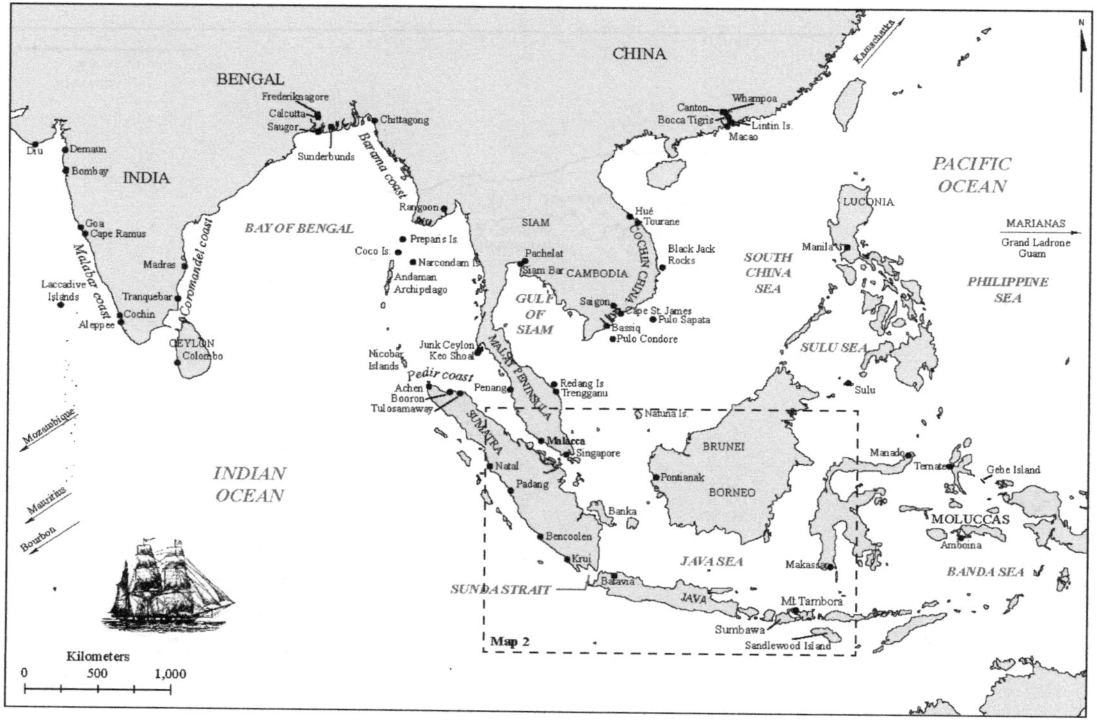

Map 1: The Malay Archipelago and surrounding countries, with places mentioned in the text.

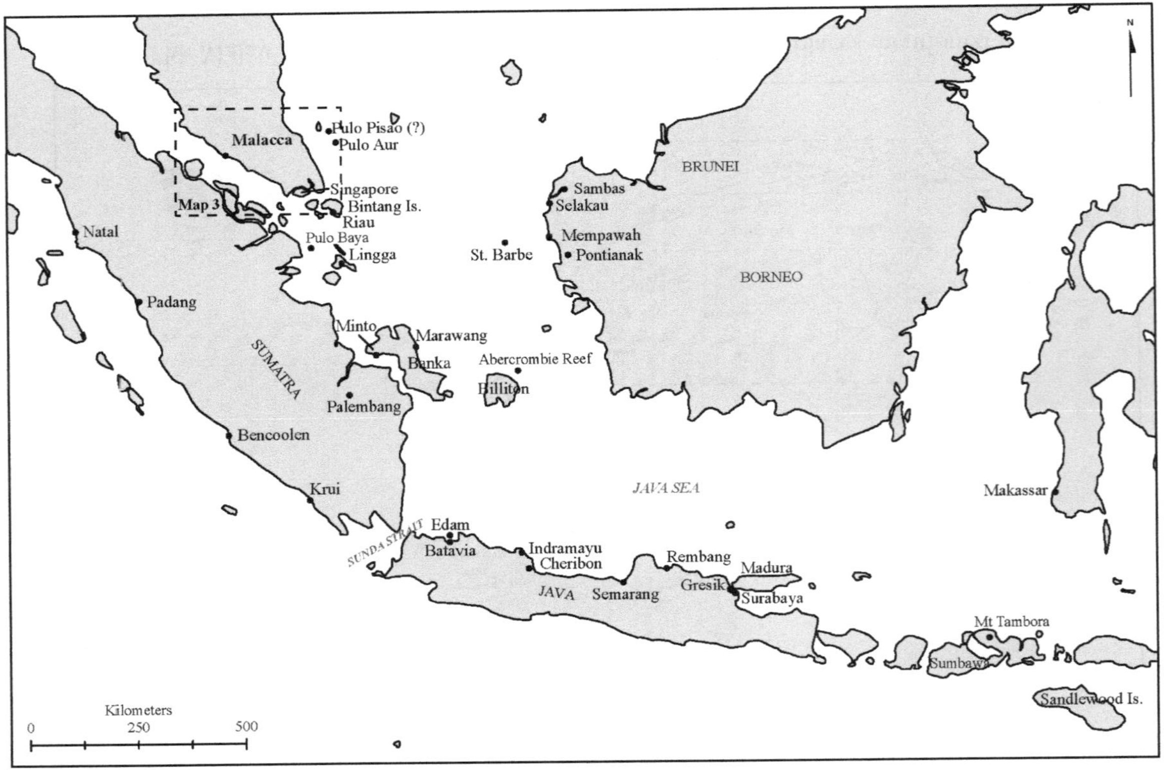

Map 2: The Java Sea, with places mentioned in the text.

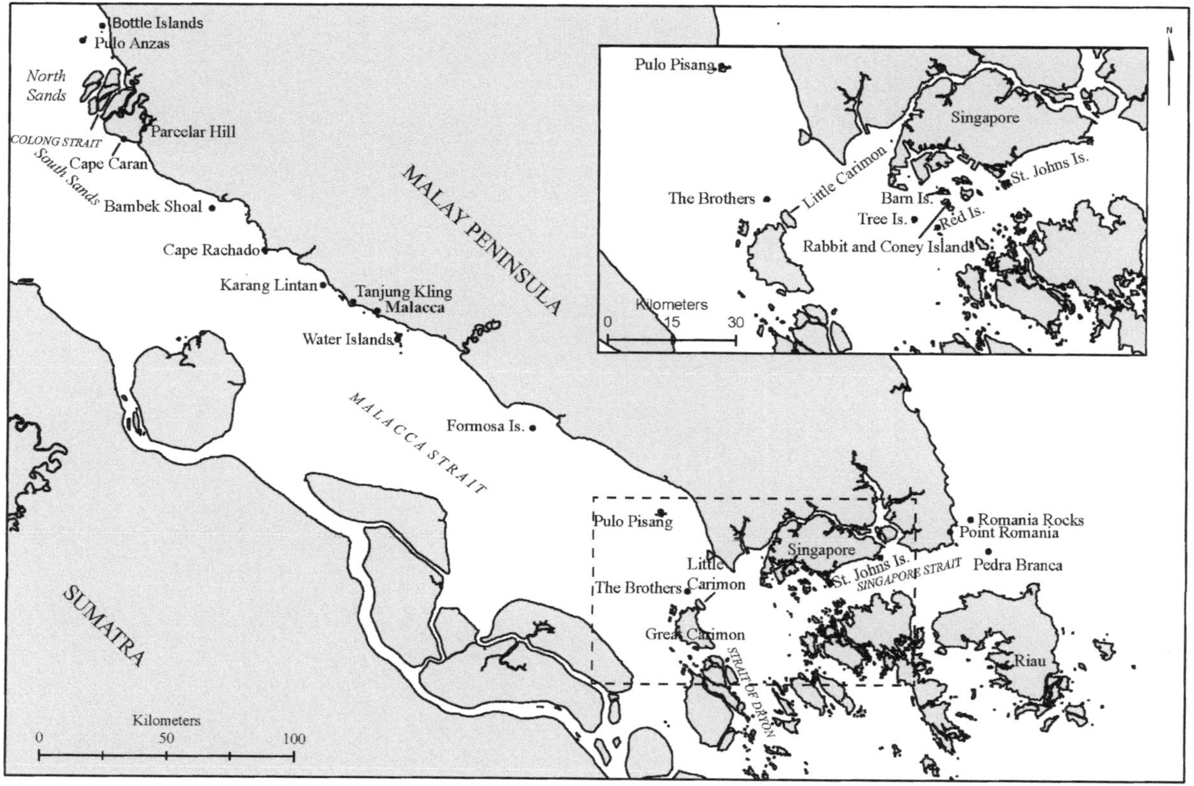

Map 3: The Malacca and Singapore Straits, with places mentioned in the text.

INTRODUCTION

By the turn of the nineteenth century European country traders were well established in the East Indies.

British trade in the Malay Archipelago had increased dramatically during the second half of the eighteenth century as a result of Britain's expanding trade with Canton (now Guangzhou). Tea was the main product purchased by Europeans from the Chinese and, in the case of the British, paid for increasingly by the sale of opium and cotton from British India, together with tin and the 'exotic' products of the islands of the East Indies. This trade between England, India and China was dominated by the English East India Company (EIC) within an arena of commercial rivalry with other European nations and Americans, inter-Malay altercations and 'piracy'. From 1792 until the end of the Napoleonic Wars in 1815, which itself prompted further interest in commercial activities, much of the business was complicated by war with France.

British private or 'country' traders, also referred to as free mariners, were quite distinct from EIC employees. Independent, risk-takers and pioneers, they were among the leading seamen who collected and carried the opium, cotton, tin and exotica to Canton under licence from the EIC whose own vessels could not keep up with the demand nor openly carry illegal cargoes of opium. Not all country traders sailed to China; many confined their trade to the archipelago, dealing in Indian rice and textiles, pepper, spices, betelnut, benzoin, dammer, tin and opium. Sometimes a country trader would load a cargo for China onto another ship *en route* to Canton.[1] A select few traded to England at first under special dispensation from the EIC and then more freely after the passing of the East India Company Charter Act in 1813, though a licence from the EIC was still required.[2]

Considerable recognition and analysis of the British country trade in general, as a commercial and political phenomenon, has long been available.

1 H. M. Elmore, *The British Mariner's Directory and Guide to the Trade and Navigation of the Indian and China Seas …* (London, 1802), pp. 166–7; C. Northcote Parkinson, *Trade in the Eastern Seas 1793–1813* (Cambridge, 1937), p. 351; Reinout Vos, *Gentle Janus, Merchant Prince: The VOC and the Tightrope of Diplomacy in the Malay World, 1740–1800* (Leiden, 1993), p. 125.

2 Anne Bulley, *The Bombay Country Ships, 1790–1833* (Richmond, 2000), p. 58.

Parkinson wrote about it in 1937 and Furber further discussed it in 1976. Bassett advanced the study, particularly relating to Southeast Asia.[3] At the same time, there is still much to be learnt about the individuals involved because, unlike captains of EIC and British naval vessels, few left personal accounts of their experiences (one of the few being Robert William Eastwick who bequeathed us his memoirs). It is true that several of the more prominent of the hundreds of country traders have been investigated by historians. For example, H. P. Clodd, and subsequent authors, have related the life of Francis Light, the country trader turned EIC official, and Bassett gave valuable insight into the role of Thomas Forrest in the country trade. Anne Bulley published and analysed the letters of John Adolphus Pope, a junior officer on a British country trader in 1786–8.[4] More recently, F. Andrew Smith has published a series of articles on specific country traders and their exploits around the Malay Archipelago. W. G. Miller, using European and local sources, has described how they operated at the turn of the nineteenth century, and how they related to British, Dutch and indigenous powers, while Miller and Smith have examined the few cases where women were found on board country trader vessels.[5]

Nevertheless, most of the country traders remain quite elusive figures. Logbooks of their voyages are rare; those most likely to be extant, according to Bulley, being those the captains kept when their ship was employed by the EIC as an 'extra'.[6] Furthermore, individuals are mentioned only briefly and serendipitously in Company records. However, certain documents in which the voice of country traders themselves is heard are the 'Protests' lodged with officials at the first port of call after a misadventure, in this case Malacca (now Melaka). These turn-of-the-century records, part of the Dutch Malaccan *Prothocol Books* now held in the British Library, allow a glimpse into a dramatic moment in the lives of these men, a vignette, and provide a starting point for further investigation of their activities.

In this period shipping was the vital sinew for personal travel, trade of goods and communication. It entered into every aspect of society and

3 Parkinson, *Trade in the Eastern Seas; Holden Furber, Rival Empires of Trade in the Orient 1600–1800* (Minneapolis MN, 1976); D. K. Bassett, *British Trade and Policy in Indonesia and Malaysia in the Late Eighteenth Century* (Zug, 1971).

4 Robert William Eastwick, *A Master Mariner; Being the Life and Adventures of Captain Robert William Eastwick*, ed. Herbert Compton (London, 1891); H. P. Clodd, *Malaya's First British Pioneer: The Life of Francis Light* (London, 1948); Bassett, *British Trade; Anne Bulley, Free Mariner; John Adolphus Pope in the East Indies 1786–1821* (Putney, 1992).

5 F. Andrew Smith, (various); W. G. Miller, *British Traders in the East Indies 1770–1820: 'At Home in the Eastern Seas'* (Woodbridge, 2020); W. G. Miller and Ann G. Smith, 'European wives and local concubines: Women on board English country trader vessels in the Malay Archipelago and beyond, from the 1770s to the 1830s, with some reference to life on board other contemporary sailing vessels', *International Journal of Maritime History*, 32:3 (2020), 596–615.

6 Bulley, *Bombay Country Ships*, p. 210.

sailors were far more significant in people's lives than they are now. In the context of the broad historical movements of the time – particularly the spread of British imperialism in India, China and the Malay world – while each individual country trader may be said to have played only a small part, collectively their role was immense. The misadventures that the group was prepared to endure and the cost they and their superiors were prepared to pay, as reflected in the Protests, not only allow us to deduce the extensive rewards that were a possible consequence of their trading activities; they also reiterate the cumulative value of their voyages to the imperial enterprise.

This study provides a guide to the Protests within the *Prothocol Books* by extracting the country traders' reports from these opaque Malacca records and describing each one. It attempts to provide basic details about little-known individuals, to reveal, classify and arrange the accidents that befell them, to describe the seafaring practices used in such calamities and the extent of any losses and damages. It places these events historically within the growing body of scientific information about navigation, particularly among the English-speaking community, as well as within the broader, but relevant, context of European wars of the period. The work touches on the colonial bureaucracy of Malacca and the sometimes tense relations between different ethnic and social groups. Footnotes with additional information are used extensively to aid in fleshing out the mariners and their ships. However, while the details in the study may help illuminate the conditions of seamen in general, as portrayed, for example, in Peter Earle's work on sailors in the merchant service,[7] the emphasis is on the Protests and the misadventures described therein, rather than on a broader portrayal of the country traders as a group.

The British were not the only foreigners to participate in the country trade. Representatives of other European nations, particularly the Portuguese,[8] were also involved. While the main focus is on the British in this study, attention is also paid to the Protests of Danish, Portuguese and ships of other nations. It is possible to draw comparisons between the form and content of these and those submitted by the commanders of British ships.

Protests

What is a Protest? In the context of this work a Protest does not mean a statement of dissent, as in common usage, but rather a statement of events that have occurred and the associated non-culpability of the declarant. The word has been used in a maritime context since the medieval period.[9] In the

7 Peter Earle, *Sailors: English Merchant Seamen, 1650–1775* (London, 1998).

8 For an account of the Portuguese country trade see Celsa Pinto, *Trade and Finance in Portuguese India: A Study of the Portuguese Country Trade 1770–1840* (New Delhi, 1994).

9 Giada Pizzoni, 'British Power in the Mediterranean: Sea Protests and Notarial Practice

period related to the present study Protests were an integral part of maritime insurance procedures and reference to them can be found in government administrative records in various countries or, as is the case in Malta, in collections of private notarial papers.[10]

According to A. B. Leonard, few British cargoes went to sea in the late eighteenth and early nineteenth centuries without insurance cover.[11] At first Lloyds underwrote the East India country trade from London. Private, then corporate insurance based in India, followed, the business eventually becoming dominated by the European controlled agency houses in Calcutta (now Kolkata). This was alongside a flourishing indigenous insurance practice. In the case of misadventure, country trader ships' captains were obliged to report the details, as a Protest, at the nearest port. This same obligation was not visited upon East India Company captains as the EIC carried its own risks and had its own reporting responsibilities,[12] but the Protest procedure was followed by other, non-British ships.

Also associated with insurance was the method adopted by some country captains of financing the goods aboard ship by a loan on respondentia, a centuries-old way of financing trade without the need for large initial capital. Anne Bulley suggests that respondentia was widely used by country traders undertaking long voyages and gives several examples.[13] Under this system the money was lent on the personal responsibility of the borrower with the goods 'hypothecated', or pledged as security, to the lender. With the safe arrival and sale of the goods at the designated port the lender received his payment together with the stipulated amount of marine interest and the borrower kept the remaining profit. In the case of misadventure at sea, the loss was borne by the lender, as long as the captain had conducted his voyage in the manner specified.[14]

---

in Nineteenth-century Malta', *The Journal of Imperial and Commonwealth History*, 50:5 (2022), 829–59, at p. 833.

10 For example in a NSW list dated 28 October 1811 of 'Fees to be received in the Notarial Department in the Judge-Advocate's Office' we have the item 'For ship's Protests of Occurrences at Sea, Extracted from the Log-Book £3.3.0': *Historical Records of Australia*, Series 1, vol. 7, p. 451; Notarial Archives Valetta, *Sea Protests of Notary Stevens*: Pizzoni, 'British Power in the Mediterranean', p. 851, fn 18. Today the information found within Protests can be valuable in new ways. For example, the Protests held in the Bermuda Archives in Hamilton, Bermuda, have been used in weather analysis: Louis K McNally, K. A. Maasch and K. A. Zuill, 'The Use of Ships' Protests for Reconstruction of Synoptic-Scale Weather and Tropical Storm Identification in the Late Eighteenth Century', *Weather*, 63:7 (2008), 208–13, at p. 208, <https://digitalcommons.library.umaine.edu/ers_facpub/105>.

11 A. B. Leonard, 'Underwriting British Trade to India and China, 1780–1835', *The Historical Journal*, 55:4 (2012), 983–1006, at pp. 987–94.

12 C. Ernest Fayle, 'Shipowning and Marine Insurance', in C. Northcote Parkinson (ed.), *The Trade Winds: A Study of British Overseas Trade During the French Wars 1793–1815* (London, 1948), pp. 25–48, at p. 40.

13 Bulley, *Bombay Country Ships*, pp. 109, 202–3.

14 Joseph Arnould, *A Treatise on the Law of Marine Insurance and Average* ..., ed. David Ma-

Nicolaus Magens in his 1755 *An Essay on Insurances* stated:

> [The Protest] is a Declaration upon Oath, usually made by the Master, and some of his People, before a Justice, Notary, or Consul, at any Place where they first arrive; setting forth whatever bad Weather they met with in the Voyage, or any other Accident that befel them: As also what Precautions they took, to guard against the ill Consequences to be apprehended from those Accidents, with the Motives they had for going into any other Harbour than that they were bound to: Which Sort of Protests are now become almost a mere Matter of Form, as a Notion is propagated in some Places, that if the Masters neglect protesting, immediately after Arrival, against the Damages that have resulted from any bad Weather, they make themselves answerable for those Damages that shall be found in any of the Goods aboard, from which they believe a Protest frees them. But this cannot be sufficient to clear them on all Occasions.

Over and above the Protest an inspection and 'a particular Examination of the Crew' might be taken to ascertain 'whether the Damage did not proceed from [the Master's] own Carelessness, bad Stowage or Defect in Caulking his Decks'.[15]

Writing in the middle of the nineteenth century it was stressed by British lawyer Joseph Arnould, later judge of the Supreme Court in Bombay (now Mumbai), that before making any sacrifice for the general safety the master should, if possible, consult the most experienced of the crew and supercargo and, where time allowed, make a detailed entry in the logbook that he should note and if possible extend in his Protest. Arnould also stressed that Protests had their limits. For example, he stated that when it came to proof of a ship's capture, the Protest of the captain was of little evidential use.[16]

Protests could be used as evidence in the determination of whether a general average contribution was applicable in particular cases. This arrangement, still in use today, applies where a loss has been caused by the deliberate actions of the captain, performed in a situation of danger, as a successful means of saving the ship and the remaining cargo. Jettisoning part of the cargo to prevent a ship being completely overwhelmed by a severe storm is

---

clachan (2 vols, London, 1877), vol. 1, pp. 87–8. As there was risk involved the lender could insure the loan. In the case of *Ewart v Bengal Insurance Company*, Supreme Court of Calcutta (1790), the plaintiff tried to recover the value of a respondentia bond when the ship *Argyle* was lost at sea. The suit was lost because the captain had deviated from the agreed course: *India Gazette*, 15 February 1790. For the intricate relationship between respondentia and insurance and an examination of some respondentia cases brought before the Mayor's Court in Bombay, see Lakshmi Subramanian, 'Seths and sahibs: negotiated relationships between indigenous capital and the East India Company', in H. V. Bowen, Elizabeth Mancke and John Reid (eds), *Britain's Oceanic Empire: Atlantic and Indian Ocean Worlds, c. 1550–1850* (Cambridge, 2012), pp. 311–39.

15 Nicolaus Magens, *An Essay on Insurances* (2 vols, London, 1755), vol. 1, pp. 87–8.

16 Arnould, *Treatise*, vol. 2, pp. 884–5. Nevertheless, Captain Daniel Smith (q.v.) protested at Malacca on 9 July 1810 about the capture of his ship the *Mary* the previous year.

an example of such an action, and in fact was resorted to by several captains registering a Protest at Malacca. The general average is a legal adjustment where the burden of the loss is shared by all parties with an interest in the ship and cargo rather than leaving such loss to be borne solely by the person or persons whose property has been directly affected.[17]

Protests could also be made in their own defence by persons responsible for the cargo, such as supercargoes or agents, where possible losses were perceived as being occasioned by the inappropriate actions of the captain or crew. The Malacca examples are dealt with in Chapter 7.

While it was rare for a captain to be sued on the grounds of negligence, cases of barratry (which had to be brought by the ship owner) were not unheard of. Barratry in marine law is defined by the *Oxford English Dictionary* as 'Fraud, or gross and criminal negligence, on the part of the master or mariners of a ship, to the prejudice of the owners, and without their consent; e.g. dishonestly sinking, deserting, or running away with the ship, or embezzling the cargo'.[18] In the much quoted case of *Heyman v Parish* of May 1809 concerning the wreck of the ship *Canopus* at Plymouth, Devon, Lord Ellenborough said that if the captain had sailed in a foul wind contrary to the pilot's direction, had disobeyed other directions and had cut the cable allowing the ship to drift onto the rocks, this would be barratry.[19] According to Arnould, fraud or criminal knavery on the part of the master is barratry even though not intended for the owner's prejudice and in fact even if taken to advance the owner's interest.[20]

In a Protest the captain had an opportunity to justify his decisions and clarify his actions. For example, if a ship was lost because the captain cut the cables, the loss might be recovered not as a loss by barratry but as a loss by perils of the seas; where a ship was captured by the enemy through an agreement between the captain and an enemy party, this might be recovered not as a loss by barratry but as a loss by capture.[21]

'Protests', with the associated terms 'Sea protests', 'Protest notes', 'Letters of protest' and 'Notes of protest', continue as an accepted part of maritime law; the definition remains the same. The *Treatise of the Law Relative to Merchant Ships and Seamen*, first published in 1802 and still in use in the twentieth century describes a Protest as 'a declaration or narrative by the master of the particulars of the voyage, of the storms or bad weather which the

17 This study does not investigate any general average claims that might apply in regard to the Malacca Protests. However, a late nineteenth century Amsterdam case concerning the ship *Jan Maria* that suffered a mishap in the Baltic in 1883 is discussed in detail by Sabine C. P. J. Go, 'Shared burdens: The General Average adjustment of the *Jan Maria*', *International Journal of Maritime History*, 33:2 (2021), 322–43.

18 *Oxford English Dictionary* ([8 vols, Oxford, 1933]; repr. Oxford, 1961), vol. 1, p. 680.

19 *Heyman and other v. Parish* (1809), 170 E.R. 1111B.

20 Arnould, *Treatise* (1848), vol. 2, pp. 821–8.

21 *Ibid.*, p. 829.

vessel encountered, the accidents which have occurred, and compelled him, if at an intermediate port, to resort to it, and the conduct which, in cases of emergency, he had thought proper to pursue'; the mechanism to be used if necessary by the master against the charterers of the ship or the consignees of goods and by the merchant against the master for breach of contract and other irregularities.[22]

While the reason for lodging a Protest at Malacca in the late eighteenth and early nineteenth centuries may have been for legal, insurance or other financial purposes, such arrangements surrounding voyages could be complicated and often involved numerous parties. This study does not go into the use made of the Protests for legal claims or the success or otherwise of insurance claims. Rather it concentrates on the risks to which country trade voyages in Southeast Asia were exposed and the actions reportedly taken by the participants in the face of mishaps.

The Records

The Protests are to be found in the *General Prothocol Books (Registers of Legal Deeds) 1786–1825*, part of the Dutch and British records from Malacca now located in the British Library.[23] This collection of records is from the Malacca Orphan Chamber (*Weeskamer*) and the Malacca Court of Justice (*Raad van Justitie*) and is extensive, occupying 44 feet of shelving in ninety-eight boxes. It has been described and discussed in general terms in a number of articles, mostly in *JMBRAS*.[24]

The *Prothocol Books* (part of the Court of Justice archives and given by the British Library the call number R/9/22) contain a wide variety of legal documents, not only marine Protests. Indeed, the Protests form only a small percentage of the documents, making them difficult to locate within the large collection of assorted legal deeds, including wills, bills and receipts for the sale

22 Charles Tenterden, Lord, *Treatise of the Law Relative to Merchant Ships and Seamen*, ed. James Perronet Aspinall *et al.*, 14th edn (London, 1901), pp. 575–6.

23 British Library, Asia, Pacific and Africa Collections, *Malacca, General Prothocol Books (Registers of Legal Deeds) 1786–1825*, IOR: R/9/22/1–75 [referred to in this study as *Prothocol Books*].

24 F. R. J. Verhoeven, 'The Lost Archives of Malacca 1641–1824', *JMBRAS*, 37:2 (1964), 11–27; Ian Baxter, 'Records of Dutch Malacca: India Office Library and Records, London', *BISEA Newsletter*, 9 (1982), 5–6; Ian Baxter, 'Dutch Records from Malacca in the India Office Records', *JMBRAS*, 56:2 (1983), 105–33; Geoff Wade, 'Some Sources for the Economic History of the Chinese in the Malay Archipelago – 1780s–1820s', Paper presented to the 15th Biennial Conference of the Asian Studies Association of Australia, Canberra 29 June–2 July 2004 (Canberra, 2004), pp. 11–50; M. R. Fernando, 'The Lost Archives of Melaka: Are They Really Lost?', *JMBRAS*, 78:1 (2005), 1–36; Annabel Gallop, 'Malay Documents in the Melaka Records in the British Library', *Itinario*, 30:2 (2006), 54–77.

of slaves, property transactions, powers of attorney and other affidavits, all of which provide 'a wealth of socio-economic information' on contemporary events and inhabitants. The condition of the *Prothocol Books* covering the end of the period is poor, probably because of the collection 'lying, neglected, for many years in the basement of the Court House at Malacca'.[25]

Given the state of the manuscripts it would be easy to overlook a Protest, however we believe the earliest Protest relating to a European vessel (the *Swift*) is that of Jacob Van Kal on 21 April 1791 and the last that of Captain John Marchant of the *Matilda* on 27 June 1821.

The following table gives the Protest date ranges within their specific call numbers.[26]

Prothocol date	**Prothocol call no.**
3 Jan–30 Jun 1791, Nos 1–60	R/9/22/9
1 Jul–29 Dec 1791, Nos 61–206	R/9/22/10
3 Jan–28 Dec 1792, Nos 1–200	R/9/22/11
2 Jan–20 Jul 1793, Nos 1–95	R/9/22/12
20 Jul–30 Dec 1793, Nos 100–200	R/9/22/13
3 Jan–30 Jul 1794, Nos 1–128	R/9/22/14
1 Aug–29 Dec 1794, Nos 1–247	R/9/22/15
5 Jan–15 Aug 1795, Nos 248–313	R/9/22/16
12 Jan–31 Dec 1795, Nos 1–154	R/9/22/17
2 Jan–23 Jun 1796, Nos 1–78	R/9/22/18
4 Jul–28 Dec 1796, Nos 79–157	R/9/22/19
11 Jan–23 Dec 1797, Nos 160–346	R/9/22/20
4 Jan–14 Dec 1798, Nos 348–524	R/9/22/21
7 Jan–14 Dec 1799, Nos 525–701	R/9/22/22
1 Jan–13 Jun 1800, Nos 708–828	R/9/22/23
5 Jul–30 Dec 1800, Nos 832–938	R/9/22/24
5 Jan–31 Dec 1801, Nos 940–1,047	R/9/22/25
11 Jan–24 Dec 1802, Nos 1,048–1,176	R/9/22/26
6 Jan–23 Dec 1803, Nos 1,177–1,305	R/9/22/27
1 Jan–30 Jun 1804, Nos 1,309–1,396	R/9/22/28
3 Jul–31 Dec 1804, Nos 1,397–1,469	R/9/22/29
5 Jan–6 May 1805, Nos 1,470–1,506	R/9/22/30
19 Jun–30 Dec 1805, Nos 1–113	R/9/22/31

25 Baxter, 'Dutch Records', pp. 107, 105.
26 *Ibid.*, pp. 124–5 (with amendments).

7 Jan–6 Sep 1806, Nos 116–191	R/9/22/32
18 Jul–8 May 1807, Nos 1–122	R/9/22/33
28 May–29 Dec 1807, Nos 126–202	R/9/22/34
11 Jan–30 Dec 1808, Nos 203–301	R/9/22/35
9 Jan–28 Dec 1809, Nos 302–435	R/9/22/36
8 Jun–22 Dec 1810, Nos 506–615	R/9/22/37
9 Jan–29 Jun 1811, Nos 619–687	R/9/22/38
1 Jul–26 Dec 1811, Nos 688–750	R/9/22/39
4 Jan–30 Dec 1812, Nos 753–860	R/9/22/40
13 Jan–23 Dec 1813, Nos 861–950	R/9/22/41
1 Jan–28 Dec 1814, Nos 951–1055	R/9/22/42
6 Jan–28 Sep 1815, Nos 1,056–1,109	R/9/22/43
2 Oct–30 Dec 1815, Nos 1–61	R/9/22/44
3 Jan–24 Jun 1816, Nos 62–149	R/9/22/45
3 Jul–30 Dec 1816, Nos 151–235	R/9/22/46
9 Jan–31 Dec 1817, Nos 237–380	R/9/22/47
2 Jul–19 Dec 1818, Nos 458–565	R/9/22/48
5 Jan–29 Oct 1819, Nos 566–816	R/9/22/49
1 Nov–17 Nov 1819, Nos 814–1020	R/9/22/50
18 Nov–30 Nov 1819, Nos 1,223–1,299	R/9/22/51
1 Dec–31 Dec 1819, Nos 1,149–1,572	R/9/22/52
4 Jan–4 Feb 1820, Nos 1,683–57	R/9/22/53
15 Feb–29 Mar 1820, Nos 1–56	R/9/22/54
7 Apr–27 Jun 1820, Nos 57–122	R/9/22/55
1 Jul–28 Dec 1820, Nos 123–227	R/9/22/56
13 Jan–30 Jun 1821, Nos 4–98	R/9/22/57

Administration of Malacca and the Malacca Protests

Malacca was a historic port on the Strait of the same name, which had been controlled since 1641 by the Dutch from their headquarters in Batavia (now Jakarta). Reinout Vos describes the settlement in the mid-eighteenth century as 'a port of call favoured by all English ships' with its pleasant climate, social diversions and facilities for provisions and repairs.[27] The attractions of the port for the British waned during the 1780s first with the progression of the fourth Anglo-Dutch war (1780–3) which broke out because of the Dutch

27 Vos, *Gentle Janus*, p. 125.

trade with the rebels in the American Revolutionary War, and second because of the Dutch war with Riau (Rhio) (1783–4) which resulted partly from the reluctance of the Malaccan government to share the spoils of the captured English opium ship the *Betsy* with Raja Haji of Riau. The eventual destruction of Riau led to an insurgence of so-called piracy in the area and the related disruption of Banka (now Bangka) tin production, the tin trade a mainstay of Malacca as an entrepôt port. Nevertheless, in 1786 when the records containing the Protests (if not the Protests themselves) commenced, Malacca had a population of between 14,000 and 20,000 people, rising to 25,000 in 1816,[28] and was still an important Dutch entrepôt and victualling port on the route between India and China and in voyages within the Malay Archipelago. After the British takeover in 1795 it became increasingly popular with British traders from India because of the contact that it provided with the Bugis and other traders from the south and east. Nearly 300 ships and square-rigged vessels and some 400 to 500 prahus anchored offshore annually from 1795 to 1805 and for the four years leading up to 1816 the annual average was still 208 ships.[29] By the mid-1790s it was a major outlet for Bengal merchants trading in opium.[30]

The founding of Penang by the British in 1786 did not sound the death knell of Malacca. While Penang had a superior harbour, comparatively low prices and low tolls, it was too far to the north of Malacca, with the obstacles of climate and piracy added to distance, to attract indigenous trade from the southern Archipelago.[31] Malacca would have maintained an initial superiority over Penang as a port for provisioning and repairs, given its long tradition in these aspects of shipping.[32] It certainly continued as an established legal and

28 Andaya, Barbara Watson, 'Melaka under the Dutch, 1641–1795', in K. S. Sandhu and P. Wheatley (eds), *Melaka: the Transformation of a Malay Capital c.1400–1980*, vol. 1 (Kuala Lumpur, 1983), pp. 195–241, at p. 207; C. M. Turnbull, 'Melaka under British Colonial Rule', in K. S. Sandhu and P. Wheatley (eds), *Melaka: the Transformation of a Malay Capital c.1400–1980*, vol. 1 (Kuala Lumpur, 1983), pp. 242–96, at p. 242; Nordin Hussin, *Trade and Society in the Straits of Melaka: Dutch Melaka and English Penang, 1790–1830* (Singapore, 2007), p. 166; Nadia H Wright, *William Farquhar and Singapore: Stepping out from Raffles' Shadow* (Penang, 2017), p. 30.

29 Farhquar to H. J. Pearson, quoted in *Ibid.*, p. 31; Brian Harrison, *Holding the Fort: Melaka Under Two Flags, 1795–1845*, Malaysian Branch of the Royal Asiatic Society Monograph No. 14 (Kuala Lumpur, 1985), pp. 13, 86.

30 Anthony Webster, 'British Expansion in South-East Asia and the Role of Robert Farquhar, Lieutenant-Governor of Penang, 1804–5', *Journal of Imperial and Commonwealth History*, 23:1 (1995), 1–25, at p. 20.

31 Turnbull, 'Melaka', pp. 245–6; Dianne Lewis, *Jan Compagnie in the Straits of Malacca 1641–1795* (Athens OH, 1995), p.123; Webster, 'British Expansion', pp. 19–20; Anthony Webster, *Gentlemen Capitalists: British Imperialism in South East Asia 1770–1890* (London, 1998), pp. 40–8.

32 Anthony Reid, and Radin Fernando, 'Shipping on Melaka and Singapore as an Index of Growth, 1760–1840', *South Asia: Journal of South Asian Studies*, 19 (1996), 59–84, at p.66ff; though there are examples in the Protests of ships heading to Penang for repairs.

Fig 1. *View looking over George Town* [Penang] *to the Queeda Coast* by James Wathen. London, J. Nichols, son, and Bentley, 1814.

Fig 2. *Malacca, with the Hope at anchor in the Roads* by James Wathen, 1814.

administrative centre for which ships in distress would head. In comparison, Penang did not seem to have the requisite facilities for the lodgement of Protests. To take some examples from the Malacca Protests: although the Portuguese ship *Mercurio* had reached Penang after taking in water in August 1800, Captain Ramos continued to Malacca to lodge his Protest; likewise, Captain William Hammond, near Penang when his ship (*Lady*?) *Flora* ran aground on Keo Shoal in 1817 and, even though he despatched the chief officer in the jollyboat to Penang to get boats to lighten the ship; most tellingly, Captain Ribeiro of the *Ulysses* spent several days in Penang in August 1814 after a much-delayed voyage, searching for a replacement for his sick first pilot, yet he too lodged his Protest at Malacca.

The governance of Malacca alternated between the Dutch and the British during the period 1786–1825. This was the result of the fortunes of war. In 1793, as a progression of the French Revolutionary Wars in Europe (1792–1802), France declared war on Great Britain and the Dutch Republic, and two years later, in January 1795, defeated Holland. In August of that year, as a response, the British took possession of Dutch Malacca under the terms of the Kew Letters, missives written in January and February by William V, Prince of Orange, from his refuge in Kew Palace, England, whereby the Dutch colonial governors were ordered to surrender their colonies to the British in order to maintain resistance against the French. This was intended to be a temporary arrangement and after the Treaty of Amiens between England and France was signed on 25 March 1802 England was expected to hand back its Dutch territories in the East Indies. Implementation of policy was always complicated by the fact that it took some months for news of European outcomes to reach India, and slow communications were amplified by a British policy of procrastination when it came to accommodating the Dutch. Thus, Malacca was still in British hands on the resumption of war between England and France in May 1803, although Amboina (now Ambon), for example, had been transferred to the Dutch in February.

Initially the administration of Malacca was answerable to Madras (now Chennai), which was the nearest EIC presidency and the home base of the occupying Company regiments. When Penang was elevated to the fourth presidency in 1805 it took over responsibility for Malacca.[33] Finally restored to the Dutch under the Treaty of Vienna (9 June 1815), Malacca was formally handed back on 21 September 1818, an arrangement that proved to be short-lived as in 1825 the British returned under the terms of the Treaty of London (1824) whereby a line was drawn between Singapore (where the British had founded a settlement in 1819) and Riau, with British interests to the north of the line and Dutch interests to the south.

33 Wright, *William Farquhar*, p. 32.

During the British interregnum period (1795–1818) – the years that are most pertinent for the present study – Britain retained much of the Dutch administration in place in Malacca. Admiral Rainier, who determined the initial form of administration, after a short trial of joint Anglo-Dutch governance, removed the Dutch governor, Abraham Couperus, and the Dutch military.[34] At least by 1800 the traditional office of *syahbandar* (harbour master) had been replaced with British harbour officials led by a master attendant.[35] The Dutch land and legal systems, managed through the Political Council, the Council of Justice and the Orphan Chamber, however, remained intact and it was therefore to a Dutch official, a 'notary', that the captain of a country trader vessel (or officer in command if the captain was for some reason no longer in charge) presented himself and submitted his Protest in conformity with the legal requirement that a captain should lodge a Protest at the first 'European' port he came to after experiencing a misadventure. Even after Malacca had been restored to the Dutch in September 1818 British country traders continued to lodge Protests at Malacca, as did the captains of Portuguese ships, until the depositions petered out around 1820–1. Several entries in the *Prothocol Books* in 1819 refer to a legal regulation passed in the Netherlands Indies on 1 October 1818 (Article 15) under which Protests could be included in the Dutch records after the handover of British rule in Malacca.[36]

Notaries played an important role in the Dutch administrative system with authority in civil law to draw up and receive legal documents and accept and administer oaths, keeping a file of the documents in 'notarial protocols' or archives. The holders commonly belonged to the top influential circle of wealthy, Malaccan-Dutch slave-owning families, often related to each other through marriage and from whom, even with British intervention, the local administrators were drawn. The notaries during the period covered in this study were Jacob van Haak (from 1786 to 1795 when he probably went to Batavia), Johannes Hamel (from 1795 to 1805), Francois Adam Lefevre (from 1805 to 1806 when he became justice of the Portuguese), Jan Hendrik Stecher (from 1806 to 1815 when he became president of the Orphan Chamber), Anthonij Stecher (from 1815 until his death in 1820) and Daniel Koek (from 1820 to 1825).[37] Anthonij Stecher who succeeded his brother, Jan Hendrik Stecher, was concurrently clerk of the Court of Justice and Dutch inter-

34 Walter Caulfield Lennon, 'Journal of a voyage through the Straits of Malacca on an Expedition to the Molucca Islands … 1796', *JSBRAS*, 7 (1881), 51–74, at pp. 68–9.

35 Wright, *William Farquhar*, p. 34. See also the Protest of Captain Neegaard, No. 838, 10 July 1800, when Charles Wallace Young was master attendant.

36 For example, *Prothocol Books*, No. 618½, 31 March 1819. Later Protests refer to Article 15 being passed on 16 October 1817.

37 Baxter, 'Dutch Records', pp. 124–5. The notaries are referred to in Dutch in the Protocol Books variously as 'Eersten Gezwooren Klerk van Politie', 'Beampt beschrijver', among others.

preter.[38] He was son-in-law to Abraham Velge, later president of the Court of Justice and through his brother's wife was a member of the important Tessensohn family. Daniel Koek was half-brother to both Adriaan Koek, president of the Council of Justice, and to Catharina Koek, wife of the deposed governor, Abraham Couperus.

The idea of one regime leaving a mark on a succeeding, foreign, regime within an area, either through remnant administrative forms or through the influence of individuals, or both, is an idea recently explored by James Wilson in relation to the Dutch and British empires in the Indian Ocean and Southeast Asia during the years 1795 to 1820, with particular reference to Cape Colony, Ceylon and Java.[39] In the case of Malacca during those years the 'entanglement', as Wilson calls it, was more a pragmatic arrangement. While William Farquhar, commandant from 1803, was a champion of Malacca, and while the British appeared reluctant to give up the port (to reiterate, they failed to do so in 1802–3 after the Treaty of Amiens and took three years, from 1815 to 1818, to implement the decision of the Treaty of Vienna), the higher EIC authorities never seemed to cherish the possession. In the last resort, faithful to the original agreement, Malacca does seem to have been regarded as a temporary stewardship and the retention of the underlying Dutch administrative/legal system was probably a money-saving convenience. The fact that the Protests dwindled away after the Dutch regained control in 1818 has less to do with the once-again changed regime than with the fact that the British had by then instituted Singapore as the epicentre of British Southeast Asian trade and, after 1824, as the administrative head of the Straits Settlements. Malacca was no longer a preferred port of call.

An official, documented Protest at Malacca could have up to three constituent parts: a notarial document, or note, describing the Protest in general terms, always written in Dutch and usually signed by the captain (we refer to this as the Protest note); the Protest itself, with details of the mishap, sometimes written in Dutch but as time went on more commonly written in English or Portuguese, signed by the captain or by officers and occasional crew members; and, lastly, a short statement in Dutch, signed by the declarant attesting that the Protest had been entered into the records.

An examination of the records shows that the early Protests, beginning with that of Jacob Van Kal on 21 April 1791, when Malacca was under Dutch control, are almost always recorded only in Dutch; occasionally extracts from an English on-board journal are included, but often the log or journal extracts, while alluded to, do not form part of the record. This situation remains unchanged even after the EIC take over in 1795. It is not until

38 *Ibid.*, p. 127.

39 James Wilson, 'The Anglo-Dutch Imperial Meridian in the Indian Ocean World, 1795–1820' (Unpublished PhD thesis, University of Cambridge, 2019), <https://doi.org/10.17863/CAM.38350>.

1805 when British Malacca was governed through the newly formed Penang presidency of the EIC that the submission in English commonly forms the larger part of the Protest. Nevertheless, any introductory and closing sections continue to be written in Dutch. Portuguese-language Protests or statements in Portuguese appended to a Dutch Protest note are common from 1800 onwards.

The Protest was often described as an extract from the ship's log and some of the Malaccan Protests do follow a standard log format. It is difficult to compare a Protest with the actual wording in the log entry as very few logs of private vessels have survived and are almost impossible to locate. An exception to this is the log of the *Hammudy* whose commander, Captain Henning, a former naval lieutenant, made a gift of the log of his journey from Bombay to Siam to the British Admiralty. His meticulous entries follow the regular Navy pattern and his Protest is indeed an extract from the log.[40] In many of the cases to be found in the Malacca records the Protests are a more informal chronological description of events, with some inclusion of recorded wind directions and depth readings. Some even seem to be a transcription of a verbal account.[41] This fits well with James W. Frey's description of the typical log of a private merchantman as 'a vague record of navigational data' unlike a detailed log of regular East Indiamen.[42] The Protest usually describes the environment and events leading up to the disaster, explains how the incident occurred, lists the subsequent actions of the captain and crew to try to mitigate or overcome the misadventure and provides a conclusion to events.

In keeping with their purpose, the Protests describe in factual terms the physical impact of a storm or a grounding; they do not have the literary licence of a Tobias Smollett to capture the human drama of being caught in a monsoon storm in the Bay of Bengal or a typhoon in the South China Sea ('I was wakened by a most horrible din, occasioned by … the cracking of cabins, the howling of the wind through the shrouds, the confused noise of the ship's crew').[43] When the *Vulcan* weathered a severe storm in the Bay of Bengal in 1806,[44] for example, the captain reported the loss of catharpins,[45] fore and top sail ties, fore topmast stay and rigging with no mention of distress to the crew; whereas when the *Penang Government Gazette* of 13 December that year reported on a second disaster that soon after befell that ship the emphasis

40 The National Archives (London), Public Record Office, ADM 55/144.

41 For example, David Dunlop (q.v.), *Prothocol Books*, No. 41, 14 September 1805; George Bateman (q.v.), *Prothocol Books*, No. 1062, 7 January 1815.

42 James W Frey, 'Getting Away with Murder: The Wrongful Deaths of Lascars Aboard the *Union* in 1802', *International Review of Social History*, 59, Special Issue 22 (2014), 45–88, at p. 61. According to Aaron Jaffer, *Lascars and India Ocean Seafaring, 1780–1860: Shipboard Life, Unrest and Mutiny* (Woodbridge, 2015), p. 24, some country traders kept no records whatsoever.

43 Tobias Smollett, *Roderick Random* (London, 1927, orig. 1748), p. 165.

44 *Prothocol Books*, No. 12, 19 September 1806.

45 Short ropes or iron clamps that helped tie the shrouds. Also known as cat-harpings.

was on the human element: 'Captain Perkins was severely wounded in the head; Mr Ewen, second officer, had both legs broke, and several of the lascars dangerously bruised, (seven of whom are since dead) by the falling of the masts.' The request by Admiral Pellew that EIC officials instruct country ship captains to edit their logbooks as a precaution against their capture and use by the French[46] might also have had an effect on the tone of the reports. Yet, even without hyperbole, the accumulated effect of so many accounts of catastrophe as are revealed by the Protests can, in itself, elicit an emotional response.

Notwithstanding the large number of Protests lodged at Malacca, one cannot take for granted that the report of a mishap where Malacca was the subsequent port of call will always be found in the *Prothocol Books*. For example, there are no Protests in the books for 1804. In particular, the loss of the *Fanny* (captain William Robertson) in the South China Sea in November 1803 is not present in the books even though a Protest-like account of the misadventure was written at Malacca after the arrival of the survivors in February 1804. For details of the loss of the *Fanny* as reported by the second mate, see Appendix C.

The statistics and types of misadventure

The exact number of country traders operating between India and China and in the Malay Archipelago during the period under discussion is not known, but there were probably several hundred a year. Parkinson estimated the total number of country ships to be 128 in 1783 and 575 in 1791.[47] Reid and Fernando state that thirty-seven English ships called at Malacca in 1785, a decline from the higher figures of the late 1770s given by Lewis,[48] perhaps reflecting the disruptions stemming from the Anglo-Dutch War and the Dutch war with Riau. A subsequent recovery in numbers is demonstrated by Nordin Hussin's analysis of Malaccan shipping statistics that show that by 1791–3 there were almost twice as many European ships (which would have included country traders) visiting Malacca than in 1780–2.[49] This was all part of the great expansion that took part in the 1790s of British country trade to the 'Eastward' described by Holden Furber.[50]

46 Jaffer, *Lascars*, pp. 22–3.

47 Parkinson, *Trade in the Eastern Seas*, p. 336.

48 Reid and Fernando 'Shipping', p. 66; Dianne Lewis, 'The Growth of the Country Trade in the Straits of Malacca 1760–1777', *JMBRAS*, 43:2 (1970), 114–30, at p. 117, fn 27.

49 Nordin Hussin, 'Trading Networks of Malay Merchants and Traders in the Straits of Malacca from 1780 to 1830', *Asian Journal of Social Sciences*, 40:1 (2012), 51–82, at p. 72.

50 Furber, *Rival Empires*, pp. 296–7. It is hard to compare the statistics given by different authors for different years. For our purposes they simply give an indication of numbers.

Between 1786 and 1815 a yearly average of twenty-five private British vessels made the hazardous trip from India to China and back,[51] 1806 being a particularly busy year with sixty-four country trader arrivals recorded at Whampoa. Twenty-four of these were rice ships that unloaded their grain but left China with little profit and without a return cargo, the result of a misunderstanding between the captains and the Chinese officials.[52] One of these rice ships, the *Cartier*, registered a Protest on the way home. Of the ninety-seven British ships involved in a protested incident recorded in the *Prothocol Books* at Malacca at least forty-two were voyaging to or from China with at least another twenty-one Portuguese ships making the trip to or from Macao.

Irrespective of the type of vessel or who owned it, whether a country trader or an EIC ship, sea voyages in the Bay of Bengal, the Malacca Strait and South China Sea were dangerous. At the extreme end of disaster was the total loss of the vessel. The available statistics, such as those compiled by John Phipps in 1823 and 1840, by Evan Cotton in 1949 and by Ed Cumming in 2016, concentrate on these fatalities rather than on less serious mishaps. The most complete fatality statistics relate to EIC ships, but they are not irrelevant to country shipping seeing as the same risks were shared by all. Given the high number of total losses, misadventures of a lesser kind must have been common.

Writing of the dangers faced by EIC ships, Evan Cotton said East Indiamen faced 'not only the peril of storm and tempest on the high seas, but also the risk of attacks by pirates, and in wartime, those of enemy men-of-war or armed merchantmen and privateers … [I]n Eastern waters they had generally to depend on their own armaments and the fighting qualities of their officers and sailors'.[53] According to Cotton, between 1700 and 1818, no fewer than 160 East Indiamen were totally lost by wreck, burning or capture, with ten ships lost in the years 1782 and 1783 alone.[54] Statistics compiled more recently by Ed Cumming in his compendium of EIC ship incidents show Cotton's figures to be an underestimation. For the same period (1700 to 1818) he lists 212 'major' EIC ships lost. In the years covered by the *Prothocol Books*, 1786 to 1825, there were ninety-four major EIC ships lost, including twenty-four captured by the French between 1796 and 1810. There was barely a year when there wasn't at least one loss, and Cumming asserts that the loss of five ships in a year (presumably a war year) would have been 'acceptable'.[55]

51 Paul A. Van Dyke, *Whampoa and the Canton Trade: Life and Death in a Chinese Port* (Hong Kong, 2020), Appendix 1.2b.

52 *Ibid.*, p. 15.

53 Evan Cotton, *East Indiamen: The East India Company's Maritime Service* (London, 1949), p. 13.

54 *Ibid.*, p. 135. For a description of misadventures suffered by East Indiamen, as opposed to country traders, see *Ibid.*, pp. 126 *et seq.*

55 Ed Cumming (ed.), *A Compendium of Incidents Incurred by the Major Ships used by the English (later British) East India Company c.1600–c.1834* (MIBEC Publications, 2016), p. 427,

Fig 3. *Whampoa Anchorage.* Oil on copper, artist unknown, c.1810. Wikimedia Commons.

Spectacularly, in the years 1808–9 seventeen EIC ships were lost, including four captured, most within a twelve-month period. There were no more EIC ships captured after 1810, when the English takeover of Mauritius neutralised the French fleet in the East Indies, and after 1816 there were fewer ships wrecked, perhaps because of an improvement in navigational aids.

Private trading vessels faced the same dangers and more, without the institutional backup of a formidable enterprise such as the EIC. Phipps' 1840 register of ships built on the Hooghly, a mixture of Company ships and free traders, shows that of the 303 vessels built between 1781 and 1825 about 30% were lost by 1839 due to wreck or burning, with another twenty captured by the French. Of the eighty-six ships built between 1817 and 1825, twenty, or 23%, were lost by 1839.[56] The shorter period doesn't allow for an exact comparison, but it is possible that the ships themselves, as well as their navigational aids, were improving in quality. Another of Phipps' lists, that of casualties to ships belonging to Calcutta[57] (no matter where built), show average losses from wreck or burning between 1800 and 1825 of about six

<https://www.nauticalarchaeologysociety.org/east-india-company-incidents> [Accessed 15 April 2025].

56 John Phipps, *A Collection of Papers, Relative to Ship Building in India … also A Report, Comprehending all the Ships and Vessels Built in India to the Present Time …* (Calcutta, 1840), pp. 96–115.

57 *Ibid.*, pp. 137–46.

vessels per annum, ranging from fourteen in 1811 to none in 1822. Against the trend, there were nine lost in 1823, ten in 1824.

Fourteen of the British Malacca Protests relate to the total loss of a vessel: eight were wrecked, two destroyed by fire and four were captured. The rest record a variety of misadventures that, in light of the fact they are those submitted at only one port, is telling evidence of the fraught nature of sailing at that time.

Note on arrangement of chapters

In his book on marine insurance Arnould listed seven risks of loss at sea against which an owner could be insured, namely:

> 'perils of the sea',
> 'fire',
> 'hostile capture or seizure',
> 'detention, arrest and embargoes',
> 'pirates, robbers and thieves',
> 'barratry of master and mariners',
> 'other perils and misfortune'.[58]

The following presentation of the Protests recorded at Malacca has been divided up using this list as a basis, with some changes that reflect the reality of the data. Thus, the Protests emanating from British country traders and the occasional EIC ship are dealt with in Part I under the following heads: perils of the sea (bad weather); perils of the sea (groundings and strandings); fire; other accidents and failings of the ship; pirates, robbers and thieves; and coercion, imprisonment and detention. Protests from individuals who made complaints about the British captains, regardless of their own nationality, are dealt with as 'accusations against master or crew (commercial problems)'.

Within these divisions the Protests are presented in a format resembling a calendar of documents. This is in keeping with our primary aim to provide a means of access to the Protest records that, as explained earlier, are not archived as a group within the *Prothocol Books* but are scattered among other legal and administrative documents with no readily distinguishable means of identification. Each record is summarised in our text, with an unwritten invitation for the reader to consult the source if he or she wishes to pursue more detail on the reason for the Protest or on whatever other aspect may be of interest. In general, the aspects are varied and many. To name a few: the route taken; the detail of the bearings; the nomenclature of geographical features; the weather and other hazards; the cargo carried; the losses sustained and the means taken to reduce these; the presence of other ships

58 Arnould, *Treatise* (1848), vol. 2, p. 792.

Fig 4. Sketch of types of vessels that feature in the Protests.

1. Ship, three masts square rigged.
2. Barque, two masts square rigged with fore-and-aft sails on the third, aftermost, mast.
3. Schooner, two or three masts fore-and-aft rigged.
4. Brig, two masts square rigged.
5. Snow, similar to a brig but with a separate mast for the spanker.
6. Grab, similar to a brig, but with a hull and pointed prow derived from the Arab ghurab.

and the aid that might be rendered; the roles of the different components of the ship's company; the attitude towards lascars; the clash of cultures in various trading areas; the effect of the European wars on the country traders in the East Indies; the relationship between the Royal Navy and the country traders; and the way in which the Protests are written – the handwriting, the spelling, the phrasing, the nautical terms used. The Protests form a cornucopia of maritime treasure. The findings gleaned from our perusal of these fascinating documents are presented in the Conclusion.

The calendar approach and the division of cases based on Arnould's list of risks necessarily means that some chapters will be much shorter than others. For example, the most common reason for lodgement of a Protest was damage caused by bad weather. Chapter 1 deals with the forty-one relevant cases. By contrast there are only four cases dealing with fire, so Chapter 3 is extremely brief.

Where we have been able to locate further information about the captains and ships we have decided not to intersperse these findings as side issues within the main text but to place them in footnotes.

Mariners of nationalities other than British who also registered Protests of misadventure at Malacca are discussed in Part II. We have dealt with these nationalities separately partly because the political situation of the time places them in a position different from the British, and also, with regard to the Portuguese, the look and feel of the Protests is different. In addition, the eighteenth-century version of the Portuguese language presented special challenges that we could not always meet. The complete deciphering of these awaits an expert.

The most common of the foreign Protests were the Portuguese followed by the Danish. All the Danish protests, clustered around the turn of the century when Danish neutrality was regarded with suspicion by the British, are listed. We include a large selection of the Portuguese Protests, with brief comments; further study is required to do justice to the totality of these. We also include the rare Protests from captains of an American ship (the *Putnam*), a Dutch ship (the *Carolina*), one from Hamburg (the *Charlotte*) and one Malay ship (the *Tiriwinaga Cany*) flying the flag of the Sultan of Riau.

PART I
PROTESTS: BRITISH SHIPS

1

Perils of the Sea (Bad Weather)

The most common misadventures recounted by country traders at Malacca in the period under consideration were caused by bad weather in the Bay of Bengal and the South China Sea. While bad weather accidents were also common in the seas off the Coromandel and Malabar coasts these were not often the subject of Malacca Protests. Such cases, especially when related to coastal shipping, were presumably more likely to be recorded at Bombay (now Mumbai), Calcutta or Madras. Mishaps could also be caused by stormy conditions in the Malacca Strait, but the Protests recorded at Malacca by ships in trouble in the Strait were usually associated with the destructive force of reefs, rocks or sandbanks rather than with bad weather alone: these incidents are listed in Chapter 2. Many of the ships reporting storm damage were from Calcutta and on their way to or returning from China. Bombay country ships feature less commonly, perhaps because there were fewer of them in the first place. Nevertheless, several Bombay ships did report storm damage, particularly on the outward voyage to China. Whether these ships sailed through the Bay of Bengal and down the Malacca Strait or used the alternative route to China down the west coast of Sumatra and through the Sunda Strait, Malacca would still be their port of recourse.

The weather patterns were all-important to the maritime traders of India and the Archipelago. The mariners were dependent on the southwest monsoon winds to convey them 'to the East' and the northeast monsoons to bring them back home again and had to take their chances with the accompanying storms, planning their voyages to avoid the worst of the typhoon months in the South China Sea and preparing to battle hurricanes in the Bay of Bengal. Within the archipelago they had to be *au fait* with the hazards of the sandbanks and manage, with frequent anchoring, unexpected squalls and contrary currents.

The monsoonal weather patterns are now explained scientifically in terms of the flow of air from high to low pressure areas towards the equator and the movement of the resulting Inter-Tropical Convergence Zone north and

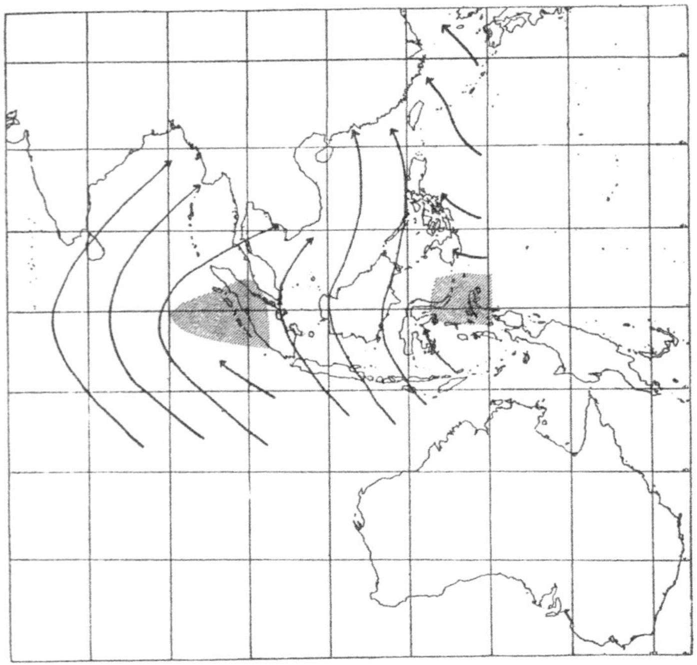

SW Monsoon—June.

Fig 5. Chart of the Southwest Monsoon for June. Shaded areas in Figs 5 and 6 denote light and variable winds.

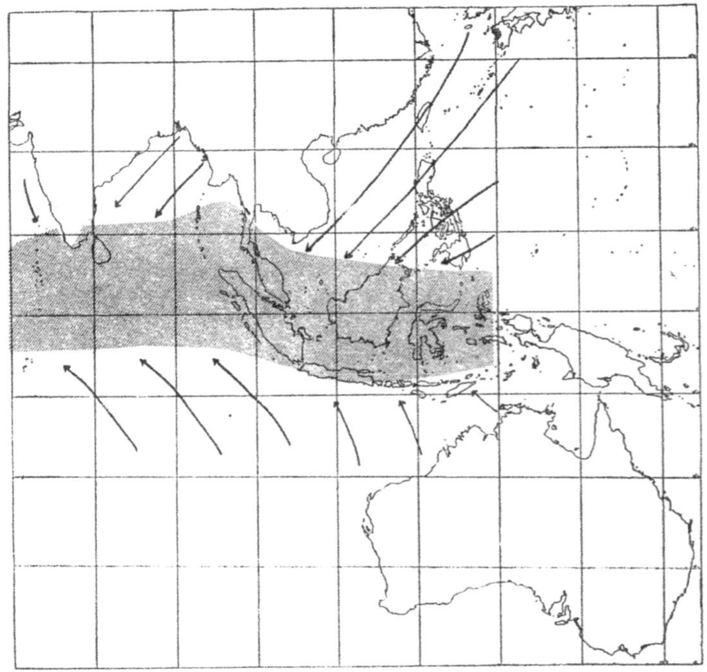

NE Monsoon—November.

Fig 6. Chart of the Northeast Monsoon for November.

south across the equator, following the sun.[1] The complicated combination of the underlying northeast to southwest trade winds overlaid by the monsoons, with multiple variations caused by the intrusion of the land masses and by the ocean currents in the different regions has been systematically explained by P. J. Rivers.[2]

Non-European sailors of the region had understood the weather systems in practical terms from time immemorial. In the late eighteenth and early nineteenth centuries British sailors, relative newcomers, could begin to take advantage of the expert weather advice offered in navigational works. These guides warned of the hazards and advised on the best routes to take at particular times of the year. The country trader Thomas Forrest published a treatise specifically on the monsoons in 1783.[3] Later, the most popular aid was the ex-country trader Horsburgh's two-volume *India Directory, Or, Directions for Sailing to and from the East Indies, China, New Holland, Cape of Good Hope, Brazil, and the Interjacent Ports*, published in 1809 and 1811, and updated in 1817, 1826 and 1836, with updates continuing after Horsburgh's death in the latter year.

Horsburgh's method, following the example of predecessors such as Joseph Huddart in *The Oriental Navigator* (1794), was to give a general description of the weather over large geographical areas followed by particulars relating to more specific regions with precise sailing instructions, the latter embellished with examples of shipping disasters and pitfalls, updated with each new edition. For example, in his general discussion of 'Monsoons, Winds, Ty-foongs and Currents' in the South China Sea, in the 1817 edition, he described the southwest monsoon as running from the middle or end of April to the beginning or middle of October, strongest in June, July and August. '[I]n these months, and also in May, sudden hard squalls blow sometimes out of the Gulf of Siam, as far as Pulo [Pulau] Condore, and Pulo Sapata. When dense clouds are perceived to rise, indicating the approach of these squalls, sail ought to be reduced without delay.' He gave various examples of mercury readings from the years 1804 to 1812 of ships caught in the 'unpredictable' typhoons, most likely from June to September, the September equinox being 'a very precarious period'. He described the northeast monsoon as commencing about the end of September or early October, becoming strongest in December and January, and petering out in February to March. The currents he described as 'very mutable, their direction and velocity depending upon local circumstances' that he proceeded to outline.

1 See Friedhelm Goltenboth, *et al.* (eds), *Ecology of Insular Southeast Asia: The Indonesian Archipelago* (Amsterdam, 2006), p. 18.

2 P. J. Rivers, 'Monsoon Rhythms and Trade Patterns: Ancient Times East of Suez', *JMBRAS*, 77:2 (2004), 59–93.

3 Thomas Forrest, *A Treatise on the Monsoons in East-India* (London, 1783).

Then followed his 'Instructions for Sailing Through the China Sea, to, or from Canton River, at all Seasons'.[4]

Horsburgh paid particular attention to the Bay of Bengal as 'more frequented by navigators than any other part of the Indian Seas', noting that the southwest monsoon blew strongest throughout the bay in June, July and August, with the northeast monsoon generally bringing severe storms between October and December. He detailed the lag in the onset of the monsoons at different parts of the bay, the local variability of the prevailing winds, the likelihood of severe storms at particular locations and the local patterns of the currents. His directions for sailing covered all parts of the bay.[5]

Particular years went down in the annals for the notoriously bad weather in the Bay of Bengal. On 5 October 1811 the *Sydney Gazette* published an account given by a passenger aboard the *Indian*, captain Andrew Barclay, describing the scene on 3 May 1811 when:

> the Indian passed by Madras Roads and beheld the most dismal spectacle that could be conceived being persuaded that out of 50 or 60 vessels the Vancouver must have been the only one saved. The Dover was perceived with her stern out of water and at a distance 49 wrecks were counted along shore. The Dover's and Chichester's crews only 3 men and a boy were [lost], but that unhappily out of 49 sail of country craft not a mast was saved.[6]

The Malacca Strait and the Malay Archipelago had their own micro-weather patterns that were generally less severe than in the Bay of Bengal and the South China Sea. There were storms but as Forrest wrote in reference to the southwest coast of Sumatra in 1783, 'I never knew a severe gale of wind on that coast … These squalls seldom last above seven or eight minutes with violence … Storms are never frequent near the Line; and the changing of the monsoons, on this coast, is never accompanied with that violence that we find in the Bay of Bengal, and the China seas.'[7] Tony Reid has stated that the sea-lanes in the archipelago were, weather wise, 'remarkably kind to seamen' and 'Storms were not a major hazard to mariners'.[8] This is borne out by the present study: in the Protests citing storm damage, only a small minority of the mishaps occur in the Malacca Strait.

Horsburgh considered the northeast monsoon the 'fair season throughout Malacca Strait'. The southwest monsoon, repelled by the mountains and

4 James Horsburgh, *India Directory, Or, Directions for Sailing to and from the East Indies, China, New Holland, Cape of Good Hope, Brazil, and the Interjacent Ports …*, 2nd edn (2 vols, London 1817), vol. 2, pp. 200–5.

5 *Ibid.*, vol. 1, pp. 422–7.

6 Quoted in <https://www.freesettlerorfelon.com/convict_ship_indian_1810.htm> [Accessed 15 April 2025].

7 Forrest, *Treatise*, p. 95.

8 Anthony Reid, *Southeast Asia in the Age of Commerce 1450–1680: Volume One, The Lands Below the Winds* (New Haven CT, 1988), p. 2.

high land stretching from Achen (now Aceh) along the coast of Pedir, he described as characterised by 'light variable winds and calms, with sometimes land breezes, or hard sudden squalls from the Sumatra coast in the night'. The danger to shipping came from these 'Sumatras', 'sometimes sudden and severe, accompanied with loud thunder, lightning, and rain' – particularly in the vicinity of the Pedir coast, and between Parcelar Hill (now Jugra) and the Carimons (now Palau Karimun). The north-westers that, while not so prevalent as the Sumatras, also blow in the northern part of the Strait, and may affect the Carimons or even Singapore Strait, 'are mostly preceded by a black, cloudy arch, rising rapidly from the horizon toward the zenith, allowing not more than sufficient time to reduce sail', though sometimes they arise more slowly. Like the Sumatras they were sometimes accompanied by thunder, lightning and heavy rain.[9]

Other writers referred to the sudden local squalls in the Malacca Strait as 'storms' because of their, albeit brief, intensity. In 1811–12 the painter James Wathen made a round trip from England to Madras and China in the EIC ship *Hope* captained by his friend James Pendergrass. They entered the Strait of Malacca on 24 October 1811. Wathen wrote:

> During our voyage down the Straits, we encountered much disagreeable and unsettled weather – almost continual rain, with thunder storms, accompanied by lightning of the most dangerous kind. These storms are prevalent in the Straits, and are occasioned by the high mountains of Sumatra on the one side, and of Malacca [Malaya?] on the other, attracting and breaking the clouds, and producing the electric phenomena of thunder and lightning, often doing much damage to the shipping.[10]

Another artist voyager, M. Le Vicomte de la Touanne, lieutenant aboard the French frigate *Thétis* in 1824 also described the hazards of the Strait of Malacca. This was in August. After warning of the irregular breezes and storms, the sandbanks and rocks that riddle the strait he continued: 'The surface of the sea, so unified and calm a moment before, wrinkles, breaks into foam; lightning and claps of thunder follow one another without cease; torrents of rain fall; the storm passes and the sky becomes clear until the arrival of the next storm, already brewing in the distance.'[11]

The following Protests against stormy weather and rough seas show a consistency with the hurricane and typhoon seasons. They describe the

9 Horsburgh, *India Directory* (1817), vol. 2, pp. 146–7.

10 James Wathen, *Journal of a Voyage in 1811 and 1812, to Madras and China: Returning by the Cape of Good Hope; In the H.C.S. The Hope, Capt. James Pendergrass* (London, 1814), p. 157.

11 E. B. de La Touanne, Vicomte, *Album pittoresque de la frégate La Thétis et de la corvette L'Espérance: collection de dessins relatifs à leur voyage autour du monde en 1824, 1825 et 1826, sous les ordres de M. le baron de Bougainville, … / receuillis et publiés par M. le vicomte de La Touanne* (Paris, 1828), p. 13.

damage wrought by the adverse conditions and also demonstrate the actions performed by the captains and crew to ensure the survival of their vessels and cargo.

The Protests (forty-one cases in chronological order)

Sometimes it is impossible to establish from a Protest whether the damage to a vessel said to have been caused by bad weather was in fact owing to the poor condition of the ship itself. A captain was unlikely to cast blame on the state of repair of the ship, which might have been attributed to his negligence. The numerous cases where a ship reported storm damage are grouped in this chapter, apart from those that also ran aground, which are dealt with in Chapter 2. The cases where leaks have occurred in less stormy conditions are described in Chapter 3.

The earliest misadventure caused by bad weather as recorded in the *Prothocol Books* took place in 1793. Joseph Maurel, captain of the country ship *Fictum Eyzac* lodged a Protest at Malacca on 9 July that year after a voyage from Bengal that had begun on 6 June.[12] During the trip the ship ran into a heavy storm and water entered the hold. Twenty-six gunny sacks[13] of the cargo (not specified) were water-damaged and because of the danger that this posed to the vessel, were thrown overboard. The Protest was against not only the lost cargo but also all other losses sustained because of the storm. The text of the Protest is in Dutch, signed by Maurel and two of the ship's officers.

The following year there are two Protests concerning the *City of Goa* (600 tons)[14] commanded by John Collie. They are both recorded in Dutch but have the feel of translations from Collie's English-language originals that have not been retained. The *City of Goa* departed Bombay on a voyage to China on 28 July 1794 as part of a fleet commanded by George Smith. Earlier in the month the ship had had an accident in the Bombay docks whereby part of the false keel and a few feet of the sheathing were torn off. Following repair she was ascertained as in good condition, 'not making a drop of water'.[15] After departing Bombay, however, the ship soon ran into heavy seas and lost contact with the rest of the fleet. It lost two of its anchors in the storm

12 British Library, Asia, Pacific and Africa Collections, *Malacca, General Prothocol Books (Registers of Legal Deeds) 1786–1825*, IOR: R/9/22/1–75 [referred to in this study as *Prothocol Books*], No. 93, 9 July 1793.

13 According to *Hobson Jobson: a Glossary of Colloquial Anglo-Indian Words and Phrases, and Kindred Terms, Etymological, Historical, Geographical and Discursive* by Henry Yule and A. C. Burnell, new edn by William Crooke (London, 1903), p. 403, gunny sacks were made from jute and 'much used in all Indian trade'.

14 Paul A. Van Dyke, *Whampoa and the Canton Trade: Life and Death in a Chinese Port* (Hong Kong, 2020), Appendix 1.2b.

15 *Bombay Courier*, 5 July 1794.

and on arrival at Malacca, on 11 September 1794, Collie lodged a Protest against this and all losses suffered to the cargo.[16] Nevertheless, Collie must have determined to continue the voyage to Canton, as by 7 November he was back in Malacca to lodge his second Protest.[17] The *City of Goa* was a poor sailer even in fair weather, and as explained by the captain, at about lat. 20°N to the west of the Grand Ladrone (part of the Marianas) on 3 October it ran into a strong northeasterly wind and rough seas. The ship began to leak, taking water at about 20 'duimen' [inches] an hour. Collie lodged this second Protest against all costs and losses suffered during the voyage.

By way of parenthesis, it is interesting to note that Captain Collie continued to have an eventful time, delayed even further by shipboard disputes. The *City of Goa* remained at Malacca until at least January 1795 as on 20 January Collie made another lengthy statement to the notary van Haak.[18] This was not a Protest, but a witness account surrounding the circumstances of a physical altercation between two of his officers, James Granville Windsor, first mate, and Peter Smart, second mate. Windsor, who had previously deserted, had arrived back at Malacca on 9 January from Pontianak on the *Carnatic*, commanded by Robert Scott, and Collie described Windsor's visit to the *City of Goa* with Captain Scott. Smart was later drowned while he and Windsor were proceeding to the shore in the ship's boat. Collie asked the Dutch authorities to go on board and arrest Windsor, which they agreed to do. Another witness account of events surrounding the dispute and physical fight between the two men and the subsequent death of Smart was given by Manuel Franciscus and William Jordan, both helmsmen on the *City of Goa*. This was entered into the records in Dutch,[19] though it is stated that Franciscus's version was originally given in Portuguese and Jordan's in English. These must have been verbal accounts as both men signed the Dutch entry in the records with a cross. While not a misadventure caused by the weather or the seas, disputes between crew members were a regular feature of shipboard life, and this incident demonstrates yet another problem that captains had to deal with on their voyages.

Meanwhile, the rest of the fleet having arrived at Whampoa, the *City of Goa* was supposed a missing ship before its eventual arrival at Whampoa in June 1795.[20]

The *Armenia* (300 tons)[21] was on a voyage to Trengganu in November 1794 when it met with 'squally weather' in the South China Sea during the night of

16 *Prothocol Books*, No. 181, 11 September 1794.
17 *Prothocol Books*, No. 224, 7 November 1794.
18 *Prothocol Books*, No. 262, 20 January 1795.
19 *Prothocol Books*, No. 271, 4 February 1795.
20 *Bombay Courier*, 15 November, 13 December 1794; Van Dyke, *Whampoa*, Appendix 1.2b.
21 Walter Caulfield Lennon, 'Journal of a voyage through the Straits of Malacca on an Expedition to the Molucca Islands … 1796', *JSBRAS*, 7 (1881), 51–74, at p. 61.

the 2nd. The masts were struck by lightning and damaged to the extent that it was impossible to continue with the voyage. Captain John Sands, concerned also about the imminent northeast monsoon season, consulted with his crew before deciding to return to Malacca. They reported their Protest to the Dutch officials as a note on 8 November and the English version was tabled in the records on 11 November 1794.[22]

The 1,000 ton ship *Travancore* (*Travankoor* in the Dutch spelling) similarly suffered storm damage, as a result of which Captain Henry Frost and First Officer Patrick Gardner (who became her captain the following year)[23] lodged a Protest note in Dutch on 16 December 1794 and a Protest in English the next day.[24] In their submission Frost and Gardner protested against the damage to the ship and the cargo that occurred on 1 December during a voyage from China to Bombay, as specified in the ship's journal, though the journal itself is not included in the records. The *Travancore* had run into a heavy gale south-southeast of the Grand Ladrone. As nearly 5 feet of water entered the hold necessitating the pumps, it was suspected 'that great part of the Cargo is damaged'.

It was probably the same gale that ruined the cargo of the *Anna* (749 tons),[25] also returning to Bombay from China, commanded by John Horn with Chief Mate James Johnston. Captain Horn tabled his Protest note on the same day, 16 December 1794, with further details on the 17th comprising both an English and a Dutch version.[26] The *Anna* was 30 miles from the Grand Ladrone when the storm struck. During the storm water entered the hold and the pumps were manned, but a strong smell of arrack was detected from the hold, suggestive of breeched casks. Consequently, Horn and Johnston protested against all loss and damages the cargo may have sustained.

Company ships did not usually lodge Protests in the same way as country traders. However, while not couched in the wording of an actual Protest, a detailed account is given on 8 July 1795 of the misadventures of the EIC ship *Surprize* (395 tons, built 1780) during a voyage from Sydney to Bengal.[27] The ship had arrived in Sydney with a cargo of convicts on 25 October 1794 and had left Port Jackson the following December. The vessel lost masts and sails in the Coral Sea on 30 and 31 December. It laboured through the Java Sea and on 22 April, just north of Semarang on the north coast of Java, met the *Zeenimph*. After receiving water and provisions from the *Zeenimph*, the *Surprize*

22 *Prothocol Books*, Nos 225, 8 November 1794; 228, 11 November 1794.

23 Van Dyke, *Whampoa*, Appendix 1.2b.

24 *Prothocol Books*, Nos 241, 16 December 1794; 243, 17 December 1794. The *Travancore* made five trips to China between 1792 and 1797 and carried armaments supplied by the EIC. In 1791 it was listed as having a crew of 150 men and twelve guns: Anne Bulley, *The Bombay Country Ships, 1790–1833* (Richmond, 2000), pp. 63–4.

25 Van Dyke, *Whampoa*, Appendix 1.2b.

26 *Prothocol Books*, Nos 242, 16 December 1794; 244, 17 December 1794.

27 *Prothocol Books*, No. 60, 8 July 1795.

reached Cheribon (now Ceribon) and then anchored off Indramayu, having lost an anchor, rope and a buoy. Concerns about the monsoon, the French frigates in the area and the difficulties of repairing the mast caused further delays. It was not until six months after setting out that the first mate, John Burnet, third mate Hugh Meehan and the ship's carpenter Richard Graham appeared before the Dutch official at Malacca, the former two signing a statement in Dutch outlining the events of the voyage. The statement mentions that the captain, Patrick Campbell, sought advice from his officers. It is not known why the captain did not sign the statement; he was still in command of the ship when it left for England from Calcutta in November 1795.[28]

On 1 December 1801 Captain Robert Shepherdson lodged a Protest note concerning events that had occurred on the *Faz Soobhany* (600 tons) on a voyage from China in November.[29] In his statement the captain confirmed that a copy of part of the ship's journal had been submitted to the authorities (this is not included in the records). The subsequent Protest (in Dutch) signed by the first and second mates, Thomas Merriman and Richard Tate,[30] explained that on 17 and 18 November off the head of Macao the vessel had been swamped by high seas 'in and over the ship'. They protested against the circumstances and any possible damage.

The *Pelican*, described as a Cochin China ship in the Protest note lodged by Captain James Purefoy on 19 February 1802,[31] was probably the British country trader later referred to by Captain (Robert) Allan as built by the king of Cochin China and given as a present to Abbot & Co. of Madras.[32] The vessel had left Cochin China on 6 February 1802 and afterwards ran into bad weather, shipping much water that necessitated the use of the pumps before arriving in Malacca on 18 February. The first mate, Jorge Morgan,

28 For further information on the *Surprize*, see <https://en.wikipedia.org/wiki/Surprize_(1780_ship)> [Accessed 15 April 2025].

29 *Prothocol Books*, No. 1036, 1 December 1801. Details of the life of Robert Shepherdson and his brother Matthew in the East Indies are given in P. J. and K. L Shepherdson, *Journey to the Straits: The Shepherdson Story* (Singapore, 2003).

30 *Prothocol Books*, No. 1037, 1 December 1801.

31 *Prothocol Books*, No. 1064, 19 February 1802.

32 Alistair Lamb, 'British Missions to Cochin China: 1778–1822', *JMBRAS*, 34:3/4 (1961), 1–248, at pp. 101–2. Captain Purefoy (d. 1846) traded in Cochin China for Abbot & Co., later Abbot & Maitland, from 1800 to 1807: Lamb, 'British Missions', pp. 111, 133, 136, 151. He began his country trading career as a mate on the *Anna* in 1792. He later captained various vessels, including *Pelican*, *Griffin*, *Friendship*, *Resolution* and *William Petrie* until 1815. For Purefoy's accounts of his time in Cochin China and for his letters see James Purefoy, 'Remarques sur la Cochinchine', *Nouvelles Annales des Voyages*, ser. 2, 1 (1826), 338–53; *Asiatic Journal and Monthly Register*, July to December 1825, pp. 521–8, 621–8; *Asiatic Journal and Monthly Register*, July to December 1826, pp. 143–7, 652–5; G. C. Duggan, 'From Indian Waters: Some Old Letters', *Journal of the Royal Asiatic Society of Great Britain and Ireland*, 1:2 (1958), 1–7.

and the gunner, Nicolaas Francisco Constabel,[33] followed the Protest note of 19 February with another Protest, as requested by the captain, on the 27th against damages that the ship had suffered.[34] Both Protests are in Dutch. A copy of the ship's log was said to be tabled but is not included in the records.

Captain Simon Peterson of the *Expedition* (perhaps the 70-ton vessel owned by Hudson Bacon & Co.) lodged a Protest note on 24 February 1802[35] concerning a problem that occurred during a trip from Penang to Malacca where he had arrived the previous day. The ship's journal is mentioned but not appended to the Dutch record and with no follow-up Protest there are no more available details. One could reasonably assume that it was storm damage.

Captain Christopher Perkins of the *Vulcan* (391 tons, built in Java)[36] recounted running into bad weather in August 1806 when crossing the Bay of Bengal on a voyage to China, lodging a Protest at Malacca on 19 September 'against the severity of the winds and weather'.[37] He listed the damage the gale had done to the ship including the loss of five of the seven catharpins, the fore and top sail ties, the fore topmast stay and rigging. An Armenian trader on board, Petrus Carapat (Carapiet), also lodged a protest (in Dutch) against any losses suffered because of the delay in Malacca.[38] This was just the start of Perkins' troubles. After having had the ship repaired, he continued on his voyage, only to lose the vessel entirely at the end of October off the coast of Luconia (now Luzon) in the South China Sea. The loss of the ship, the rescue of the officers and crew by the *Trafalgar*, one of the ships taking a cargo of rice to China to relieve the then current shortage, and the subsequent generosity of Mr Carapiet towards Captain Peter Meares of the *Trafalgar* was widely reported in 1807.[39]

Following shortly after Captain Perkins' experience in the Bay of Bengal, Captain Robert Scott[40] of the *Experiment*, also on a voyage from Calcutta, expe-

33 'Constabel' could be a surname or could equally be a reference to his occupation as gunner.

34 *Prothocol Books*, No. 1070, 27 February 1802.

35 *East-India Register and Directory for 1803*, p. 97; *Prothocol Books*, No. 1068, 24 February 1802.

36 Margaret J. E Steven, 'Robert Campbell, Colonial Merchant 1769–1846' (Unpublished PhD thesis, ANU, 1962), p. 137.

37 *Prothocol Books*, No. 12, 19 September 1806.

38 *Prothocol Books*, No.13, 19 September 1806.

39 See, for example, *Calcutta Gazette*, 15 January 1807; *Naval Chronicle*, vol. 19, January to June 1808, p. 192; *London Morning Post*, 10 September 1807.

40 There were several country traders named Robert Scott round this time, but this particular Robert was most likely the Robert Scott captain of the *Carnatic* in the mid-1790s, brother to William Scott, later 6th Laird of Raeburn, and cousin once removed of James Scott, the Penang entrepreneur. He was in business with James Scott and was later a member of the firm Hutton & Forbes and its subsequent reincarnations Forbes & Scott, Forbes & Brown and Brown & Co. Well respected, he was in all probability the man referred to by Raffles in a letter to Lord Minto 22 May 1811 as one of the 'best

rienced similar bad weather in the Bay at lat. 14°26´N, 'the gale increasing with a very high confused sea lightening in every direction, with constant rain'. He had to maintain the pumps in order to reach Malacca safely and, after consultation with his officers, jettisoned 260 bags of his cargo of rice. He and his two officers signed a Protest, drawn up by the 'undersigning Notary', Jan Hendrik Stecher, on 5 October 1806.[41] Scott had made a safe voyage to China and back in the *Experiment* the previous year and, although there is no record of his having reached China in 1806,[42] that was probably his original destination considering his cargo of rice, and the fact that a record number of ships tried to take advantage of the rice shortage in China that year. The *Experiment* is listed in the 1808 *East-India Register and Directory* as of 500 tons, built in Calcutta. It is also on Phipps' list of casualties to Calcutta ships as lost in 1807.[43]

An unusual consequence of a storm occurred in the case of the *Cartier*, another of the 1806 rice ships to China, late in that year. While anchored in the Macao roads, when Captain James Macfie was ashore 'on business unknown', the ship was hit by a severe gale that caused the vessel to part from her anchors. The gale and strong current forced the ship to sea. For two days the crew attempted in vain to regain Macao. Jonas James Hart, first mate, after consulting with the second officer, serang and gunner, then 'judged it best for the good of the concern to bear up for the fleet in hopes of overtaking them or if not able so to do to make the best of our way to Malacca, the port bound for in case the Master had been on board'. As the captain had been left behind, the Protest of 10 December 1806 was signed by Hart, second mate David Walker and the gunner Nicholas Phillips.[44] Presumably Macfie joined the ship in Malacca as its arrival at Calcutta from Penang with Macfie as captain early in 1807 is recorded in the *Madras Courier*.[45] The *Cartier* was a Bombay-built ship of 400 tons, owned by Fairlie, Gilmore and Co.[46]

---

informed and most respectable of our Eastern Traders in the Malay Seas' (see C. E. Wurtzburg, *Raffles of the Eastern Isles* (London, 1954), p. 141). James Horsburgh dedicated his 1821 chart of Singapore and adjacent islands to him and the country trader and merchant James Carnegie. For Carnegie's career, see F. Andrew Smith, 'James Carnegy and the "Country Trade" in Penang, c.1802–1824', *JMBRAS*, 96:1 (2023), 51–80; and for Robert Scott, see F. Andrew Smith, 'William Scott in Penang: Missing Material, Maritime Matters and More', *JMBRAS*, 94:2 (2021), 185–97.

41 *Prothocol Books*, No. 21, 5 October 1806.

42 Not in Van Dyke, *Whampoa*, Appendix 1.2b.

43 John Phipps, *A Collection of Papers, Relative to Ship Building in India … also A Report, Comprehending all the Ships and Vessels Built in India to the Present Time* … (Calcutta, 1840), p. 138.

44 *Prothocol Books*, No. 53, 10 December 1806. Van Dyke, *Whampoa*, Appendix 1.2b records the *Cartier* as having arrived at Whampoa on 17 October 1806 and as having passed through Bocca Tigris on its way back to Bengal on 23 December 1806. This latter date must be an error.

45 *Madras Courier*, 18 February 1807, p. 3.

46 *East-India Register and Directory for 1804*, p. 96. The *Cartier* was captured by the French

Captain John Harford's Protest against the weather had its origins in his missing the prevailing monsoon.[47] His vessel, *General Baird* (350 tons, built in Surat 1793),[48] set sail from Bombay with a cargo of cotton on 31 July 1806 and reached Malacca on 9 September. It departed for China on 12 September[49] but by 15 October Harford arrived at the decision that he could not make China and he would return to Malacca. He decided it was 'too late ... to attempt the usual passage by the funnel' and he did not have sufficient supplies to sail via the Eastern Passage, or, as he put it, 'by the east of Luconia'. He returned to Malacca to 'wait for a favourable monsoon', arriving on 3 November. Even that part of the voyage proved a trial. The ship experienced a 'deep confused swell from the north east, as also from the south west, the said ship pitched so deep as to drive the rudder off her counter'. Harford was concerned that he would lose the rudder altogether as he 'experienced the most severe weather [he] ever knew' and had 'reason to suppose that some of the cargo may be damaged'. He protested against 'the wind and weather and the exceeding uncommon sea'.

Harford was careful to mention the legal requirements of a Protest but there are several peculiar features of this rather wordy one. It stated that it was made in 'the first port after the loss' and within twenty-four hours of arrival at Malacca but it was not actually signed until 29 November. It appears to have been made twice, neither time before the notary, but once before the master attendant J. M. B. Alms and again before William Farquhar, the commandant at Malacca. The English-language statement was not entered into the records by the Dutch officials until 29 January 1807.

Harford had taken the Bombay ship *Asia* (built 1797) to China in 1804 and 1805 and made a successful voyage to China in the *General Baird* in 1807. Before becoming a country trader he had had a career in the Royal Navy, serving as lieutenant. He died on 4 November 1808 at Penang.[50]

---

brig *L'Adèle* in October 1807, renamed the *Caravan* and recaptured in May 1809 by HMS Fox: *Asiatic Annual Register*, vol. 11, 1809, p. 103.

47 *Prothocol Books*, No. 67 ½, 8 January 1807.

48 *East India Register and Directory for 1808*, p. 301, though Van Dyke, *Whampoa*, Appendix 1.2b, gives the size as 600 tons. The *General Baird* had a reputation as a bad sailer. After its trip to China in 1805 the agents of the owner, Francis Wappers, told him that the ship had been damaged in a typhoon, that nobody would entrust their goods to it and that the vessel was too small for the trade: Bulley, *Bombay Country Ships*, pp. 202–3.

49 Seven days out from Malacca, near the Singapore Strait, the *General Baird* came across the shipwrecked Captain Frazer Sinclair and crew of the *Forbes*, in three boats. Sinclair recorded that Captain Harford, 'with his wonted liberality supplied them with everything requisite for their further progress to Malacca': Horst H. Liebner and David van Dyke, 'An account of the loss of the Country Ship *Forbes* and Frazer Sinclair, her late Commander', *Wacana, Journal of the Humanities of Indonesia*, 17:1 (2016), 38–67, at p. 52.

50 Van Dyke, *Whampoa*, Appendix 1.2b; *Madras Courier*, 7 December 1808; Three Decks Forum, <https://threedecks.org/index.php?display_type=show_crewman&id=8032> [Accessed 15 April 2025].

There are no more storm damage Protests recorded by British ships at Malacca until January 1812 when the *Providence*[51] was hit by a gale on 3rd and 4th of that month during the northeast monsoon as it sailed through the South China Sea to Malacca from Manila. In his Protest of 13 January[52] Captain George Mann said he had 'every reason to suppose the cargo must be damaged' and provided details of the gale and accompanying heavy seas with the ship labouring and 'taking in a great deal of water'. He described how the crew managed the sails to prevent any damage to the ship itself and how they kept the pumps going every hour, or even half hour at times.

The *Ganges* was a Calcutta-built brig of 140 tons. In a Protest dated 9 March 1812, marked by the Dutch authorities as having been entered into the books on 10 March, nearly two weeks after the initial Protest note of 24 February,[53] the ship's captain, Joseph Peters, his supercargoes J. W. Hudson and Thomas Bacon, as well as W. Winter and J. Theodore, first and second mates, protested against damage suffered as a consequence of heavy squalls, rain and 'dark weather' during a voyage from Malacca towards Surabaya on the coast of Java. This Protest is a ten-page 'Extract from the Log Book' with details of weather, bearings and damage to the ship written in paragraph form. While not always decipherable, noted landmarks include the Carimons, the Brothers, Pulo Pisang and the Water Islands.

The trouble began on 13 February near Viol Island (the Portuguese name for Rabbit, now Biola Island) when in bad weather the ship 'struck' very hard and unshipped her rudder. The main mast had to be cut away and with the vessel listing to port they had 'every reason to suppose that some part of ye cargo may be damaged'. The next day the decision was taken to head back to Malacca as the nearest port. In a strong tide carrying them towards Tree Island (now Pulau Nipa)[54] they lost the kedge anchor, but continued on their course, pumping 'as most needful' as the ship made a constant 1 inch of water per hour, to arrive at Malacca twelve days later.

Captain Peters made another Protest the following year, this time as commander of the brig *Penang*. On a voyage to Penang from Malacca it was again the main mast that failed, forcing Peters to return to Malacca to seek repairs and register Protests on 25 and 26 April 1813.[55] In strong winds and a heavy swell on the 24th several of the stays had been ripped off and sails shredded, while during the night at about 4.15 a.m. a mighty crack was heard

51 This is not the same ship as the EIC *Providence* that made a voyage to China in 1811–12.

52 *Prothocol Books*, No. 757, 13 January 1812.

53 *East-India Register and Directory for 1814*, p. 121; *Prothocol Books*, Nos 784, 9 March 1812; 776, 24 February 1812.

54 Tree Island now forms part of the Indonesian archipelagic baseline on which the Singapore-Indonesia maritime boundary is based. For a blog on the island with maps from the seventeenth century to the present, see <https://historydelocalized.blogspot.com/2015/05/> [Accessed 15 April 2025].

55 *Prothocol Books*, Nos 888, 25 April 1813; 889, 26 April 1813.

coming from the main mast. The mast had come out of the partners (the timber around the hole where the mast goes though the deck). In the morning light no breakages in the mast were seen but at 9 a.m. another loud crack was heard. Cape Rachado (now Tanjung Tuan) lay to the north-northeast and Sumatra could be sighted away to the southwest. Peters wrote in an extended note in the log:

> Found upon Examination and in the present state the main mast is in at present and the continuing hard blowing weather from NW to W that it is impossible to secure it so as to proceed on our intended voyage to Penang and after consulting together we think that for the preservation of the ship and cargo it is most advisable for us to bear up for Malacca to repair the Damage.

Peters and his chief officer R. J. Bowler confirmed their Protest 'against the wind and weather which sustained on this occasion' as entered into the records on 30 April.

Two extracts from the log of the *Little Mary* were presented to support the Protest of Captain Edward Woods concerning the misadventures of that ship which occasioned loss of time rather than damage to the vessel or cargo. While the *Little Mary* did not arrive at Malacca until 15 August 1813, the Protest being submitted the next day,[56] the first extract of the log was written on 12 July near Bintang (now Bintan), close to the Strait of Singapore. The brig, 'so small a Vessel … uncoppered … consequently very unfit to beat up against a regular Monsoon', was at that stage making a voyage from Malacca to Java but was unable to proceed further due to the strong currents and monsoon winds blowing from the east. The mast and rigging were under great strain and the captain and officers decided that, given they would not be able to complete the voyage, it was wiser to return to port rather than sustain losses and expend provisions and water.

> Under such circumstances we the undersigned have hereunto set our names, and do hereby most solemnly Protest, as far as human foresight can foresee, against the Winds, W[eathe]r and Seas, with every other impediment whatsoever, as to the hindrance of the Vessels making her passage against the present strong winds & currents.

The second extract forming part of the Protest, from Wednesday 11 August, reinforced the decision to return to Malacca after Woods was unable to obtain provisions from the vessels of the Expedition to Borneo[57] anchored under the Carimons. Many Protests were simply an outline of events and a statement

56 *Prothocol Books*, No. 919, 16 August 1813.

57 These vessels, commanded by George Sayer, were returning from the Punitive Expedition of June 1813 against the Sultanate of Sambas, designed by Raffles to break the power of the Sambas 'pirates': John Bastin, 'Raffles and British policy in the Indian Archipelago, 1811–1816', *JMBRAS*, 27:1 (1954), 84–119, at pp. 94–5.

of Protest. By contrast, Captain Woods' Protest from the log for 11 August gives the position, the conditions every hour and the actions that were taken.

Captain John Laird of the *United Kingdom* (an ex-EIC ship of 850 tons, launched in London in 1801) followed his Protest note with a Protest of 30 June 1814 also in the form of a log entry, with extensive remarks in addition to the formal details of hour, distance, course, winds, and so forth. The Protest was confirmed as entered and witnessed on 2 July.[58] Laird described how on the night of 13 June, on a voyage from India to China, in the Bay of Bengal between Sauger Roads (at the mouth of the Hooghly) and the Strait of Malacca the vessel was hit by a gale from the west-southwest. At 9.30 p.m. when they sounded the depth of water in the hold they found it to be 3 feet 10 inches, although the crew had been manning the pumps since the commencement of the gale. Laird outlined the actions taken to counter the impact of the storm and successfully contain the leaks. He did not record possible damage to the cargo, but only that to the sails. The ship arrived safely at Malacca on 30 June where Laird and two officers, J. Brokeley, the first mate, and Joseph Paraysens, protested against 'Winds and weather'. Paraysens signed only with a cross. The *United Kingdom* continued its voyage to China, arriving at Whampoa on 21 July and then heading for Batavia where it arrived on 5 November.[59]

Another Protest submitted in the form of a logbook was that of Captain William Dew of the *Hope* (650 tons, built in Brazil)[60] that also ran into a severe storm in the Bay of Bengal on a voyage from Calcutta to China in July 1814. Dew and his first and third officers lodged their Protest after they made landfall at Malacca on 31 July 1814, later continuing to Whampoa where they arrived on 22 August.[61] The Protest, entered into the *Prothocol Books* on 1 August, included pages of the log for 2, 3 and 4 July as evidence of the foul weather and the action taken to preserve the ship and cargo.[62] The crew battled strong gales and rain from the southwest and were continually adjusting the sails and pumping the ship. Dew concluded that the gale 'occasioned the ship to labour very much from the violence of the weather [and] thinking the cargo may Damage thereby. We the Commander and officers do protest against the same'.

58 *Prothocol Books*, Nos 991, 992, 30 June 1814.

59 Van Dyke, *Whampoa*, Appendix 1.2b. On 7 January 1815 the *United Kingdom* embarked from Batavia for England with a cargo of coffee but, having sprung another leak in another gale, was forced to return to port on 24 January. It re-embarked on 20 March but foundered off the Cape of Good Hope on 4 August: *Java half-yearly almanac and directory for 1815*, n.p.; <https://en.wikipedia.org/wiki/United_Kingdom_(1801_EIC_ship)> [Accessed 15 April 2025].

60 *East India Register and Directory for 1816*, p. 128.

61 Van Dyke, *Whampoa*, Appendix 1.2b.

62 *Prothocol Books*, No. 999, 1 August 1814.

On 10 April 1815 Mount Tambora on Sumbawa Island erupted.[63] It was the most destructive explosion on earth for 10,000 years. Apart from the total devastation in the immediate area where 10,000 people were killed, the effects of the eruption were felt right around the world, particularly in the northern hemisphere, for the next three years. This was a result of the 'Tambora cloud' of pulverised mineral matter, gases and sulphate aerosol particles that had been blasted into the upper atmosphere. This blanket caused the earth to cool by 3° Celsius, disrupting the monsoonal patterns and triggering unseasonal droughts and floods, widespread crop failure and starvation.

The number of weather-related accidents associated with storms, groundings, strandings, leaks and collisions, reported at Malacca by British and other Europeans during the period June 1815 to September 1818 (a total of thirty-two) was two to three times higher than in any other three consecutive years.[64] Although this is a small sample it shows a definite trend: there must surely be a connection with Tambora. Yet the Protests continued to be couched in the same dead-pan language as before. That of Captain Richard Ballard of the *Asia Felix* is a good example.

In his Protest of 18 July 1815 Ballard wrote:

> Having had a very tempestuous passage from Bombay towards Malacca & the Ship having laboured much and being also much by the head I apprehend that some part of the Cargo may be damaged … & do hereby protest [against] winds and weather.[65]

The *Asia Felix* (374 tons) was a Bombay grab built at Demaun (now Daman) in 1807. At the time of the Protest it was on its way to China laden with 900 bales of Bombay cotton. It arrived at Whampoa on 5 August 1815.[66] The Protest was one made when only doubt about any damage existed, a measure to ensure that in the event the captain would be covered.

Captain Francis Balston was in a similarly cautious frame of mind when he and his first and second officers lodged a Protest, replete with irregular spelling, on 4 September 1815.[67] When sailing down the Eastern Channel (presumably the Saugor or Eastern Channel at the entrance to the River Hooghly) from Calcutta bound for China they experienced heavy swells breaking over their 680-ton cotton ship the *James Drummond* (built Demaun

63 The information on the Mount Tambora eruption is taken from Gillen D'Arcy Wood, *Tambora: The Eruption That Changed the World* (Princeton NJ, 2014).

64 See Appendix B.

65 *Prothocol Books*, No. 1101, 18 July 1815.

66 Phipps, *Collection of Papers*, p. 170; *Asiatic Journal and Monthly Register*, July to December 1815, p. 103; Van Dyke, *Whampoa*, Appendix 1.2b.

67 *Prothocol Books*, No. 1105, 4 September 1815. Before Captain Balston arrived at Malacca he had come to the rescue of Captain Daniels (q.v.) and crew of the wrecked *Athena*. Balston also lodged a Protest in 1818 as captain of the *Lady Flora*.

1800 as *Adam Smith*).[68] Water entered the vessel through the 'rudder hole' and later 'very heavy seas came in at the cabin windows which fitted the steerage'. As a result, Balston and his officers were 'of opinion the Cotton … may be dammaged by water arised from the heavy sea shipped while working down and at anchor in the eastern Channel'. He went on to state that 'we in Justification of any loss that may arise from any damage oughth to be repayed by the underwriters or those persons concerned in the cargo of the ship'. Balston need not have been too despairing. After they arrived at Whampoa on 25 September they sold 3,700 bales of their cotton.[69]

Most captains wrote their Protests in prosaic terms. Captain Kidd (or Kyd) used a more flowery turn of phrase. He began:

> To all before whom these presents shall come be it known by this Publick Instrument of Protest that on the Twenty Second day of November in the year One Thousand Eight Hundred and Fifteen, I, David Kidd, Commander of a certain ship called the Duchess of Wellington of the burthen of six hundred tons or thereabouts declared and averred for truth as follows.[70]

His ship, he went on to say, had been 'freighted by individuals for a voyage from Canton to Calcutta, and that the said ship being stout, staunch, tight and strong manned with a crew of eighty men and boys …' and well stocked with supplies, had, on the 2 November (five days after leaving Whampoa)[71] encountered a gale in the middle of the South China Sea (lat. 19°N and long. 117°E). Kidd further wrote that:

> the said declarant is of opinion that part of the cargo may be damaged from the violence of the late gale and therefore doth publickly protest and hereby protesteth for the owners of the said ship and shippers of the cargo for recovery of losses, costs, charges, expences and damages in the said ship or cargo that may arise.

He and the third officer, Kenne Volsteedt, signed the Protest.

Two months later, in January 1816, after embarking on a voyage from Calcutta to Batavia with a cargo of saltpetre, the *Duchess of Wellington* was burnt in Saugor Roads, a suspected case of arson on the part of some of the

68 126 *East-India Register and Directory for 1814*, p. 301. The *James Drummond* had also been used as a transport in the Java invasion fleet of 1811, <https://en.wikipedia.org/wiki/Transport_vessels_for_the_British_invasion_of_Java_(1811)> [Accessed 22 October 2020].

69 Van Dyke, *Whampoa*, Appendix 1.2b; *Asiatic Journal and Monthly Register*, July to December 1816, p. 103.

70 *Prothocol Books*, No. 39, 22 November 1815.

71 Van Dyke, *Whampoa*, Appendix 1.2b.

lascars. Fourteen lives were lost, including that of the captain's young nephew. Captain Kidd himself was not on the ship at the time.[72]

When the English country vessel *Experiment* (300 tons, built in Aleppee (now Alappuzha))[73] was hit by 'continuous heavy gales' in the Philippine Sea east of Luzon between 22 and 29 September 1815, Captain Silv Ramsey and his officers wrote their Protest on board on the 29th, but only lodged it at Malacca on 15 December.[74] It is not stated where they had been in the meantime but perhaps the damage was so extensive as to impede almost all progress. Some unusual features pertain to this Protest. First, the ship had departed from Guam, which in the Protest is also referred to as 'Spannse Eyland'; second, the cargo was copper; and third, there was an independent report of the *Experiment*'s distress.

During the gale that hit the ship in September 1815 Ramsey reported that the copper shifted in the hold, causing the vessel to tilt. This suggests that insufficient dunnage, or no dunnage, had been employed. With waves breaking over the ship, water rose to a depth of 4 feet in the bilge. The masts, cables, anchors and the ship's boats were damaged, as was the rudder. Sheathing too had come loose. On 25 September the crew were able to get into the hold, 'shifting the copper to bring the ship upright'. This appears to have not been totally successful for by the 28th the copper in the 'twist decks' was threatening to 'make its way thro' the sides'. The captain went on to report that 'our crew so exhausted with fatigue and several with wounds that we are unable to stow it below or open the hatches for that purpose, it is therefore deemed necessary to throw it overboard'. The next day, conditions having eased, the crew ceased the jettison and began repairing the wreckage. The captain and officers protested 'against the insurers, being well assured that the loss sustained arises from no defect in the vessel but solely from the severity of the weather encountered'.

The misadventure of the *Experiment* was reported in the *Asiatic Journal and Monthly Miscellany* of August 1816 as an extract from the logbook of the ship *General Brown*:

> Friday, Dec. 1, 1815 – At 4. H. 30 m. P.M. saw a ship to the eastward under jury masts, observing a signal of distress flying, hauled our wind towards her. At 5 h. 30 m. spoke her, when she proved to be the Experiment, Captain Ramsay, from Manilla, in June: was dismasted in a squall, off the Marian Islands on the 24th of September, intends going into Penang, to be remasted, and requested to be reported.[75]

72 *Asiatic Journal and Monthly Register*, July to December 1816, pp. 209–10.
73 *East-India Register and Directory for 1814*, p. 121.
74 *Prothocol Books*, No. 56, 15 December 1815.
75 *Asiatic Journal and Monthly Miscellany*, July to December 1816, p. 208.

Fig 7. *The Country Ship Upton Castle in Two Positions* by Thomas Luny, 1796.

As we have seen, most ships, if not confined to the archipelago, were sailing between India and China, as Captain Ramsey himself had done in the *Experiment* in 1814.[76] From Manila to Guam suggests special circumstances. In May 1815 the *Rey Fernando* was one of the last Spanish galleons to call in at Guam for supplies, plying the old route between Acapulco and Manila. Traditionally, copper destined for Manila was shipped from Acapulco as flat, round ingots. Is it possible that Captain Ramsey obtained such a cargo from the *Rey Fernando* or had he also sailed to somewhere other than Guam?[77]

A Protest could be a very brief statement indeed. A mere eleven-lines were submitted on 21 June 1816 by Captain Warren of the brig *Jane* concerning a voyage from Bengal via Penang where on 27 May 1816 'heavy squalls' led to 18 inches of water entering the 'well'. Therefore, Captain Warren protested 'against any damage the cargo may have suffered hereafter'.[78] This was the first of a flurry of Protests registered in 1816, suggesting the middle months of the year to have been very bad for storms.

Captain Forrest Hamilton of the *Earl Kellie* made a Protest concerning events on 8 June 1816 that he submitted on 24 June, but the events described are unfortunately too faint to read.[79] The *Earl Kellie* was a new ship of 520 tons built that year in Calcutta and carrying 4,000 bales of cotton to China.[80]

The *Upton Castle* from Bombay, unlike the *Earl Kellie*, was an old ship of 675 tons built in 1793.[81] Also bound to China, it ran into 'heavy squally weather' in mid-1816. Captain Henry W. Beyts 'found the ship to have made two and a half feet of water' when off the Malabar coast (lat. 9°45′N, long. 75°53′E). He described, in the extract from the log (without the exact date) that he presented as the Protest in July, all the actions the crew had taken to prevent any harm and did 'hereby Protest against all damages likely to arise from the above cause'.[82]

76 Van Dyke, *Whampoa*, Appendix 1.2b.

77 See <https://www.guampedia.com/manila-galleon-trade-route-la-nao-de-china-a-legacy-in-the-marianas/> [Accessed 15 April 2025]; 'Philippine Historical Documents in the National Archives of Mexico' (1966), p. 187. Copper had traditionally been used in the making of small denomination coinage and for bronzes, as well as for household utensils and artillery. But there may have been an increased demand as the sheathing of ships' hulls became more common in the shipbuilding industry in India.

78 *Prothocol Books*, No. 144, 21 June 1816.

79 *Prothocol Books*, No. 149, 24 June 1816.

80 Phipps, *Collection of Papers*, p. 107; *Asiatic Journal and Monthly Register*, January to June 1817, p. 79. The eventual demise of the *Earl Kellie* in 1835 after foundering, but not sinking, with the crew subsisting in the freezing North Atlantic on nothing but rats for seventeen days, is discussed by Neil Hanson, *The Custom of the Sea* (London, 1999), p. 190.

81 Phipps, *Collection of Papers*, p. 168.

82 *Prothocol Books*, No. 152, 5 (or possibly 8) July 1816; This was the last of the *Upton Castle*'s many trips to China as the ship fell a victim to arson at Saugor shortly after her return, on 16 February 1817: *Asiatic Journal and Monthly Register* July to December 1817, p. 309. Beyts was a native-born country captain who was at the time working for Forbes and

About the same time in mid-1816 the *Bombay Castle* (another new ship, 602 tons, built in 1816 at Cochin) ran into bad weather soon after departing Calcutta with 5,000 bales of cotton aboard.[83] On 14 July in lat. 21°21′N and long. 88°29′E the vessel began pitching and labouring badly. The pumps were started and continued to be used for several days. The vessel was still shipping much water on 21 July. In a brief ten-line statement submitted on 23 August 1816,[84] supposedly 'an abstract from the log book of the ship', Captain Walter Cleland and Second Officer P. Campbell were obliged to protest 'against all such damage as may have happened to the cargo during the bad weather'.

The *Ruparell* (318 tons, built in Demaun 1807)[85] also ran into bad weather on 9 November 1816 soon after leaving China on the voyage back to Bombay during the northeast monsoon. The following morning at 10 o'clock, when off Cochin China and in sight of Black Jack Rocks (lat. 13°15′N, long. 109°37′E), Captain (F. D.?) Briggs wrote a Protest in the ship's log in the presence of the first and second mates 'against the said gale of winds which have occasioned such damages … [and] losses to the ship and cargo'. He described 'a Mountainous confused swell', with the water continuing to come in and gaining on the pumps as the ship almost lay over on her side. He tabled two pages of the log in Malacca on 23 November as evidence of the conditions, the actions taken and the damage inflicted.[86]

The year 1817 also provided challenges.

The *Charlotte* (650 tons, built in Bombay 1803),[87] *en route* to China from Bombay, seems to have run into bad weather in the Strait of Malacca in May 1817. Captain C. James Stevenson, in a now barely decipherable record, protested on the 28th against any damage to the ship and cargo.[88] The faintness of the entry does not enable us to establish the full details of the conditions and the voyage, but the damage probably ensured that the ship proceeded no further than Malacca. Bulley, who provides many details of the ship's career up until 1825, does not record it as going to China in 1817.[89]

Company. He went on to purchase his own country trader ship and later became superintendent of the floating establishment of the Custom House and a commissioner of the Court of Requests at Bombay: Bulley, *Bombay Country Ships*, p. 201; *Bombay Calendar and Almanac,* 1843, p. 45.

83 Phipps, *Collection of Papers*, p. 170; *Asiatic Journal and Monthly Register*, January to June 1817, p. 79.

84 *Prothocol Books*, No. 174 (?), 23 August 1816.

85 The *Ruparell* was still operating in the 1840s and was listed in the *Bombay Calendar and Almanac* for 1842 as a barque of this description.

86 *Prothocol Books*, No. 213, 23 November 1816.

87 *East-India Register and Directory for 1804*, p. 269.

88 *Prothocol Books*, No. 290, 28 May 1817.

89 Bulley, *Bombay Country Ships*, pp. 127–8. The *Charlotte*, which in 1804 had taken part in the Battle of Pulo Aur, was one of the few ships to have had a long working life. It was finally driven ashore and wrecked in June 1851 after losing its anchors about 30 miles

Captain Robert Graham made a short Protest on 12 August 1817 concerning the bad weather his ship *Cornwallis* (784 tons, probably built in Surat in 1790) ran into on a voyage from Bombay to China.[90] The ship had left Bombay on 12 July, presumably carrying cotton. Graham spoke of the 'frequent severe squalls' and very high Westerly swells on the Malabar Coast on 13 July that resulted in 'much water' entering the ship, requiring pumping every two or three hours. He protested 'against the abovementioned weather should any damage accrue to ship or cargo thereby'.

July 1817 resembled the tempestuous July of the previous year. Two other captains, Atkinson and Ramsey, lodged Protests against the damaging seas at that time. Captain Thomas Jasper Atkinson and Chief Officer Kirton of the relatively small brig *Hibernia* of Bombay (156 tons, launched 1808) tabled an extract from the ship's log for 19 July on 16 August 1817 when they reached Malacca.[91] Disappointingly, the details are unreadable.

---

south of Bombay, while carrying a cargo from Calcutta: <https://en.wikipedia.org/wiki/Charlotte_(1803_ship)> [Accessed 15 April 2025]. The newspaper report of the time refers to the ship as a barque: *Indian News and Chronicle of Eastern Affairs*, 1851, pp. 349, 350.

90 *East-India Register and Directory for 1816*, p. 321; *Prothocol Books*, No. 325, 12 August 1817. The *Cornwallis* was listed as a Bombay ship in the *East-India Register and Directory* from 1803 onwards. Captain Graham had been the commander on at least three previous voyages to Whampoa, 1809–10, 1811–12 and 1812. It is not known if the ship arrived in Whampoa in 1817: as with the *Charlotte*, Bulley does not record it as going to China that year. The *Cornwallis* was also similar to the *Charlotte* in having a long career. Laden with cotton for China, it was burnt in Bombay harbour in 1841, perhaps wilfully set on fire: Van Dyke, *Whampoa*, Appendix 1.2b; Bulley, *Bombay Country Ships*, p. 124; *Nautical Magazine and Naval Chronicle*, 1847, vol. 16, p. 588. There is confusion in the Wikipedia article <https://en.wikipedia.org/wiki/Cornwallis_(1789_ship)> [Accessed 15 April 2025] between two separate private ships called *Cornwallis*. It is clear that the country trader *Cornwallis*, with Captain Graham battling a storm on the Malabar coast in July and recording his Protest in Malacca in August 1817, could not have been the *Cornwallis*, Captain Brown, at Madras on 10 July 1817 *en route* for London, supposedly for the EIC. This latter *Cornwallis* was actually a transport ship carrying invalids and 'limited' HMS and EIC servicemen. There was also a third *Cornwallis* at the time, Captain Huntley, operating between London and the Cape of Good Hope: *Asiatic Journal and Monthly Register*, January to June 1818, pp. 99, 199, 211, 517.

91 Phipps, *Collection of Papers*, p. 103; *Prothocol Books*, No. 327, 16 August 1817. Three years later Captain Atkinson and the *Hibernia* fell victim to the great storm of the 8, 9 and 10 May 1820 that ravaged both the Malabar and Coromandel coasts. The storm was reported round the world: 'The weather was uncommonly tempestuous in the Bay of Bengal at the change of the monsoon and it was supposed that the destruction of vessels and loss of property and lives was greater than had ever before been experienced in one season', the gales 'equally severe on the western coast of the peninsula': *Norwalk Gazette*, vol. 3, No. 38, 17 January 1821, p. 2. Atkinson, who had left Bombay on 8 May was drowned off Cape Ramus, near Goa. His young wife and infant daughter had embarked on the same day for Madras and Bengal on the *Hope*, Captain Denman, which was also lost, though the passengers were saved. Unusually, Atkinson had been headed for Kamschatka. He belonged to a successful London merchant family (two

Captain S. Ramsay of the *Good Hope* (388 tons, built in Calcutta 1806) tabled a short Protest on 26 August 1817[92] concerning that which befell the ship on a journey from Calcutta during the last weeks of July:

> From the leaving the Pilot till the 3rd August a continuance of Blowing Stormy weather with a most destructive sea. This labouring greatly shipping at times heavy seas, and making water, from which there is every reason to apprehend that the cargo must be damaged. We the undersigned note this as a Protest against the Insurers for what injury the Ship or Cargo may have sustained.

In October 1817, having survived a grounding four months earlier (described in the following chapter), the brig *Christina* sank off the Carimon Islands during a voyage from Calcutta to Java. Captain Robert Deans having drowned, the Protest on 24 October 1817 was signed by First Officer James Galway and Thomas Vaughan, the second mate.[93] The sinking of the vessel occurred rapidly when hit by a sudden squall in the Malacca Strait, perhaps more forceful than usual: 'the violence & suddenness of said squall of wind totally overset & sunk the said Brig Christina in so short a time as to render all affords useless for the preservation of the said Brig & Cargo.' The two officers, having arrived at Malacca on the *Hope* under Captain Kidd, solemnly protested 'against the Winds & Weather, and do hold the Insurers of the said Brig & Cargo responsible for all losses, costs & Damages that have been sustained by the said Wind and Weather'. They declared they and ship's company had done all in their power to prevent the damages.

The loss of the *Christina* was reported in detail by the *Asiatic Journal*, the report providing the 'human element' that the Protest, typical of its kind, lacked. Not only was Captain Deans drowned, but so were his wife and child and about thirty of the crew, some of whom 'were going round to join the new ship building works at Java for Messrs. Deans, Scott and Co.'.[94] Presum-

of his brothers were knighted) but one wonders whether there was also a connection with another less elevated London Atkinson family of the time who called themselves Russian merchants: *Asiatic Journal and Monthly Register*, July to December 1820, pp. 399, 502–3; *Asiatic Journal and Monthly Register* January to June 1821, p. 85; John Burke, *A Genealogical and Heraldic Dictionary of the Landed Gentry of Great Britain and Ireland*, vol. 3 (London, 1850), pp. 9–10; Sally Hayles, 'Charles Atkinson', <https://siberiansteppes.files.wordpress.com> [Accessed 15 April 2025].

92 John Phipps, *A Guide to the Commerce of Bengal for the Use of Merchants, Ship Owners, Commanders … Resorting to the East Indies* (Calcutta, 1823), p. 91; *Prothocol Books*, No. 334, 26 August 1817. The captain is given as S. Ramsay in *East-India Register and Directory for 1819*, p. 134, while a Sylvester Ramsay is listed as mariner of Calcutta on page 164, suggesting that Captain Ramsay of the *Good Hope* is probably the same man as Captain Silv Ramsay (q.v.) of the *Experiment*.

93 *Prothocol Books*, No. 355, 24 October 1817.

94 *Asiatic Journal and Monthly Register*, January to June 1818, p. 607.

ably Captain Robert Deans was a relative of John Deans who had established Deans, Scott and Co. a few years earlier with Robert Scott.

Unfortunately, while there are two entries for 1818 that initiate Protests before the notary Anthony Stecher, the detailed Protests themselves are not included. Captain George Hammett of the *Shah Byramgore* (550 tons, built in Calcutta 1800, also known as *Byramgore*)[95] lodged a Protest note on 12 August, before the British handover of Malacca to the Dutch,[96] and John Gray Duncan, captain of the *Lady Sophia* (319 tons, built in Calcutta 1813), did the same on 10 September, after the handover.[97] Both ships had departed Calcutta (the *Shah Byramgore* on 1 June)[98] and had reached China by October when both captains signed a testimonial in Canton to James Horsburgh for services rendered to navigation.[99] It is most likely that both Protests concerned bad weather in the Bay of Bengal.

On 15 February 1819 Captain James Thomas Anderson, commander of the *Mary Ann* submitted a copy of the ship's log, after the initial Protest note, in respect of the damages suffered on a voyage from Manila destined for Madras.[100] Squally weather, rain and high seas made the ship 'roll her gunnels', 'labor and strain very much', and to ship a great deal of water on 28 January 1819. Anderson described the various manoeuvres employed to deal with the storm. In the middle of his copy of the ship's journal of 29 January he wrote:

> A Noted Protest. I Jas. Thos. Anderson Master of the Ship Mary Ann, do solemnly Protest and declare in consequence of the violence of the sea, it apparently has done considerable damage to the hull, masts & Yards etc. of the aforesaid ship which caused her to make water in various places and I the

95 *East-India Register and Directory for 1816*, p. 322. The *Shah Byramgore* was featured unfavourably in an article of the time arguing for the superiority of Bombay-built ships over those built in Calcutta: 'The *Byramgore*, a ship built in Calcutta in 1797 or 1798, had a complete repair in Bombay in 1815, without which she must have fallen to pieces': *Asiatic Journal and Monthly Register*, July to December 1819, p. 447. In April 1820 it was severely damaged in a tremendous storm off Madras, probably the same weather system that destroyed the *Hibernia*, and next year it was condemned and broken up in Calcutta: *Asiatic Journal*, July to December 1820, pp. 391–3; Phipps, *Collection of Papers*, p. 144. Phipps and *The East-India Register and Directory* give a build date of 1800. Confusingly, there were other ships with the same name. For a discussion of these, particularly the one built in 1818, see Ross Shardlow, 'The Byramgou Cup and the Extermination of Pirates', *Maritime Heritage Association Journal*, 19:3 (2008), 12–19.

96 *Prothocol Books*, No. 484, 12 August 1818.

97 Phipps, *Collection of Papers*, pp. 105, 144; *Prothocol Books*, No. 499, 10 September 1818.

98 *Asiatic Journal and Monthly Register*, July to December 1818, p. 647.

99 *Asiatic Journal and Monthly Register*, January to June 1819, p. 673.

100 *Prothocol Books*, Nos 587, 588, 15 February 1819. Anderson died on 12 February 1847 in Jaffna, Ceylon, aged sixty-eight: *Allen's Indian Mail*, 1847, p. 301; <https://cdfhs.org/the-anderson-name-in-the-british-ceylon-widow-and-orphans-fund-records/> [Accessed 19 May 2023].

> aforesaid Jas. Thos. Anderson do verily believe that some part of the Cargo must have received considerable damages from the violence of the Sea, causing the ship to make water in several parts of the upper works and I the aforesaid do further positively declare that all losses and damages that has now or may hereafter be found shall, must and ought to be borne by the Freighters, Owner or underwriters, of the aforesaid ship and I the aforesaid do further Protest & declare that it is neither through the Negligence of Him, his officers, or crew as the aforesaid Ship set sail from Manilla well manned & sound, her hatches closely covered and fit to Proceed to execute her Present voyage. Witness our hands this 29 Day of January 1819.

The pumps were manned but water continued to enter the ship and by 30 January, for the safety of the ship and the crew, it was found necessary 'to throw part of the Cargo over board'. After dispatching 400 bags of sugar in this way and by keeping the ship before the wind the vessel did not 'labour so much nor make so much water'. The Protest was confirmed as entered in the records by the captain, the first mate, John Williams and the supercargo, Abraham Tyndall.

The *Indian*[101] was on a somewhat different course to most of the other vessels when it ran into foul weather crossing the Pacific from South America. Captain John Reid and his officers lodged Protests at Malacca on 12 and 13 November 1819 concerning the damage the ship had suffered between 23 and 27 October 1818 when travelling in a westerly direction.[102] The exact location is not given as it was impossible to take an observation. But the gale meant the loss of boats, sails, rigging and copper sheathing with the ship 'plunging and rolling very much'. The pumps were used continually during the five days of severe storm.

Captain W. P. (William Peacock) Fulcher of the *Asia* (492 tons, launched in Calcutta 1816) made a far shorter, one-page Protest on 22 November 1819 after his ship arrived at Malacca on 21 November following a rough passage from China.[103] He wrote of the 'confused' and 'heavy' seas that made the ship 'lurch very deep in the water to strike her with great violence'. Apprehensive that water had entered the hold, he and his officers protested against the above causes should any cargo be found damaged.

The voyage from Bombay *en route* to Canton in 1820 in the *Shah Byramgore* (791 tons, launched Calcutta 1818) was sufficiently arduous for Captain (John

101 Not the same *Indian* as the ship of that name which had been involved in the Protest of Ally Goelam (q.v.) in 1811 (Protest No. 737) and that had sprung a leak in 1813 (Protest No. 342) as that ship had been lost in 1817.

102 *Prothocol Books*, Nos 944, 12 November 1819; 945, 13 November 1819.

103 Phipps, *Collection of Papers*, p. 107; *Prothocol Books*, Nos 1298, 1299, 22 November 1819. William Peacock Fulcher died at Calcutta on 22 July 1820: *Asiatic Journal and Monthly Register*, January to June 1821, p. 180; Holmes & Co., *Bengal Obituary or a Record to Perpetuate the Memory of Departed Worth …* (London, 1851), p. 139 <https://wellcomecollection.org/works/u973e2dw> [Accessed 15 April 2025].

C.) Crockett to lodge a Protest at Malacca on 23 May of that year.[104] In the Indian Ocean at lat. 9°23′N, according to the copy of the ship's log for 7, 8 and 9 May which he tabled in evidence, the ship ran into 'Fresh gales with severe squalls and high Sea from the SSE'. He spoke of the 'confused' sea and of the damage to the ship and cargo over three days. Crockett had fallen foul of the renowned storm of May 1820, which crippled the other *Shah Byramgore* and destroyed the *Hibernia*.[105]

Captain Robert Carter tabled his ship's log from 29 June to 3 July 1820 as evidence for his Protest at Malacca on 19 July against bad weather and rough seas.[106] His ship, described in Dutch, not as a 'particuliere' vessel as in most of the earlier Protests but as 'het Engelsch koopvaardij schip' (the English merchant vessel), the *Sulimany* (679 tons, built in Demaun 1799),[107] ran into 'frequent squalls' with 'constant rain' near the Great Coco Island (just north of the Andamans) on her voyage from Bengal to China. The squalls developed into strong gales with heavy rain so that by Sunday 2 July the ship was 'pitching very deep at times', causing the pumps to be employed. Carter and his second officer, Richard R. Down signed the Protest into the records. The safe arrival of the ship in Canton with the first of the Bengal cotton crop was recorded on 5 October.[108]

The *Matilda* was a new ship of 250 tons, launched in Calcutta on 23 November 1820.[109] It was travelling in a southeasterly direction through the South China Sea on 9 May 1821 when it was struck by a 'very hard squall' from the northwest that caused the ship to 'labour' very much and become 'very crank' (that is, liable to capsize). Action was taken with the sails to ease the situation and the pumps were used to reduce the 'great quantity of water in the twixt decks rolling about'. Captain John Marchant and his officers included in the log for that day a Protest against the wind and weather 'as the cause of whatever damage may be found in the twixt decks or the Hold'. Matters did not improve, however, and in the abstract of the logbook for 31 May, submitted as part of the Protest on 27 June,[110] the ship was still

104 Phipps, *Collection of Papers*, p. 109; *Prothocol Books*, No. 85, 23 May 1820. This was a different ship to that captained by George Hammett in 1818. Bulley, *Bombay Country Ships*, in her numerous references to the *Shah Byramgore* has confused the two ships.

105 Crockett's *Shah Byramgore* was lost on 17 November 1827 on a coral reef off Laccadive Island when returning from China with a valuable cargo. Crockett himself died on 25 June 1837, aged fifty, at Macao where he was in command of an opium stores ship at Lin Tin. See the short biography of Crockett given by Ross Shardlow, 'Byramgou Cup'.

106 *Prothocol Books*, No. 138, 19 July 1820.

107 Phipps, *Guide*, p. 85. This ship with its many spelling variations is the same ship as the *Soolymany* captained by Thomas Dixie Finey (q.v.) in 1811. For more on the *Sulimany*, see Bulley, *Bombay Country Ships*, p. 126.

108 *Bombay Courier*, 16 December 1820.

109 Phipps, *Collection of Papers*, p. 110.

110 *Prothocol Books*, No. 97, 27 June 1821.

'laying over very much' and was 'Labouring very heavy' with the pumps still employed. It was then that the foremast 'sprung' about six feet above the deck because of the ship 'pitching very heavy'. Captain Marchant consulted with his officers, T. R. Court and Charles Fox, as to whether they should struggle on to Calcutta or 'proceed to the first port' to purchase a new mast. The latter course of action decided upon, the ship called at Malacca where the Protest of 27 June against the wind and the weather for the loss of the foremast was confirmed on 30 June.[111]

Taken together, the Protests relating to bad weather provide a clear picture of the severity of the storms in the Bay of Bengal, the squalls in the vicinity of the Malacca Strait and the typhoons in the South China Sea, sometimes including very detailed meteorological observations. The timing of the 'weather' accidents during the voyages to and from China clearly delineates the sailing patterns. *En rout*e to China, almost all the ships that ran foul of storms did so in the Bay of Bengal between the months of May and August, when the southwest monsoons were strongest. They made their Protests at Malacca, undertook any necessary repairs and continued to Whampoa. The *City of Goa* stands out as an anomaly, being forced to abandon the trip to China and return to Malacca from the Philippine Sea in October 1794, having been caught in storms around the Great Ladrone. This was only a little earlier in the year than the *Anna* and the *Travancore* caught in similar storms on their return trip from China. The gamble taken by the captain of the *City of Goa* to continue to China after considerable early delays had not paid off. The idea was for the ships to arrive at Whampoa in time to sit out the worst of the typhoon season and depart around November or December with the northeast monsoon. The storm damage reported by ships at Malacca returning from China almost invariably occurred somewhere in the South China Sea or Philippine Sea in the months of November to January. (The *Matilda* is another anomaly. Why it was headed south when it suffered storm damage in the South China Sea in May 1821 is not specified in the Protest.)

The Protests also describe the actions of the commanding officers in keeping their vessels afloat and preserving, as far as possible, their cargoes. Many of the captains and other declarants described the specific damage sustained by their ships – loss of anchors, ropes and buoys, damaged or lost masts and sails, loss of boats, loss of copper sheathing, unshipping of the rudder, leaks and water in the hold. The amount of water entering the ship was often specified and emphasis placed on the efforts put into pumping. To forestall any suggestion of weakness in the ship itself the captains frequently

111 The *Matilda* was lost in April 1823 when it hit a rock at the entrance to the port of Mozambique. Marchant, himself from Mozambique, died a few months later: *Asiatic Journal and Monthly Register*, January to June 1824, pp. 286, 561; *Oriental Magazine*, July to December 1823, p. xxix.

designated their vessels as initially sound and well-manned. Solicitous of their cargo, they were careful to report in general terms any possible damage to it.

The Protests, however, are not a good source of information about the specifics of the cargoes. Of the forty British Protests against the weather, eleven made no mention of damage to cargo; twelve cited 'possible' cargo damage, including two to a cargo of cotton; nine stated positive damage to the cargo without giving any details. Only in four cases do we learn from the Protests what the damaged cargo was: from the smell of arrack coming from the hold of the *Anna*, and the jettisoning of rice from Captain Scott's *Experiment*, copper from Captain Ramsey's *Experiment* and sugar from the *Mary Ann*. (The remaining four cases are unreadable.)

2

Perils of the Sea (Groundings and Strandings)

A grounding is when a ship strikes the seabed, while a stranding is when the ship then remains there for some length of time.

Running aground could be one of the most disastrous misadventures to befall a ship, the situation requiring prompt and strong action by the officers as the vessel could quickly break up. Furthermore, as the crisis evolved the crew could become disorderly. Sailing across the open seas of the Bay of Bengal presented few dangers of groundings. But weaving one's way through the Andaman Archipelago, the South China Sea and the straits of the Malay Archipelago was a different matter. It was a beautiful region of verdant tropical islands, sandy beaches and azure seas but presented numerous navigational challenges. Between 1805 and 1819, there were fourteen Protests lodged by British country traders at Malacca relating to groundings or strandings, ten of which occurred in the Malacca Strait or the Singapore Strait.

Surprisingly, in his *India Directory*, starting from the first edition of 1809–11, Horsburgh downplayed the dangers in the Malacca Strait: 'To persons unacquainted, Malacca Strait appears an intricate navigation, but as the channels are mostly spacious, with good anchorage, it is certainly not dangerous, if common prudence is observed. Many ships keep under way day and night, in most parts of the strait, and often pass through, without anchoring above once or twice.'[1]

Why then, at the turn of the nineteenth century were vessels still running aground in Malay waters? What were the navigation tools available?

Indigenous charts and navigation techniques existed in the Malay world well before European seamen arrived.[2] The Chinese compass was widely used and local nakhodas made use of maps. In fact, 'maritime trade networks'

1 James Horsburgh, *India Directory, Or, Directions for Sailing to and from the East Indies, China, New Holland, Cape of Good Hope, Brazil, and the Interjacent Ports …*, 2nd edn (2 vols, London 1817), vol. 2, pp. 147–8.

2 Anthony Reid, *Southeast Asia in the Age of Commerce 1450-1680: Volume Two, Expansion and Crisis* (New Haven CT, 1993), pp. 43–7; J. V. and J. V. G. Mills, 'Arab and Chinese Navigators in Malaysian Waters in about A.D. 1500', *JMBRAS*, 47:2 (1974), 1–82.

had existed in Southeast Asia for at least 2,000 years.[3] However, there is no evidence in the Protests that the country traders sailing between India and Canton were routinely making use of local navigators, although it is possible that such guides were used but rate a mention only when their advice was interpreted as having had a disastrous outcome. In the case of the 1818 loss of the *Vestal*, Captain Elliott did attempt to use the local knowledge of a Malay *datuk* to return to recover his vessel, but the Malay chief proved unreliable. Captain Deans was equally misled by the Surabaya pilot who guided the *Christina* to a grounding in 1817. Neither is there any evidence in the Protests that the British country traders made use of Spanish and Portuguese charts and navigation aids *per se*. These had been published since the sixteenth century using pilots' logbooks and 'reconnaissance charts'. The charts were accompanied by 'rutters', which 'gave pilots advice and instructions on the different routes in the Atlantic Ocean, the Indian Ocean and the Asian waters'.[4]

It may be helpful to distinguish between country traders who sailed between India and Canton, mostly on larger vessels and passing through the Strait of Malacca only twice a year at the most, and those country traders who sailed regularly within the Malay Archipelago. The latter had established a long tradition of employing people from the region as guides or cooperating with them to safely navigate the waterways: Thomas Forrest recruited the knowledgeable and well-connected Tuan Haji as guide for his voyage to the Moluccas (now Maluku) in 1774–6, though it was probably as much for the contacts and introductions as for the nautical directions. In 1795 Robert Lauder with his vessel the *Duchess* resided for eight months on the eastern Indonesian island of Gebe under the protection of the local ruler Nuku. He continued to trade and sail in the Moluccas for the next ten years under Nuku's protection.[5] Forrest and other pioneers such as Francis Light, James Scott and Thomas Sadler had built up a personal knowledge of the seas of the archipelago. They could make sinuous voyages throughout the islands calling at minor ports with an apparent degree of certainty. For example, Sadler on his final voyage in the *Transfer* in 1795, after twelve years' experience as a country trader, called at Penang, Natal, Padang, Bencoolen (now Bengkulu), Batavia, Pontianak, Mempawah, and Banka.[6] This expertise did

3 Geoff Wade, 'The Pre-Modern East Asian Maritime Realm: An Overview of European-Language Studies', in Satish Chandra and Himanshu Prabha Ray (eds), *The Sea, Identity and History: From the Bay of Bengal to the South China Sea* (Singapore, 2013), pp. 93–136, at pp. 93, 96.

4 Kees Zandvliet, *Mapping for Money: Maps, plans and topographic paintings and their role in Dutch overseas expansion during the 16th and 17th centuries* (Amsterdam, 1998), p. 18.

5 W. G. Miller, *British Traders in the East Indies 1770–1820: 'At Home in the Eastern Seas'* (Woodbridge, 2020), pp. 65–6.

6 W. G. Miller, 'Why Did Syarif Kassim Kill Captain Sadler at Mempawah in 1795?', *JMBRAS*, 85:1 (2012), 63–84, at p. 71.

not go unrecognised: captains of East Indiamen and even the British Navy depended at times on the experience and knowledge of the 'local' country traders. The British attack on Padang in 1781 using East Indiamen would not have been successful without the acknowledged guidance of local country trader William Kerton along the west coast of Sumatra.[7] It is also well-established that the route used by the British fleet that invaded Java in 1811 was surveyed and recommended by 'local' country traders.[8]

Although published guides were available to everyone, the captains who sailed the larger country trader vessels between India and China might not have had as much practical experience of the section of the route between the eastern rim of the Indian Ocean and Canton that local country traders might have had. The most spectacular loss by stranding reported at Malacca was that of the *Abercromby*, which sank off Billiton (now Belitung) in 1812. It was a large ship, 1,280 tons, brand new, built at Bombay the previous year and on its maiden voyage to China. The captain, David Brown, had taken the *Thomas Henchman* to China and back twice in 1809–10;[9] otherwise he remains elusive. Horsburgh labelled his night-time navigation in an area of known dangers as imprudent. The tragedy was regarded as a major nautical event at the time and the detailed report of the loss in the *Calcutta Monthly Journal* for November 1812 was republished verbatim as a lengthy note by John Purdy in his *Tables … to accompany the 'Oriental Navigator'*.[10] The 800-ton *Triton* was another China ship lost in a similar way. However, it is only fair to say that the larger ships more commonly reported a misfortune at Malacca because of storm damage rather than grounding.

For determining the exact position of their ship at any one time, the India-China country traders appear to have depended on the currently available European navigation methods. However, while the late eighteenth century saw a number of significant improvements in methods of determining a ship's position, at the beginning of the nineteenth century there were still many gaps in navigational knowledge in general and an understanding of the seas of the Malay Archipelago in particular. This would certainly help account for those misadventures where a ship ran aground or was wrecked on a reef.

The chronometer had been perfected during the 1780s. It improved the ability of seafarers to determine their longitudinal position much more reli-

7 Miller, *British Traders*, pp. 101–4.

8 C. E. Wurtzburg, 'Who Planned the Sea Route of the Java Expedition in 1811?', *The Mariner's Mirror: The Journal of the Society for Nautical Research*, 37 (1951), 104–8, at p. 104; Miller, *British Traders*, p. 137.

9 *Calcutta Monthly Journal*, July 1809, p. 23; Paul A. Van Dyke, *Whampoa and the Canton Trade: Life and Death in a Chinese Port* (Hong Kong, 2020), Appendix 1.2b.

10 Horsburgh, *India Directory* (1817), vol. 2, p. 358 fn; John Purdy, *Tables of the Positions, or of the Latitudes and Longitudes of Places, Composed to Accompany the 'Oriental Navigator', or Sailing Directions for the East Indies, China, Australia Etc …* (London, 1816), note 16, p. 128.

ably than by the traditional method of 'dead reckoning' that was complicated as well as in lacking accuracy.[11] However, it is probable that country traders only adopted the use of chronometers gradually. Captain Alexander Henning of the *Hammudy* stated in a letter attached to his 1818–19 log that he did not have one aboard. No doubt a few of the traders may have been able to acquire one, for there had been approximately 5,000 instruments manufactured by 1815.[12] The *Diana*, for example, is said to have had 'chronometers' on board when she was wrecked in 1817, being among the priority items rescued when the ship began to sink.[13] As the *Diana* belonged to John Palmer, the wealthy 'Prince of Merchants', it may have been better equipped than many other country traders, though other evidence suggests that captains had to buy their own chronometers.

Chronometers were expensive, costing between £65 and £80 at that time. Even British naval officers had to pay for a chronometer out of their own pocket and ships of the Royal Navy were not officially issued with them until 1825.[14] Captains of East Indiamen could buy a chronometer in England, but not all did. Captain George Simpson of the *Ariston*, for one, could not afford it. His ship, when acting as a troop transport, became separated from its convoy during a voyage from Ceylon to England in May 1815 and owing to navigational error was wrecked on a reef near Cape Agulas, South Africa. An officer from the convoy later wrote: 'This valuable ship and all the lives on board of her, were actually sacrificed to a piece of short sighted economy. That they might have been saved, had she been supplied with the worst chronometer that was ever sent to sea, is also quite obvious.'[15]

According to Pearson, there was a 'technology lag', which meant that 'the average seaman didn't benefit until chronometers became more affordable in the mid nineteenth century'.[16] Even naval officers continued to rely on 'lunars', or dead reckoning, into the nineteenth century.[17] Dead reckoning was difficult and time consuming, and 'a complicated piece of mathematical computation was needed to ascertain the correct local time and compare it with that of the prime meridian' (Greenwich mean time). 'To do so was beyond the skills of many ships' officers, and, according to Pearson, inaccuracy in longitude calculation remained common'.[18] It can be concluded

11 Michael Pearson, *Great Southern Land: The Maritime Exploration of Terra Australis* (Canberra, 2005), p. 12.

12 Dava Sobel and William J. H. Andrewes, *The Illustrated Longitude* (London, 1998), p. 193.

13 Dorian Ball, *The Diana Adventure* (Kuala Lumpur/Groningen, 1995), pp. 14, 85.

14 Sobel, *Illustrated Longitude*, p. 192.

15 Ed Cumming (ed.), *A Compendium of Incidents Incurred by the Major Ships used by the English (later British) East India Company c.1600–c.1834* (MIBEC Publications, 2016), pp. 368–9, <https://www.nauticalarchaeologysociety.org/east-india-company-incidents> [Accessed 15 April 2025].

16 Pearson, *Great Southern Land*, p. 13.

17 Sobel, *Illustrated Longitude*, p. 192.

18 Pearson, *Great Southern Land*, p. 13–14.

therefore that, despite the appearance of chronometers and notwithstanding that Europeans had been sailing in southeast Asian waters for nearly 300 years, a number of country captains could well have been less familiar with their actual positions than one might have expected.

There was also always the possibility of the over-confidence of the officer responsible for determining the ship's position; Captain Simpson of the *Ariston*, for example, had compounded his errors by not taking soundings.[19] Such omissions might have been common: Smollett in his novel *Roderick Random* (a work based on his personal experience) describes how his fictional first officer was 'so infatuated as to neglect sounding', resulting in the ship 'striking'.[20]

To add to the poor navigation equipment available, the charting of the seas at the time, while improving, was still in an incomplete state. In 1796 Walter Caulfield Lennon on the British Navy expedition with Admiral Rainier to the Moluccas could write after the *Shah Munshy* had been lost on Pedra Branca[21] in the Strait of Singapore that 'the loss of this fine ship is the consequence of the want of proper survey of these straits'.[22] As Parkinson has said, 'That maze of islands stretching from the Malay Peninsula down to New Holland itself formed in those days a world of mystery and complexity … Vast areas were unsurveyed, ill-surveyed, or even unexplored'.[23]

During the late eighteenth century both the Dutch and French were far more organised than the British in their collection and distribution among themselves of their knowledge of the sea routes,[24] but the findings were not necessarily readily available to others. The Dutch in particular, at least earlier in the century, kept secret their hydrographical knowledge.[25] However, East Indiamen captains did have a number of published guides at their command. John Thornton's *The English pilot, describing the sea-coasts …* first appeared in 1703 and was republished regularly. According to Andrew Cook, it was used alongside Cornwall's 1720 pilot book, *Observations upon Several Voyages to India.* But these compilations were not infallible and 'owed more to commercial opportunism than to systematic analysis'. Other guides, several of which were severely criticised, included Huddart's *The Oriental Navigator …* and Elmore's *The British Mariners Directory*.[26]

19 Cumming, *Compendium*, p. 368.

20 Tobias Smollett, *Roderick Random* (London, 1927, orig. 1748), p. 209.

21 Variations on this name include Pedra Blanca, Pedro Banco and Branco.

22 Walter Caulfield Lennon, 'Journal of a voyage through the Straits of Malacca on an Expedition to the Molucca Islands … 1796', *JSBRAS*, 7 (1881), 51–74, at p. 74.

23 C. Northcote Parkinson, *Trade in the Eastern Seas 1793–1813* (Cambridge, 1937), p. 347.

24 Andrew S. Cook, 'Surveying the Seas: establishing the sea routes to the East Indies', in James R. Akerman (ed.), *Cartographies of Travel and Navigation* (Chicago IL, 2006), pp. 69–96, at p. 71.

25 Howard T. Fry, *Alexander Dalrymple (1737–1808) and the Expansion of British Trade* (London, 1970), p. 14.

26 Andrew S. Cook, 'Establishing the Sea Routes to India and China: Stages in the Development of Hydrographical Knowledge', in H. V. Bowen, Margaret Lincoln and Nigel

Alexander Dalrymple had begun undertaking surveys and collecting information about the Malay waters from the 1750s when he first arrived in India as writer to the EIC at Madras. He undertook a voyage on the *Cuddalore* to Canton in 1759 and made several other trips in the East Indies.[27] Like the country traders, he made use of local informers, in particular for his early maps of Sulu and Borneo.[28] In 1777, by about which time he had become the unofficial hydrographer to the EIC, he commenced the systematic collection of data using EIC shipping records.[29] Perhaps emphasising the danger to shipping on the route from London to Canton posed by the Malay region, one of his earliest intentions (not realised at the time) was to produce maps of the Strait of Banka, the Strait of Singapore and the Parcelar Banks in the Strait of Malacca.[30]

Based in London, Dalrymple had to depend on information from the captains of East Indiamen as well as from country traders;[31] there were few, if any, actual surveys undertaken. Dalrymple himself was aware of the limitations of this method and was not an unquestioning recipient of all the data received. In his 1782 'Memoir concerning The Passages to and from China',[32] an analysis of a wide range of routes in the Eastern Archipelago, he went to elaborate lengths to explain that his charts based on a number of outside sources were not perfect. For example, he was critical on a number of occasions about the information Thomas Forrest sent him, stating, 'It is much to be regreted that Capt. Forrest's attention has not been equal to his ability'.[33] On another occasion Dalrymple wrote, 'although I regret [Forrest's] want of accurate attention, I do not suspect his fidelity, and therefore these plans may be of use'.[34]

Succeeding Dalrymple as hydrographer to the EIC in 1810, James Horsburgh was the most prominent of the new generation of country traders in respect of navigation information compilation. Having sailed first with the EIC in 1762, he had been a country trader from 1784 until 1804 and had developed an interest in charts and sailing directions. Several charts were

Rigby (eds), *The Worlds of the East India Company* (Woodbridge, 2002), pp. 119–36, at pp. 122–3.

27 Fry, *Alexander Dalrymple*, p. 23.

28 Thomas Suarez, *Early Mapping of Southeast Asia; The Epic Story of Seafarers, Adventurers, and Cartographers Who first Mapped the Regions between China and India* (Singapore, 1999), p. 238.

29 Cook, 'Establishing the Sea Routes', pp. 128–9.

30 *Ibid.*, p. 131.

31 Fry, *Alexander Dalrymple*, p. 255.

32 Quoted in C. H. Philips and B. B. Misra (eds), *Fort William-India House Correspondence and other Contemporary Papers Relating Thereto, Vol. XV Foreign and Secret 1782–1786* (Delhi, 1963), p. 23.

33 Quoted in *Ibid.*, p. 35.

34 Introduction to *Collection of Plans of Ports in the East Indies 1779 and 1780*, 2nd edn (London, 1787) (in British Museum).

issued from 1805 in his *Memoirs*. The most comprehensive directory at the time of its publication in 1809 and 1811 was his two-volume *Directions for Sailing to and From the East Indies, China*. It was updated and republished until the eighth edition in 1864. Shortcomings continued, however. Ball states that the cause of the sinking of the *Diana* in 1817 was the inaccuracy of Horsburgh's chart of the Malacca Strait;[35] Captain Henry Elliott blamed the *Vestal*'s grounding in 1818 on misleading Horsburgh directions; and Captain Daniels believed his ship the *Athena* was lost in 1815 on rocks not 'laid down' on the (unspecified) charts.

Horsburgh's work was constantly improved by information received from country captains or officers. In this way the misfortunes of one ship could be the saviour of many. Some of those who registered Protests at Malacca had their experiences used in this way. For example, the loss of the ship *La Paix* on Bambek Shoal on 28 November 1805 was described by Horsburgh, as was its experience of shallow water in July of that year between Red Island and Tree Island, Horsburgh marking that passage 'very unsafe'.[36] In the supplement to the 1817 edition Horsburgh reinforced his recommendation to avoid Bambek Shoal citing the 1816 wreck there of the *Caroline*.[37] Abercromby Reef was named after the sinking of the forementioned country ship *Abercromby* on that reef off the east coast of Billiton in July 1812, the ship's dismasting in a tempest south of Sandalwood Island (now Sumba) in January of that year also rating a mention.[38] In his entry on Preparis Island, part of the Andaman Archipelago, Horsburgh emphasised the dangers of the reef on the west side 'which extends much further from the south end of Preparis Island than is generally represented'.[39] As evidence he related the fate of the *Athena*, which was wrecked on a rock there on 10 August 1815.

In spite of its imperfections, Horsburgh's publications were understandably highly valued by the country traders, twenty of whom presented him (albeit *in absentia*) with a piece of plate on 18 October 1818 in Canton in recognition of his services to the navigation of the Indian seas. Seven of these men were among those who had registered Protests at Malacca: Francis Balston, Robert Graham, George Nicholls, John Gray Duncan, James Stevenson, George Hammett and Thomas Dixie Finey. The letter accompanying the gift read:

> We the undersigned commanders of the ships now lying in the port of Canton, and belonging to the country service of India, being impressed with the highest respect and veneration for your zeal, ability, and arduous undertaking in compiling and amending the Indian Charts and Directory, so essential and beneficial to all classes of men trading to British India, and from which navi-

35 Ball, *Diana Adventure*, p. 84.
36 Horsburgh, *India Directory* (1817), vol. 2, pp. 174, 185.
37 *Ibid.*, vol. 2, supplement, p. 3.
38 *Ibid.*, vol. 2, pp. 358, fn 523.
39 *Ibid.*, vol. 2, p. 26.

> gators individually and generally have benefited; we do solicit your acceptance of a piece of plate … as a memorial of the regard we all entertain for your personal talents in this laudable and indefatigable work.[40]

Thus, the hydrographers and the country traders played a reciprocal role in the improvement in navigational directions.

Reliance on the input of ships' captains was gradually replaced by actual surveys undertaken for the express purpose of compiling charts. For example, charts based on the work from 1810 of navigators such as Daniel Ross of the Bombay Marine began to be published and were more accurate.[41] But it was not until the end of the nineteenth century that scientific hydrographic knowledge, in the service of colonial expansion, developed to the extent required to give adequate security to mariners in the area.[42]

The following Protests confirm the still inadequate nature of the navigational tools available and the actions taken to overcome critical situations. They also reveal instances of cooperation between ships, or the lack of it, as well as crew behaviour in times of crisis and salvaging (or scavenging) by Malays.

The Protests (fourteen cases in chronological order)

From an unclear Dutch entry in the *Prothocol Books* dated 6 June 1798,[43] it would appear that the snow *Nancy*, which had arrived at Malacca on 5 June from the coast of Borneo under the command of Captain Hugh Drysdale, had suffered a grounding at lat. 2°8′N. Although the vessel was extricated from this position, it was found to have sprung a leak necessitating constant pumping. Drysdale reported the incident and protested against any further consequences to cover himself in the event of any loss suffered.[44]

The stranding that occurred during the 1805 voyage from China to Bengal of the country ship, *La Paix* (500 tons, originally a French ship from

40 *Asiatic Journal and Monthly Register*, January to June 1819, pp. 672–3.

41 F. Andrew Smith, 'Mercantile Life in Early 19th Century Asia: the Ross Brothers', *JMBRAS*, 96:2 (2023), 49–75, at p. 55; Cook, 'Establishing the Sea Routes', pp. 135–6.

42 Eric Tagliacozzo, *In Asian Waters: Oceanic Worlds from Yemen to Yokohama* (Princeton NJ, 2022), p. 346.

43 British Library, Asia, Pacific and Africa Collections, *Malacca, General Prothocol Books (Registers of Legal Deeds) 1786–1825*, IOR: R/9/22/1–75 [referred to in this study as *Prothocol Books*], No. 430, 6 June 1798.

44 Drysdale was massacred in July 1803 during a surprise attack on the country ship that he was then commanding, the *Calcutta*, by the people of the Sambas. See Smith, F. Andrew, 'Piracy against the Sambas "Pirates"? The case of Captain Burnside – and What Happened to him Afterwards in the Antipodes', *Borneo Research Bulletin*, 40 (2009), 67–80, at p. 68. An account by J. D. Richardson was published in 1805 by the *Bombay Gazette Press*.

Bordeaux),[45] bears out the ferocity of the conditions. During the outgoing voyage to China in June, *La Paix* had experienced severe weather and had had to undergo repairs at Penang.[46] This time, on the return trip, things were worse. Commander John Wright tabled his very detailed Protest on 4 December 1805.[47] The ship had departed Malacca after the voyage from Canton at 3 a.m. on 27 November 1805 and by noon the next day was becalmed, lying at anchor off Cape Rachado. When the winds sprang up the ship tacked southwest but at 5.45 p.m. on that evening struck a shoal of sand and rock (Bambek Shoal) situated between Cape Rachado and Parcelar Point. Captain Wright's account then describes the efforts made to get the vessel off the reef by trimming the sails, casting the anchors, getting the boats out, manning the pumps and lightening the ship. He goes on to relate that he 'saw two small craft in the offing to which sent our jolly boat and cutter to procure assistance in taking out our cargo to lighten the ship, but they being loaded was of no service to us'. Wright then sent 'Captain Eggleston, a passenger from China' on one of the small craft to Malacca to engage other vessels to come and assist in unloading and lightening the ship. On board, efforts continued to try and preserve the vessel, but it remained aground, at the same time taking water and leaning on its side. On 30 November, with heavy seas, the ship was still stuck fast and 'strained herself' while continuing to take water. That afternoon a brig was sighted to which they sent a boat and made a signal of distress. It was the *Tweed* from Penang sailing eastwards. Wright agreed with the brig's Captain, Mr Valence, to pay him for remaining with *La Paix* whatever loss the underwriters agreed the *Tweed* would suffer from the detention. The situation further deteriorated and by 10 o'clock at night the ship fell further on its side and water in the hold had risen as far as the hatches on the gun deck. Very little of the cargo, supposed to be a valuable 'horde of chinaware',[48] could be saved; what little could be rescued was transferred to the *Tweed*. No assistance having arrived from Malacca and the *Tweed* being required to continue its voyage, the decision was made to cut away the masts in the hope that the wreck might not break up before Wright could get back from Malacca. The Captain went with the *Tweed* to Malacca, arriving on 1 December where he found Captain Eggleston had hired 'two vessels and a boat' that were about to depart for the *La Paix*. Wright cancelled

45 *East-India Register and Directory for1804*, p. 96; a French ship called *La Paix* was captured by HMS *Endymion* in May 1800. The ship was described as 'built for a ship of war and pierced for 29 pounders, is quite new, and sails fast': *Caledonian Mercury*, 24 May 1800, p. 2.

46 *Bengal Hurkaru*, 30 July 1805.

47 *Prothocol Books*, Nos 98, 99, 4 December 1805.

48 *Bengal Hurkaru*, 31 December 1805. The previous year the captain had brought back a cargo of superior quality tea: *Bengal Hurkaru*, 8 January 1805, p. 1. An attempt made in 1993 to find the wreck was unsuccessful: Ooi, Keat Gin, 'Maritime Treasures off Peninsular Malaysia', *Journal of Indo-Pacific Archaeology*, 36 (2015), 5–15, at pp. 8, 11.

the two vessels knowing that what could be saved would be very little while Captain Eggleston used the boat to go to *La Paix*, returning to report that 'Malays had taken possession of the ship and that he could not board her on that account'.

The ship *Jane* (300 tons) ran aground on 14 December 1807 off Lingga when approaching the port. A copy of the logbook was tabled at Malacca on 23 December as part of the Protest describing the events, signed by Commander Edward Masquerier and Chief Officer J. Kingsmill.[49] The *Jane* struck about 5 leagues off 'Linger' (Lingga) and action was taken to lighten her by moving the cargo and manipulating the anchors. The ship received 'some material damage' and 'the cable was very much cut by the rocks in heaving the ship off' and as a consequence 'the protest against any loss on behalf of the owners' was submitted to the notary. Aboard this ship were the survivors of an earlier piratical attack on the *Admiral Troubridge*.

A disastrous accident occurred at 7 a.m. on 8 September 1808 when the *Triton* (800 tons, built in England in 1787),[50] sailing from Calcutta to China under the command of Captain F. Patrick with a cargo of cotton, rattans and saltpetre, became stranded off Parcelar Hill, north of Malacca. The Protest of 4 October, which did not mention the opium the ship was said elsewhere to be carrying,[51] described how the longboat was lowered in an attempt to heave the *Triton* off the sand bank, 'but before an anchor could be laid out she swung across the tide and stuck fast'. The ship rolled violently and quickly began to fill with water, and by 4 p.m. the level in the ship had risen to 15 feet. It was feared the vessel would break up and in order to prevent this the masts were cut away. The second officer was dispatched to Malacca in the jollyboat. He arrived back on 12 September with the harbour master, accompanied by other boats, and took away fifty of the crew while another boat was able to save cables, ropes and sails. On the 16th Captain Patrick 'left the ship which had become a compleat wreck to go to Malacca to hire a vessel to save what property could be got at'. Meanwhile, things went from bad to worse. On 17 September 'six Malay prows, three large and three small attacked and took possession of the *Triton*'s longboat in which were the third officer, gunner and six lascars', and threatened to

49 *Prothocol Books*, No. 197, 23 December 1807; Edward Masquerier (1767–1814), who was from an English Huguenot family, died at Surabaya on 30 April 1814, and was described in his death notice as a captain of 'the country service': <https://www.genealogieonline.nl/en/indische-bikken/I12794034810.php> [Accessed 15 April 2025]; 'Deaths', *Java Half-Yearly Almanac and Directory for 1815*, n.p. He took the *Jane* from New Guinea to China in 1808 and was employed by Raffles to transport military stores to Mindanawi (Mindanao) in 1811: Van Dyke, *Whampoa*, Appendix 1.2b; Sophie Raffles, Lady, *Memoir of the Life and Public Services of Sir Thomas Stamford Raffles…* (London, 1830), p. 64.

50 Originally an EIC ship: <https://en.wikipedia.org/wiki/Triton_(1787_EIC_ship)> [Accessed 15 April 2025].

51 *Prothocol Books*, No. 277, 4 October 1808; *Asiatic Annual Register*, vol. 10, 1811, p. 89.

attack the ship. It was decided to recapture the longboat and then abandon the ship as it was thought there was little on it left to be plundered. The supply of fresh water was in the longboat. This they achieved, and despite the longboat being attacked again, the remaining fifty-two crew members in it survived for three days on 'a little raw salt meat'. They made it to Malacca on 20 September. Captain Patrick then returned to the wreck with a Malay crew, prepared to save what he could and attack the 'pirates'. All that could be saved, however, were the foresail mainyards, two 9-pounders and a few broken spars. They returned to Malacca on the 30th.

The Protest raises the matter of the degree of cooperation between country traders. Providing assistance by one vessel to another in time of distress, even before written into law, was a time-honoured principle of sailing. While the *Triton* lay helplessly stuck on the shoal, Captain Patrick reported other ships' refusal to assist in the following terms:

> five ships that were in sight to the NNW did not seem inclined to render [assistance], altho' the Triton had the signal of distress flying at the main royal mast head from the time the ship was found to be in such a situation. At the same time two guns were fired to attract their attention and the same signal kept flying until that they had disappeared. It was hoisted again on the 11th for four ships that passed to the Eastward and one gun fired, and again on the 15th September to one ship, but it was to no purpose. They did not notice it.

There is no evidence to verify that these were all British country ships – they could have been vessels from other nations, or EIC or Navy ships, less inclined to come to the aid of a private trader. It seems that country traders did have a more supportive attitude towards each other for when Captain Patrick returned to the wreck on 27 September he found 'Captain Court of the *Britannia* and Captain Smith of the *Margaret* from Penang, come for the express purpose of assisting to save the *Triton*'s cargo for the good of the owners and underwriters'.

Captain John Mayne of the ship *Batavia* (555 tons, built in 1802), made a Protest at Malacca on 16 May 1811.[52] The *Batavia* had begun as an independent trader to the East Indies but in 1810 was enlisted as an extra EIC ship to serve as a transport in the British invasion of Java. The entry explains that on 9(?) May she went aground near Cape Rachado but was able to be extricated without developing any leaks with the aid of boats from the country ship *Discovery*. The Protest was signed by Mayne and his chief officer James Day.

52 Charles Hardy, A *Register of Ships, Employed in the Service of the Honorable the United East India Company, From the Year 1760 to 1819, with an Appendix* ... revised by Horatio Charles A. Hardy, 3rd edn (London, 1820), p. 290; *Prothocol Books*, No. 658, 16 May 1811; <https://en.wikipedia.org/wiki/Transport_vessels_for_the_British_invasion_of_Java_(1811)> [Accessed 22 October 2020].

The Protests of 5 and 6 August 1812 described the loss in the previous month of the *Abercromby* (1,280 tons, built in Bombay 1811)[53] on a voyage from Surabaya to China. The account was one of those that included an entry from the ship's log. The ship had originally set out from Bombay on 21 November 1811 laden with cotton and bound for China by the Eastern passage, the route via the Moluccas first taken by the *Pitt* in 1758.[54] Dismasted by a violent storm on 3 January 1812 it proceeded to Surabaya for repairs, remaining there until 23 July when it resumed its voyage.[55] In their Protest the captain, David Brown, and his first and second mates tabled an 'Extract from the Ship *Abercromby*'s Log Book' as evidence of what occurred next. It provided a running description of events on Sunday 26 July and the early morning of Monday 27 July including, as with a standard log, time, course, winds, soundings and details of happenings on board.

The ship ran aground on what is now called Abercromby Reef within sight of Billiton.[56] Having made all attempts to get off the rocks after it first struck, using sails, pumps, anchors and the boats, it was found impossible to save the ship in the heavy seas and it keeled over and sank. Brown was critical of the lascars who would not obey orders. They were, he said, 'in a state of mutiny as they refused to pump or do any work whatsoever' and during Sunday night occupied themselves 'making rafts to quit the ship'. His extract from the log 'solemnly' made the Protest 'against the winds, weather and dangers of the sea as being the sole cause of the loss of the ship *Abercromby*'. What happened to the crew is not known, but from the Malacca records it can be established that the officers arrived at Malacca in one of the boats on 5 August where they lodged their Protest.

Captain Brown gave the latitude of where the ship struck as 2°29′S, 'the centre of Billiton bearing SW by S'. Horsburgh placed the reef near the

53 *Prothocol Books*, Nos 808, 5 August 1812; 809, 6 August 1812; John Phipps, *A Guide to the Commerce of Bengal for the Use of Merchants, Ship Owners, Commanders … Resorting to the East Indies* (Calcutta, 1823), p. 84, lists the *Abercromby* as having been built in Bombay in 1811 and Horsburgh, *India Directory* (1817), vol. 2, p. 523, writing of its dismasting in the January1812 disaster, calls it a new ship. Its launching was reported in the *Bombay Gazette*, 26 October 1811. The *Abercromby* described elsewhere, for example, in <https://en.wikipedia.org/wiki/Abercromby_(1795_ship)> [Accessed 15 April 2025], as a former EIC ship of around 600 tons built in 1795, is not the ship that sank in 1812.

54 H. B. Morse, *The Chronicles of the East India Company Trading to China 1635–1834* (5 vols, Oxford, 1926–9), vol. 5, p. 74.

55 Purdy, *Tables*, Note 16, p. 128.

56 The country trader *Forbes* had foundered in this area, described as 'the South entrance of the Straits of Billiton' on 11 September 1806: Horst H. Liebner and David van Dyke, 'An account of the loss of the Country Ship *Forbes* and Frazer Sinclair, her late Commander', *Wacana, Journal of the Humanities of Indonesia*, 17:1 (2016), 38–67, at p. 38. Though the captain and crew reached safety in Malacca in the ship's longboats, there is no evidence a Protest was lodged there.

Montaran Islands lying off the northeast part of Billiton.[57] Brown, however, also gave an incompatible longitude of 107°30′E, which positioned the ship in the Gaspar Strait to the west of Billiton. This is the reading that was promulgated in subsequent gazetteers such as the publications of Purdy and Wright.[58] The mistake in the longitude calculation bears out the difficulties faced by mariners who had to ascertain their position without the use of chronometers.

The Protest of Captain John Daniels on 4 September 1815 concerned a serious misadventure in the area of the Andaman Islands.[59] His brig, *Athena*, was lost on the rocks about 12 miles south of the Island of Preparis in the North Andamans on 10 August. The vessel had departed Rangoon for Bengal on 25 July. At a quarter past three on the morning of 11 August breakers were sighted and five minutes later the brig struck rocks. Both the longboat and the jollyboat were staved. The crew remained on the brig until daylight 'when finding the Brig going to pieces fast and sea breaking with great fury all hands left the vessel and went on the Rocks'. The captain said it was impossible to save anything from the wreck. However, eighteen lascars were able to make two rafts and, said Daniels, 'without our advice at noon left the island' (they were not heard of again). On 13 August the remainder of the crew were taken off the island by the boats of the *James Drummond* (Captain Balston), which ship, *en route* to China, had already weathered heavy seas with the possibility of damage to its cotton cargo. Aboard the *James Drummond*, on examining the charts, the officers found 'no such rocks laid down'. The *James Drummond* then brought the officers and crew of the *Athena* to Malacca where they arrived on 3 September. Captain Daniels and his chief officer, Joseph White, protested 'against the consequences', lodging their Protest the next day, when Captain Balston also lodged his against storm damage.[60]

In a now barely readable report of 11 February 1816, submitted after a Protest note, Captain John Brace of the brig *Thainstone* described the loss of the longboat and the jollyboat as well as anchors when the vessel ran aground in heavy seas on a voyage from Sumba.[61] While the document is unclear, it would seem the ship itself was saved. The mishap occurred in late December 1815. It is not specified what cargo the *Thainstone* was carrying, but the brig, a 'local' country trader based in Penang, had in the past traded in opium.[62]

57 Horsburgh, *India Directory* (1817), vol. 2, p. 358 fn.

58 Purdy, *Tables*, p. 125; G. N. Wright, *New and Comprehensive Gazetteer; being a Delineation of the Present State of the World* ... (London, 1834), vol. 1, p. 13.

59 *Prothocol Books*, No. 1106, 4 September 1815.

60 An account was also given in the *Asiatic Journal and Monthly Register*, January to June 1816, pp. 600–1.

61 *Prothocol Books*, Nos 87, 88, 11 February 1816.

62 Jan-maree Herivel, '"A Perfect Malay": James Scott, East Indies Country Trader' (Unpublished PhD thesis, Charles Darwin University, 2020), p. 356, <https://ris.cdu.edu.au/ws/portalfiles/portal/44135311/Thesis_CDU_Herivel_J.pdf> [Accessed 15 April 2025]; John Bastin, 'Raffles and British policy in the Indian Archipelago, 1811–1816',

On 27 August 1816 the *Caroline* (456 tons, built in Calcutta 1805),[63] stranded on the Bambek Shoal in the Strait of Malacca, the same place where *La Paix* had come to grief in 1805. The *Caroline* was on a voyage from Bengal to China, after having returned from Whampoa earlier that year.[64] Captain George Strut (sometimes Street) lodged his Protest on 2 September.[65] He claimed that 'At sunset [there was] a thick haze over the land which prevented us from taking the bearings distinctly'. After making attempts to get his vessel off the rocks, Captain Strut decided to abandon ship:

> It was our Opinion that all exertions to get the ship off was useless & as we had only one Boat to depend upon to save our lives we thought it necessary for the preservation of our lives to abandon the ship & proceed to Malacca as fare as possible for assistance to save the property. At 2PM left the ship with the Ensign flying Union down in hopes it might deter the Malays from boarding her until we returned'.

The *Caroline* was carrying opium, eighty or ninety chests of which were removed from the wreck before it sank and 'sold on the spot at 1500 dollars'.[66] In the extract of the log provided to the notary at Malacca the word 'Protest' is not used. It is, however, used in the Dutch Protest note.

An interesting feature of Strut's report, similar to the experience of Captain Patrick in 1808, is the lack of support from a nearby unnamed ship in whose company they had sailed the previous day. The unwritten law of the sea of assisting another vessel when in need appears not to have prevailed in this case. The captain wrote:

> from ten to fifteen Minutes after we Struck fired Guns and showed Blue lights at Intervals throughout the Night expecting the Ship would have heard us & lent us assistance. At Daylight saw the Ship at Anchor … sent the Cutter away with the 2nd Officer to endeavour to get on Board her for assistance but soon after the Cutter left the Ship it weighed and made sail owing to which the Cutter returned not being able to Come up with her.

Another ship that was totally lost was the *Diana* (300 tons, built in Chittagong),[67] which hit a submerged rock in the Strait of Malacca between Tanjung

JMBRAS, 27:1 (1954), 84–119, at p. 103.

63 Phipps, *Guide*, p. 75, though Horsburgh, *India Directory* (1817), vol. 2, p. 3, calls her 'a strong Bombay-built ship'. Two of the *Caroline*'s previous captains had undergone court proceedings in London, Captain T. D. Finey (q.v.) for fenestration, and Captain Harrower for bigamy: Bulley, Anne, *The Bombay Country Ships, 1790–1833* (Richmond, 2000), p. 226–7; *The Extraordinary Trial of Capt. Harrower* … (1816).

64 Van Dyke, *Whampoa*, Appendix 1.2b.

65 *Prothocol Books*, No. 178, 2 September 1816.

66 *Asiatic Journal and Monthly Register*, January to June 1817, pp. 509, 615; Ball, *Diana Adventure*, p. 105. A 1993 'survey' for the *Caroline* failed to find the ship: Ooi, 'Maritime Treasures', p. 8.

67 *East-India Register and Directory for 1816*, p. 127; Bulley, *Bombay Country Ships*, p. 29.

Kling and Cape Rachado on 5 March 1817. The wreck was discovered and excavated, mainly for its valuable Chinese ceramics cargo, in 1993 by Dorian Ball who published a book about the ship and its twentieth century recovery.[68]

The extract from the logbook that was entered at Malacca on 8 March 1817[69] was signed by the first and second officers, James Crichton and Thomas Hill, as well as the serang. The ship's master, Captain Alexander Lyell, had drowned. The ship was sailing from China and was, according to the officers, about three-and-a-half miles offshore when it struck at 10.30 p.m.[70] The vessel broke free from the rocks at 4 o'clock the following morning, but as an 'immense quantity of water [had] settled in the after hold', when the *Diana* set course back to Malacca 'she went down in an instant in about 20 fms'. The longboat had been launched and it 'succeeded in picking up such of the crew as were on board at the time, but unfortunately Captain Lyell with 2 Lascars, Mamet and Bechao, were drowned … The Long Boat and 2 Cutters with the remainder of the Crew arrived safe at Malacca the following day about 1 o'clock'.

The name *Diana* appears again in the *Prothocol Books* exactly twelve months after the above entry. On 7 March 1818 this second entry mentions the 'berongelukte' (unfortunate) ship and a Protest by James Crichton.[71] However, the records for the first three months of 1818 have been severely damaged by water and are virtually unreadable, so it is not known if this was another copy of Crichton's original Protest. What is discernible (to some extent) is a list of articles rescued from the wreck at the time, headed 'List (?) of Articles saved from the wreck of Ship Diana'.[72] The list is made up of a number of boxes with the owners' name on them – usually people in Madras, but someone also from Penang. One of the boxes contained silks and another fans. There were a number of 'trunks' containing silver cutlery: a ladle, a gravy spoon, nineteen tablespoons, seventeen dessertspoons, twenty-four forks and a butter knife. There was also a 'spy glass', a dressing case, boxes of tea and a tin box containing twenty-six fans.

The *Christina* was one of those fortunate vessels that was re-floated after running aground.[73] The grounding happened on the island of Banka on a voyage from Batavia. The brig had departed Java on 30 April 1817 and arrived at the port of Marawang (Pangkalpinang) to collect a cargo of tin on 11 May. When it proceeded up the Marawang River at a quarter past four in the afternoon of the 17th, guided by a 'Sourabaya Pilot' who assured

68 Ball, *Diana Adventure*, especially chapters 1, 3, 6, 7 and 9.

69 *Prothocol Books*, No. 252, 8 March 1817.

70 The rocks were only 1.2 nautical miles offshore when the wreck was discovered in 1993, Ball, *Diana Adventure*, p. 14.

71 *Prothocol Books*, No. 255, 7 March 1818.

72 *Prothocol Books*, No. 259 (unreadable), March 1818.

73 The *Christina*'s good fortune was not to last long. Four months later she was on a voyage back from Calcutta to Java when she sank off the Carimon Islands.

Captain Robert Deans that 'we were sure to have eleven feet water in the channel', the *Christina* ran aground. In his Protest taken from the ship's log and tabled at Malacca on 14 June,[74] Deans and the second mate, Thomas Vaughan, described the dire situation and the actions taken to re-float the brig. The 'sea continued to heave us bodily on the shore vessel rolling and thumping very hard'. The crew lost all their anchors in the process of trying to haul the vessel back into the channel but during the night and following day were fortunate to receive assistance from a Dutch gunboat commanded by a Mr Anicet who located the bower and sheet anchors and guided them to safety. As Captain Deans admitted, 'I consider it necessary here to mention that had it not been for the Assistance rendered us by him and his people the Brig *Christina* must inevitably have been lost, Assistance in any other way not being procurable here, and the greatest part of our own crew being sick'.

The *Flora* (perhaps the *Lady Flora*, 705 tons, built in Calcutta)[75] also managed to free itself, this time from the 'Keo Shoal' (probably near Goh Keo Jai, southwest of Junk Ceylon (now Phuket)) where it ran aground on 7 June 1817 during a voyage from Bengal. In a Protest registered at Malacca on 18 June[76] William Hammond, the commander, explained how he took successful action that included shifting the cargo, dropping the anchors and dispatching the chief officer to Penang in the jollyboat to get boats to lighten the ship. The result was that 'On 8th June about four o'clock AM had a few hauls on the capstan and at five o'clock AM after very heavy straining got the ship afloat'.

Another vessel that ran aground but managed to break free was the *Tweed*, which arrived in Malacca on 4 August 1818 and lodged a Protest the following day.[77] The *Tweed* (which had come to the aid of *La Paix* in 1805) was owned by James Scott and Co. and had a cargo of opium, hence the vaguely worded

74 *Prothocol Books*, Nos 301, 13 June 1817; 302, 14 June 1817. The Protest incident must be that described in Horsburgh, *India Directory* (1817), vol. 2, p. 131: 'A brig sent lately from Mintow to Marawan for tin, got entangled by the numerous shoals, near that place, and grounded on 1 of them, although she had a Malay pilot on board, which obliged her to lie near Pulo Panjang, distant about 10 miles from Marawan, where she took in tin'. Horsburgh attributes the accident to the 'surrounding dangers' rather than the ineptitude of the pilot.

75 Phipps, *Guide*, p. 76. The *Lady Flora*, a private ship, operating between England, India and China, was sometimes referred to as *Flora*. It seems that Captain William Hammond had previously been captain and part owner of the *Countess of Loudon* (460 tons), which operated a similar route and that, under his command, sank in November 1816 after hitting a shoal in the South China Sea: Horsburgh, James, *India Directory, Or, Directions for Sailing to and from the East Indies, China, New Holland, Cape of Good Hope, Brazil, and the Interjacent Ports …*, 3rd edn (2 vols, London, 1827), vol. 2, p. 239. There was another smaller vessel called *Flora* (261 tons) that might also have been the ship protesting at Malacca: Phipps, *Guide*, p. 92.

76 *Prothocol Books*, No. 303, 18 June 1817. This record is very faint and difficult to read.

77 *Prothocol Books*, No. 478, 5 August 1818.

'laden with a cargo consisting of sundres articles of Merchandize'. In an attempted legalistically worded Protest unusual in the records, William Spiers, commander, and Nathaniel Rogers, chief officer, explained how their small (180-ton) craft had departed Calcutta bound for Canton on 27 May in sound condition, well-manned and 'provided with all things needful and necessary for the said voyage'. However, from 27 July until 2 August they encountered 'gloomy, squally dark cloudy weather with a strong lee (?) current'. On 27 July 'in the vicinity of the north and south sands' in the Malacca Strait the ship touched the bottom. On the 29th the wild weather continued and when they lost the small bower anchor they were 'put in great danger but escaped'. They were still in danger on 2 August when they again touched ground. They denied any neglect and protested against any person concerning any loss or damage. While they believed the brig had not been damaged, they still felt it 'their duty to prepare for the worst that may possibly happen'.

The brig *Vestal* (140 tons, built in Chittagong 1817)[78] is another vessel that ran aground in the same vicinity on 9 September 1818, specifically in the Strait of Colong. This happened in spite of the captain's taking bearings, as advised by Horsburgh, from the Bottle Islands (also known as Pulo Besar and Pulo Tekolo) and Pulo Anzas (also known as Mudancoos or Mud and Goose) and steering in the strait 'according to Horsburgh Directions'. The statement entered in the Dutch records on 15 September 1818 by Captain Henry Elliott and Chief Officer Silvester William Hazlewood (though signed only by Elliott),[79] does not mention the word 'Protest'. It was, however, described as such in the Dutch Protest note.

A week before the British handover of Malacca to the Dutch, the *Vestal* was carrying stores for the British troops at Malacca and also had on board the Agent to the Bengal Commissariat, Captain Hampton, who was to supervise the embarkation of the troops. The brig ran aground at 8 p.m. and could not be got off at high tide. At daybreak the crew attempted to heave the vessel off using the anchors and when this was not successful, began to lighten the ship by throwing overboard part of the cargo, including wheat and firewood. In the end, it was decided that Captain Elliott should take the longboat to Malacca to obtain assistance.

There is an additional statement by Elliott, dated 16 September but filed with the Protest of 15 September (no. 503) that records the attempt to return to the *Vestal* to make the recovery. This account describes a number of additional challenges faced by mariners in the area at that time and

78 Phipps, *Guide*, p. 178; not to be confused with the HMC brig *Vestal* of the Bombay Marine that was operating at the same time.

79 *Prothocol Books*, No. 503, 15 September 1818. An account of the Hazlewood family in Burma records that Sylvester Hazlewood paid his £500 bond to trade on his own account as a free mariner the next year, 1819: 'Goodbye Burma', <https://www.goodbyeburma-book.com/more-about-hazlewoods> [Accessed 21 August 2021].

includes details of human responses normally excluded from the formal Protests. Captain Elliott was granted use of the tender belonging to the ship of the 'Dutch Admiral' (Rear-Admiral Wolterbeek) but decided for reasons of urgency to proceed in 'boats' or prahus. He took with him those crew members of the *Vestal* who had gone to Malacca as well as a number of sepoys under the command of a naik (naig), the non-commissioned officer of the sepoy regiment. Elliott met with some disobedience from the sepoys and was accused of violence against them.

To add to his difficulties, Elliott, under pressure from William Farquhar, commandant of Malacca, to recover the ship and the stores as soon as possible, was frustrated by the lack of urgency of the Malay crew of the prahu. Even in his own account of events, he appeared unable to command his motley company. Furthermore, the Malay leader (referred to by Elliott as *Datto*, modern spelling 'datuk', meaning 'elder' or 'chief') on whom he was dependent for navigational guidance, proved to be unreliable. When they arrived in the area of the Strait of Colong the Datto claimed that he did not know the southern entrance. At this stage Elliott admitted 'I then shoved him from me'.

The final straw in the rescue attempt came when the expedition was hit by a storm and Elliott's boat lost its rudder. It half-filled with water and was fortunate not to be engulfed. Elliott tried to attract the attention of a passing ship by firing two muskets, but the ship took no notice. Earlier he had hailed a prahu with a sail and small boat but had been informed by the naik that they were thieves. The only positive feature concerning the rescue attempt was when the crew of the *Vestal* were spotted on shore and taken aboard. In the end it was a sorry group that made their way back to Malacca:

> we now mustered twenty two in number and the boat in a leakey and very shattered condition and nothing on board to eat or drink and the Seapoys as well as my own people were complaining … and I knew it would take us two days nearly to get to Malacca And the major part of my people disposed to be very troublesome I could not by any means keep them from being noisy and two which were landsmen and who had often been punished by the Serang on board for their indolent conduct bid me defiance and refused even to bail out the boat or pull; I struck one with a rattan twice and the other three times.

The rescue bid was unsuccessful. The wreck was occupied by 'the Malays', and 'the pirates had made prize of her' as the *Asiatic Journal* put it.[80]

The above fourteen Protests illustrate the treacherous conditions that faced sailors in the East Indies, particularly in the Malacca Strait where charts could not be wholly relied upon and where hidden rocks and sandbanks could translate into a sudden grounding. The perseverance and ingenuity called for to rectify such a situation and minimise damage to ship and cargo is attested to in the examples. In the worst cases of stranding and loss of the ship one

80 *Asiatic Journal and Monthly Register*, July to December 1819, p. 96.

sees doubt cast on the reliability of the crew, and hopes of rescue by other ships sometimes realised and other times dashed; all the drama reported in a calm and factual manner typical of the Malaccan Protest.

3

Fire

Fire on board was one of the most dangerous of the misadventures faced by mariners. Outside the risks of fire associated with warfare, there were risks associated with lightning strike; the carriage of gunpowder or saltpetre or fibrous cargo such as cotton; wood fires in the galley; or a spark from candle or lantern falling into a broached keg of spirits, with tarred rope and oiled canvas always ready to burn. As well there was the possibility of arson on the part of disgruntled seamen while in port. Lascars were commonly blamed for fires, the idea being that after taking wage advances they would burn the ship and abscond. James Horsburgh was one of those who believed that 'a rage for burning ships pervaded the native sailors of India'.[1] Four of the ships that protested at Malacca in 1816 and 1817 were later destroyed by fire, attributed to arson, while in port: the *Bombay Castle* bound for China with a load of cotton burnt off Saugor Island in May 1846; the *Cornwallis* was burnt in Bombay with a load of cotton on board in 1841; the *Duchess of Wellington* burnt in Saugor with a cargo of saltpetre in 1816 and the *Upton Castle*, again in Saugor, laden with cotton in 1817, the latter after a foiled first attempt.[2] In the case of the *Duchess of Wellington* the report in the *Asiatic Journal* asserted that:

> Some of the crew belonging to the Duchess of Wellington have been apprehended, and are detained on suspicion of having set the vessel on fire. In most cases when ships are burnt in this river, there has been reason to believe that the Lascars (who receive impress money in advance for several benefits) have been instrumental in their destruction. We have lately seen an excellent plan, which is now under consideration whereby the Lascars may be protected from the iniquitous system of extortion so long practiced in Calcutta, and the owners of vessels ensured against the frequent chance of loss by fire; as it provides, that

1 Quoted in Aaron Jaffer, *Lascars and India Ocean Seafaring, 1780–1860: Shipboard Life, Unrest and Mutiny* (Woodbridge, 2015), p. 76.

2 *Nautical Magazine and Naval Chronicle*, 1847, vol. 16, pp. 588–91; *Asiatic Journal and Monthly Register*, July to December 1816, p. 209; *Asiatic Journal and Monthly Register*, July to December 1817, p. 309.

> in all cases when ships are burnt, the native seamen belonging to them shall be detained to complete their stipulated term of service in some other manner.[3]

Michael Fisher, however, in his study on Indian maritime labour and arson believes that the suspicion cast upon lascars was misplaced.[4]

A fire aboard ship that could represent catastrophic and immediate loss of life and property, a large-scale event, could also have lesser consequences that added to the uncertainties of ordinary life. Thus, William Anderson, an officer on a country trader, wrote to his father in Scotland from Madras on 30 September 1798, '[I]t is more than probable that neither my letters nor pamphlet will ever come to hand',[5] these items having been entrusted the previous April, in Bombay, to the second officer aboard the EIC ship *Princess Amelia* that soon after had been destroyed by fire off the Malabar coast.

There are only four Malacca Protests relating to fire on board vessels, but they nevertheless convey the severity of the situation, the destruction caused and the attempts employed to overcome these disasters.

The Protests (four cases)

The first Protest concerning fire in the *Prothocol Books* is that of the brig *New Endeavour* (140 tons, built in Bombay). Dated 14 March 1809, it involved not only fire but a medley of events that took place in December 1808 and January 1809.[6] The captain was Joze Antonio D'Coil. The vessel, not in the best condition, was a poor sailer and had experienced trouble sailing in convoy from Bengal to Penang, having to be towed, for example, by the 'Admiral ship' (HMS *Culloden*, the flagship of Admiral Edward Pellew). It had also been involved in an accident with the Admiral's ship, losing a mast and the jib boom;[7] it took in water and part of the cargo had to be thrown overboard. Finally, on 17 January while lying near Booron (now Bireuen) Roads on the Pedir coast where they had stopped for wood and water before attempting to reach Penang, the *New Endeavour* caught on fire:

> Mrs Yeats passenger on board called the Captn. and said look what smoke comes out of the cabin. Then the Captain went down into the cabin and found

3 *Asiatic Journal and Monthly Register*, July to December 1816, p. 210.

4 Michael H Fisher, 'Finding Lascar "Wilful Incendiarism": British Ship-Burning Panic and Indian Maritime Labour in the Indian Ocean', *South Asia*, 35:3 (2012), 596–623.

5 Aberdeen University Library, Museums and Special Collections, 'Letter of William Anderson, Madras, 30 September 1798', Papers of Seton Family of Mounie, MS2787/5/2/4/18.

6 British Library, Asia, Pacific and Africa Collections, *Malacca, General Prothocol Books (Registers of Legal Deeds) 1786–1825*, IOR: R/9/22/1–75 [referred to in this study as *Prothocol Books*], Nos 335, 336, 14 March 1809; *East-India Register and Directory for 1809*, p. 120.

7 See Chapter 4 for details of this event and the relevant Protest.

> the cabin full of smoke and took off the cabin scuttle and in doing so the fire burst out of the scuttle. He ran on deck and called out fire below and called all hands to bring water to try to put out the fire but found impossible to put it out. We were thus obliged to get into the boat as fast as possible with the clothes that we had on our body. Therefore we enter our protest to serve where necessary.

The Protest evokes the catastrophic nature of the accident and the short time afforded for escape, but does not address the cause. Nor does it mention the whereabouts of the *Culloden*.

Two months later, when the survivors finally made it to Malacca, after being held captive by the inhabitants of the Pedir coast,[8] the Protest was submitted. It was signed by the captain, the chief mate William Roach (?) and, with a cross, by two crew members.

There are three Protests registered in the *Prothocol Books* surrounding the well-documented disaster of the loss by fire, on 25 May 1811, of the ship *Thomas Henchman* (500 tons, built in Calcutta 1802). The *Henchman*'s commander, George Nicholls, and First Mate Ross submitted theirs on 3 June.[9] The ship, a country trader that had made regular trips to China between 1805 and 1808, had been hired by the EIC as a transport for the British invasion of Java and was one of the nearly 100 vessels of the fleet gathered at Malacca in preparation for the attack. Although it was still administered by the Dutch, Java was at that time under the control of, and defended by, the French. The British fleet left Malacca for Java on 11 June, but the *Henchman* was no longer part of it.

The extract from the logbook of the *Henchman* stated that at 11 p.m. on 24 May 1811 'the alarm was given of the ship being on fire in the hold and the smoke was at the same time issuing rapidly out of the fore and main hatchways and in a few minutes the twixt deck was so full of smoke that the people could no longer remain below to get at the fire or even to discover where it had first broke out'. As the transport vessel was carrying gunpowder for the invading army, the situation was critical. The crew fought the blaze from the hatchway but 'at ½ past 12 o'clock it was deemed necessary by the Commander, Officers and crew to abandon the ship'. The ship then burnt until 9 o'clock in the morning when 'she blew up with a dreadful explosion near the Roads of Malacca'.

When the *Henchman* caught fire, other country ships hired as transports and anchored nearby were also in danger. Two of the captains who recorded their actions did so as Protests. John Parrish[10] of the *Fort William* (1,236 tons,

8 See Chapter 6 for this event and the relevant Protest.

9 John Phipps, *A Guide to the Commerce of Bengal for the Use of Merchants, Ship Owners, Commanders … Resorting to the East Indies* (Calcutta, 1823), p. 75; *Prothocol Books*, No. 672, p. 3 June 1811. The ship is called either the *Thomas Henchman* or simply *Henchman*.

10 Alias David Ross, brother of Hercules Ross (q.v.). For a short biography of Parrish (alias Ross) see F. Andrew Smith, 'Mercantile Life in Early 19th Century Asia: the Ross

Fig 8. The country trader ship *Fort William*. British School, c.1806.

built in Calcutta 1806) noted on 28 May[11] that they assisted the *Henchman* 'as far as lay in our power' but being informed that the ship had powder on board and was likely to blow up, and 'our being but cable's length[12] from her and immediately under her lee the wind at the time off the land – from the dangerous situation we lay in … thought it most prudent for the preservation of the ship to cut the Best Bower Cable 65 fms from the anchor and slip the stream cable made sail and ran out to the West'. The *Fort William* later returned to the original anchorage and after a couple of hours searching recovered the lost cables and anchors, but Parrish filed a Protest explaining his actions nevertheless.

Captain James Green of the *Fleetwood* (380 tons, ex-*Jessy* built in Rangoon 1802) also submitted part of his ship's log as a Protest on 28 May,[13] justifying his actions in leaving his berth and losing two cables and anchors. Green was initially surprised to hear the *Fort William* firing shots at 11 p.m. at night and then sailing off, but being informed by a boat from another country ship, the *Windham*, that the *Henchman* was on fire, began to take evasive action. This was indeed necessary, for the burning vessel was 'not more than a cables length

Brothers', *JMBRAS*, 96:2 (2023), 49–75, at pp. 59–62.

11 Phipps, *Guide*, p. 92; *Prothocol Books*, No. 666, 28 May 1811.

12 1 fathom = 6 feet; 100 fathoms = 1 cable length.

13 *East-India Register and Directory for 1805*, p. 108; *Prothocol Books*, No. 667, 28 May 1811.

from us on our Larboard quarter'. The crew of the *Fleetwood* also thought of sending their longboat to assist the *Henchman*, but Captain Nicholls himself came on board and said he and the crew had abandoned their ship and 'he expected her to Blow up instantly'. To distance the *Fleetwood* from the burning ship, the crew 'bent the Fore and mizen top sails & Jibb and at 1 AM cut the sheet Cable of 17 inches, made sail and cut the stream cable of 11 inches and shaped the end into the Long Boat'. Green noted that all of the ships that had been anchored at Tanjung Kling were under way. He too recorded that the *Henchman* blew up at '½ past 8 AM'. They returned to their former berth but unlike the *Fort William*, were unable to locate their lost anchors. Anchors and cables – some of the latter up to 20 inches in diameter – were of considerable value and their loss had to be accounted for. Mention of them occurs in many Protests. They are discussed further in the next chapter.

The explosion of the *Henchman* excited the residents of Malacca and was recorded by the young Malay writer in Raffle's office, Munshi Abdullah, who later mentioned it in his biography.[14] He remarked that the blast from the explosion rocked the town and during the following days wreckage and debris were washed up along the shore. Providing some colour to other accounts, he said, possibly repeating local gossip, the fire was caused by seamen smoking cigars and throwing a lighted end into the ship. John Leyden, in a letter of 13 June 1811 to Dr John Hare wrote in a more pointed manner: 'A rascally Lascar is supposed to have set her on fire wilfully.'[15]

These instances of fire reported at Malacca are representative of a much-feared calamity and, in the case of the *Henchman*, of the follow-on repercussions on other ships and the suspicions cast as to the origin of the conflagration.

14 Munshi Abdullah, 'The Hikayat Abdullah, an annotated translation by A. H. Hill', *JMBRAS*, 28:3 (1955), 1–355, at p. 95.

15 *The New Scots Magazine*, 31 January 1829, vol. 1, p. 118.

4

Other Accidents and Failings of the Ship

A number of mishaps were reported at Malacca without reference to bad weather or fire. The Protests discussed here concern collisions, overturning, loss of anchors and cables, and leaks.

The Protests (thirteen cases)

Collisions

Collisions were most likely to occur in port, either during a storm or while participating in manoeuvres. Paul Van Dyke describes such occurrences in Whampoa.[1] Arthur Bowes Smyth recorded in his journal the shambles that characterised the departure of the New South Wales First Fleet from Botany Bay to Port Jackson on 26 January 1788:

> the Prince of Wales and Friendship who cd not keep in stays came foul of each other and the Friendship carried her jib-boom. The Prince of Wales had her New Main sail & her Main top mast Stay Sail rent in pieces. The Charlotte also came foul of the Friendship afterward & carried away some of the carv'd work from her stern, & it was with the greatest difficulty the Lady Penrhyn escaped the same fate.[2]

The collisions reported at Malacca, however, all took place on the open sea, though they were related to travelling in convoy.

William Colvel, Commander of 'het particuliere Engelsche schip *Saijgon*' on a voyage from Madras collided with a royal naval vessel. He presented a part of the ship's journal (not retained in the archives) to the Malaccan authorities on 26 August 1801 to convey what happened.[3] A further Protest

1 Paul A. Van Dyke, *Whampoa and the Canton Trade: Life and Death in a Chinese Port* (Hong Kong, 2020), p. 245 and Appendix 11.4.

2 National Library of Australia, Arthur Bowes Smyth, 'Journal 1787 March 22–1789 August', MS 4568, p. 130.

3 British Library, Asia, Pacific and Africa Collections, *Malacca, General Prothocol Books (Reg-*

recorded in Dutch was given on the 28th, at the request of the captain, by First Mate Edmond Barry and Second Mate Rock (or Roek) Fredath.[4] This stated that at 10 a.m. on 19 July the *Saigon* unavoidably collided with the Royal Navy frigate *Daedalus*, commanded by William Waller, when the frigate was 'lying against the wind'. According to the mates 'much damage' was sustained, but there is also much crossing out, which makes the record particularly difficult to read.

The Protest on 14 March 1809 of Joze Antonio D'Coil, captain of the brig *New Endeavour*, mentioned above, includes a logbook extract from 8 December 1808, also involving the Royal Navy.[5] In a stormy voyage in convoy from Bengal to Penang, as we have seen, the brig had had to be towed by the 'Admiral ship', HMS *Culloden*, and had also required assistance with the pumping. Then the collision occurred. '[A]t nine o'clock the Admiral's ship was taken aback and driven across our hass [hawse] and carried away our jib boom and fore royal mast and the hawser that we was towed by'. The decision was taken to throw the cargo in the tween decks overboard to lighten the ship and '[o]n the ninth at 7 o'clock in the morning the Admiral sent his boat on board with a Lieutenant, the ship's carpenter and one midshipman and 20 men to assist'.

On 7 December 1809 Captain Francis Smith of the *Anna* (899 tons, built in Bombay 1790) recorded a collision that he said occurred off Point Romania on 30 November.[6] This was on a return trip from China to Bombay[7] and was not dissimilar to the experience of the *New Endeavour*. Captain Smith, having received a signal from the leader of the British convoy[8] to anchor, proceeded to do so but before he had completed the task his ship was hit by the Portuguese ship *Activo*. The extract from the log of the *Anna* submitted with the Protest read:

> Variable Northerly Breeze at 9 P.M. rounded the Ruff [Bluff] off Point Rominia: at 10 anchored pr. Signal in 16 fathoms with the Small Bower the Ship brought up but before we had given Her the length of Cable intended to ride by, a Portuguese Ship named Ativo Captn Joze Coitano Pedro bound to Goa, came athwart Hawse [across the bow] of us and carried away the Jibboom unshipt the Starboard Bumpkin with other Damages about the Head Starboard side finding it impossible to get Her clear owing to the Strength of the Tide and

isters of Legal Deeds) 1786–1825, IOR: R/9/22/1–75 [referred to in this study as *Prothocol Books*], No. 1006, 26 August 1801.

4 *Prothocol Books*, No. 1007, 28 August 1801.

5 *Prothocol Books*, Nos 335, 336, 14 March 1809.

6 *East-India Register and Directory for 1809*, p. 301; *Prothocol Books*, No. 427, 7 December 1809.

7 *Calcutta Monthly Journal*, July to October 1809, p. 22; Van Dyke, *Whampoa*, Appendix 1.2b.

8 This was the Royal Navy vessel *Dedaigneuse*, Captain George Bell: *Calcutta Monthly Journal*, July to October 1809, p. 22; *Madras Courier*, 27 December 1809, p. 2.

> Wind cut the cable with one half of Ditto outside of the Hawse, let go the Best Bower, Cleared away the Rigging and Sails etc. about the Bowsprit and rigged out the Spare Jibboom.

The other side of the story, the point of view of Captain Pedro, discussed in Part II of this work, was also recorded as a Protest on the following day, 8 December 1809.

Overturning

The nature of the losses that befell the brig *Hammudy* in 1819 and reported as a Protest on 12 April concerned the brig's cargo boat.[9] The brig had travelled from Bombay to Siam and was preparing for the return trip. On this occasion the cargo boat had overturned in the Menam River during the transfer of goods from the shore to the boat. The accident occurred on 28 February 1819 while the brig itself was at anchor off Siam Bar, taking on a load of sugar, 'elephant's teeth' and 'sundry other species of cargo'. The unfortunate cargo boat overturned upstream 'opposite the Guard house near the village of Pachalat'[10] when the supercargo, Mohamat Bey Meya Bassache, was supervising the loading. This location was some distance from where the ship was anchored and news of the incident only reached the *Hammudy* on 2 March. The captain, Alexander Henning,[11] departed that day to investigate, writing his Protest as part of the ship's journal on 5 March when he returned to his vessel. Having checked the situation, he did not explain the cause of the incident, but wrote that he had 'ascertained the fact of the Cargo Boat's being upset part of the property had been recovered by means of divers, etc. but injured in consequence of the Wet, etc.' He protested against the loss of some of the cargo and 'the injury and Expence sustained in those recovered'.

9 *Prothocol Books*, No. 624, 12 April 1819.

10 Pachalat was probably Paklaat, a village a few miles north of Paknam. Paknam, often referred to by the English as Pakenham, where vessels trading with Siam had to leave their guns, is now Samut Prakan. For maps of this area see Larry Sternstein, 'The London Company's Envoys Plot Siam', *The Journal of the Siam Society*, 81:2 (1993), 11–95, at pp. 82, 84–5.

11 Alexander Henning had previously had a naval career, being promoted to the rank of lieutenant on the reserved half-pay list on 11 September 1815. In the 1830s and 1840s he commanded ships first for the EIC and then for Green, Wigram's & Green. In 1824 Henning sent his log of his 1819 voyage to the Gulf of Siam, 'a place which has not been much frequented by Europeans', to the Admiralty. Of the country traders making Protests at Malacca, this is the only log known to the authors: National Archives (London), Public Records Office, Admiralty Records, 'Captain Henning's Log of the ship *Hammudy*', ADM 55, File 144 item A [Available at NLA AJCP reel no. 1,600]. See also William R O'Byrne, *A Naval Biographical Dictionary: Comprising the Life and Services of Every Living Officer in Her Majesty's Navy from the Rank of Admiral of the Fleet to that of Lieutenant* (London, 1849), p. 497; *Navy List* (London, 1860), p. 56.

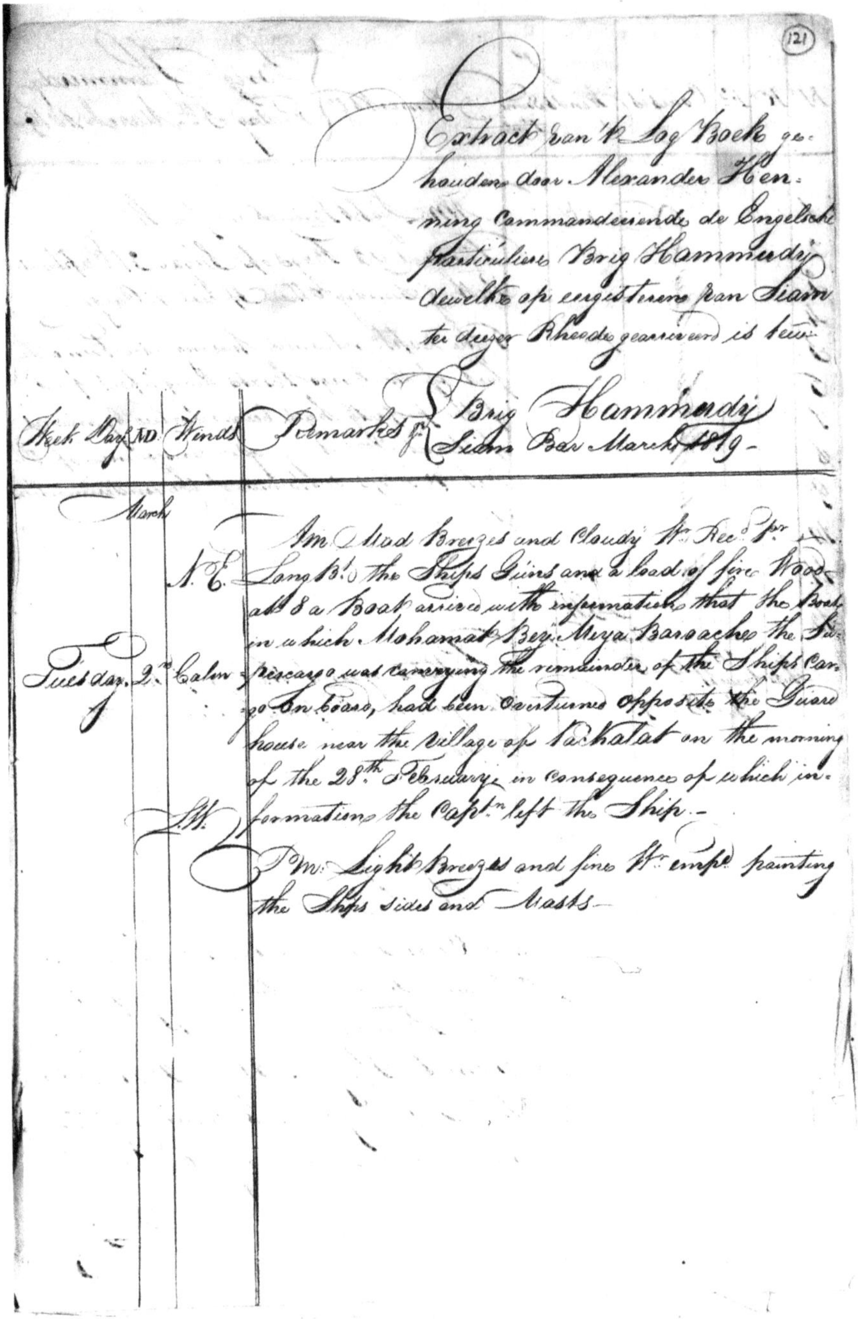

(121)

Extract van 't Log Boek gehouden door Alexander Henning Commandeerende de Engelsche particuliere Brig Hammudy dewelke op eergisteren van Siam ter deezer Rheede gearriveerd is luid

Brig Hammudy
Siam Bar March 1819 -

Week Day	D	Winds	Remarks &c
March			
		N.E.	Am Mod Breezes and Cloudy Wr Recd pr Long Bt the Ships Guns and a load of fire Wood at 8 a Boat arrived with information that the Boat in which Mohamat Bey Meya Barsaches the Supercargo was conveying the remainder of the Ships Cargo on board, had been overturned opposite the Guard house near the Village of Pachalat on the morning of the 28th February in consequence of which information the Captn left the Ship -
Tuesday	2nd	Calm	
		S.W.	Pm Light Breezes and fine Wr empd painting the Ships sides and Masts -

Fig 9. Page of the *Hammudy*'s log for 2 March 1819 entered as part of the Protest of Captain Henning on 12 April 1819 before the notary Anthonij Stecher about an accident to the brig's cargo boat on the Menam River, Siam.

Captain Henning included in his Protest 'A List of the articles lost from the Cargo Boat that was overturned in the Siam River' that demonstrates the variety and size of the load being carried by the cargo boat, some items of which appear to be unsold goods from India, *viz*:

> A Writing Desk[12], containing as follows –
> An account book of the Ships Cargo etc. receipts of several Ships Papers –
> 81 Picals. 5 Dollars. 1 watch 12 Bbay rupees 2 Ringa
> 5 Small Boxes of Jewellry.
> A Chest containing Dolls. & Picals, it was picked up broken in 2 Pieces & the Dolls. were afterwards found by the Divers, but 222 Picals were lost.
> 2 Large & 1 small pieces of Kincobs.[13]
> An embroidered Service – Some embroidered native Caps.
> An Embroidered Armenian Dress.
> A Box contg. 100 Picals weight of Monies.
> A Bale contg. 98 Pieces of Surat piece Goods.
> 1 Piece of Europe Cloth – 1 large Bottle of rose Water.1 Picul black Pepper – 2 Bags containing 49 ½ Piculs Callies Aggar Wood
> ½ Picul Puggar Wood.[14]
> 3 Chests contg. Plate Glass
> 1 Writing Desk containing 145 Picals.
> The Expences attending those things recovered, were, paid to the Divers.
> 80 Dollars & 1 Courg(?) Surat piece Goods
> 406 Picals 1 Shawl.

Loss of anchors and cables

Captain John Ross Parrish of 'het Engelsch schip' *Fort William*, which had been menaced by the fire aboard the *Henchman* in 1811 and been temporarily dispossessed of an anchor and cable, tabled a Protest in the form of a logbook entry on 23 October 1812 in explanation of another, more permanent, loss of an anchor and cable during a passage from China to Malacca.[15] The *Fort William* (1,137 tons) had left Whampoa on 1 September.[16] While off Point

12 This was a small box that opened up to reveal a sloped surface and small compartments.

13 Gold and silver embroidered cloths from India.

14 Perhaps relating to wood for a small shrine known as a Pooja mandir.

15 *Prothocol Books*, No. 840, 23 October 1812.

16 Van Dyke, *Whampoa*, Appendix 1.2b. On this list the *Fort William* is described as an EIC ship although Charles Hardy, *A Register of Ships, Employed in the Service of the Honorable the United East India Company, From the Year 1760 to 1819, with an Appendix … revised by Horatio Charles A. Hardy*, 3rd edn (London, 1820) does not list it as such for this year. The ship continued to England, arriving in March 1813. The return journey to Calcutta was a disaster, with about 100 passengers and crew dead by the time of its arrival in July 1814: F. Andrew Smith, 'Mercantile Life in Early 19th Century Asia: the Ross Brothers', *JMBRAS*, 96:2 (2023), 49–75, at p. 61.

Anchors (scale $\frac{3}{16}$in = 1ft)

1 Sheet anchor and bower
2 Anchor ring
3 Anchor stock
4 Hoops
5 Nuts
6 Anchor shank or shaft
7 Anchor flukes
8 Anchor arm
9 Anchor crown
10 Stream anchor (stock not shown)
11 Kedge anchor (stock not shown)

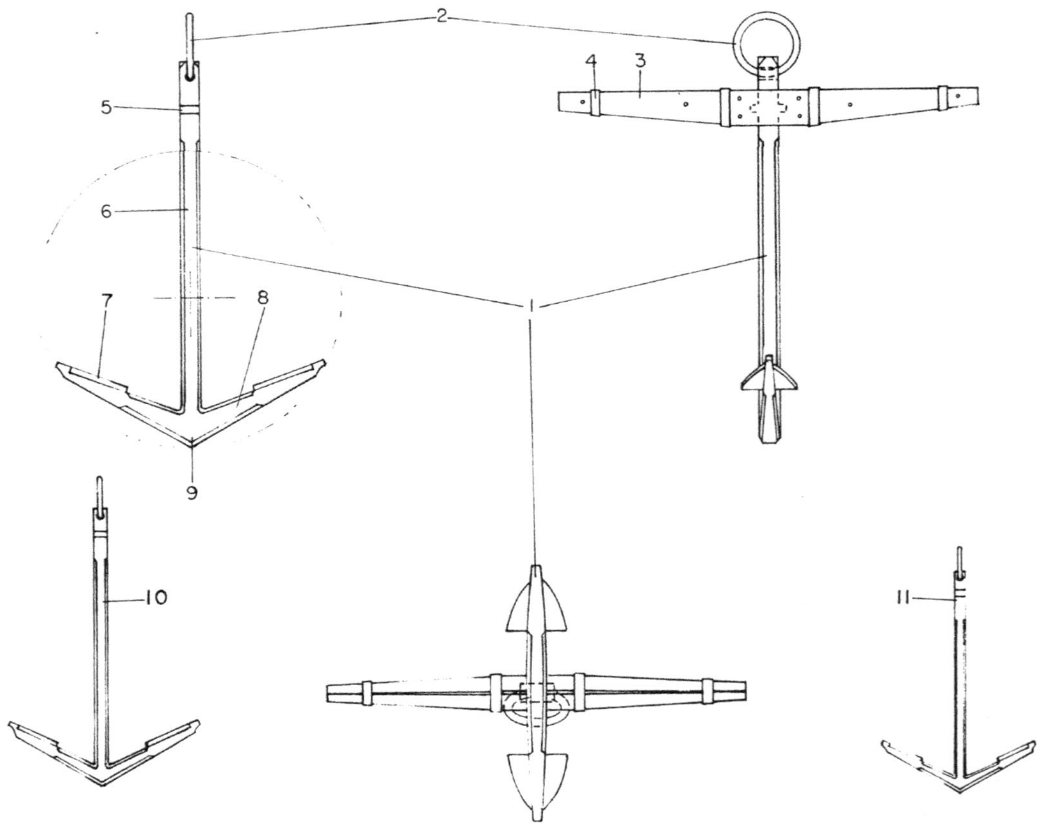

Fig 10. Sheet, bower, stream and kedge anchors.

Romania on 18 October the crew were forced to 'let go the small Bower in 12 fms stiff mud' but 'in veering away parted the Cable at about 60 fms (sixty) from the anchor outside of the hawser'. The Protest was against the loss of anchor and cable due to weather. No other losses or damage were recorded.

The loss of an anchor had considerable impact as, depending upon the type, it was used not only for holding the ship fast but for manoeuvring the vessel. A merchant ship could carry several different anchors. In addition to the two main anchors, the best bower and the small bower, which hung either side of the ship's bow, there could be two lightweight stream anchors used in shallow, tidal waters, two kedge anchors that were used for operations such as warping (or hauling) the ship and a heavy sheet anchor for emergencies. Each of these types is mentioned in the Protests as having been lost, the most common loss being that of a bower anchor.

The loss of any anchor at all was most usually associated with storms, gales and groundings although a cable was sometimes cut or slipped to facilitate escape from other dangers. Captain Parrish cut the *Fort William*'s best bower cable and Captain Nicholls cut the sheet and slipped the stream cables of the *Fleetwood* to escape the spread of fire from the *Henchman* in 1811. Also in 1811, Captain Hammett cut the small bower cable from the *Charles Baillie* after the ship struck a rock, while Captain Mackay sacrificed the *Argo*'s anchor to flee from pirates in 1814.

As cutting a ship's cable could endanger both ship and cargo the Protest sometimes not only gave an explanation of the necessary circumstances but also included the details of how much cable had been cut and what size it was. Mackay for example specified that he 'cut from the anchor of fourteen hundred weight … sixty fathoms of fourteen inch cable'.[17]

The quantity and quality of rope and cable were among the many issues of concern to a ship's captain of the period. They took up a large part of storage in a vessel and had to be kept in good repair. For example, the hemp cable of a first-class Indiaman 'took up the whole of her forehold, being over eight inches in diameter and tested up to a strain of over 50 tons',[18] while the repair of ropes and making of 'point' are recorded as occupations of lascars aboard country traders.[19]

Russian Hemp was most commonly used for cordage on European-built ships, while in India there was also the choice of rope made from coir (a

17 *Prothocol Books*, No. 1045, 25 November 1814.

18 Basil Lubbock, Basil, 'Ships of the Period and Developments in Rig', in C. Northcote Parkinson (ed.), *The Trade Winds: A Study of British Overseas Trade During the French Wars 1793–1815* (London, 1948), pp. 87–101, at p. 93.

19 See, for example, National Archives (London). 'Captain Henning's Log of the ship *Hammudy*', pp. 21, 22, 27. Point was a short piece of rope or flat braided cordage, tapering from the middle towards each end, and used to reef the courses and top-sails of a ship.

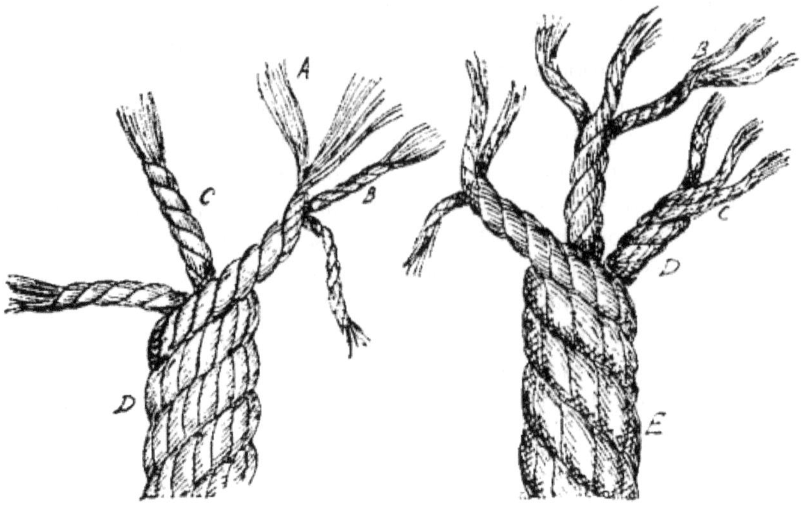

Fig 11. Construction of rope: A. Fibres; B. Yarn; C. Strand; D. Rope; E. Cable.

coconut husk product from the palm *Cocos nucifera*), ejoo (from the palm *Arenya saccharifera*, similar to the sago palm), plantain (Manilla hemp, *Musa textilis*) and sunn (Indian hemp, *Crotalaria juncea*).[20] Each type of rope had its particular qualities. Coir for instance, while not much esteemed for running or standing rigging, was said to be excellent for thick cables because of its elasticity, Manilla hemp could bear 'great strains', sunn also had the potential of significant strength, though couldn't take the hot air in the hold, while ejoo was valued for its durability.[21] The quality was not standardised though and much depended on the method of manufacture.

Coir cables were the subject of a Protest of 10 June 1811 by Captain Dixie Finey (variously Finney, Fenny, among others) of the *Soolymany* (679 tons).[22]

20 For a discussion of the different types of rope and some of the trials undertaken to test them, see John Phipps, *A Collection of Papers, Relative to Ship Building in India … also A Report, Comprehending all the Ships and Vessels Built in India to the Present Time …* (Calcutta, 1840), pp. 17–33; for a more detailed account of these fibrous plants, their cultivation and uses, including for rope, see J. Forbes Royle, *The Fibrous Plants of India fitted for Cordage, Clothing, and Paper. With an Account of the Cultivation and Preparation of Flax, Hemp, and their Substitutes* (London, 1855).

21 C. Northcote Parkinson, *Trade in the Eastern Seas 1793–1813* (Cambridge, 1937), p. 332; Royle, *Fibrous Pants of India*, pp. 115, 64, 277–8, 102.

22 *Prothocol Books*, No. 680, 10 June 1811; John Phipps, *A Guide to the Commerce of Bengal for the Use of Merchants, Ship Owners, Commanders … Resorting to the East Indies* (Calcutta, 1823), p. 85. This is the same ship as the *Sulimany* captained by Robert Carter (q.v.). Finey appears to have been an irascible man. On 5 April 1815 two members of Finey's crew, when he was captain of the *Caroline*, were imprisoned after a trial in the Old Bailey for conspiring with others to charge Finey with the murder of his steward, A.

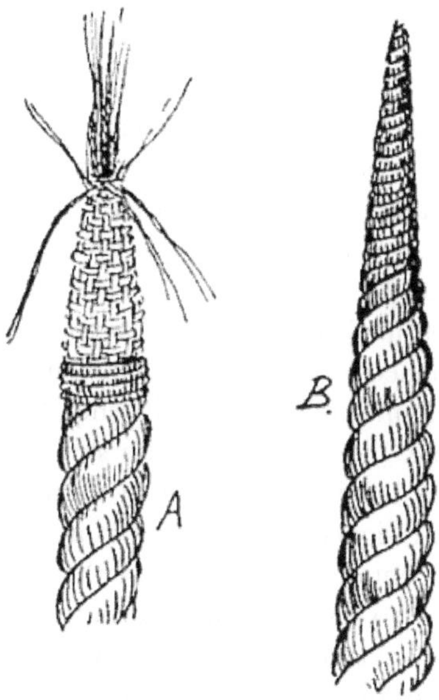

Fig 12. Pointing of rope.

On this occasion Finey drew attention to the poor quality of his coir cables and the difficulty of finding replacement cables in Malacca:

> This is to Certify, to whom it may concern, that Two cair [coir] Cables of 17 Inch purchased at Madras, one from the Honble Company, & the other of the Native Rope maker Employed by them, – have in consequence of the badness of the coir, both parted the 2nd June of letting go they being perfectly bad & useless – I do thereby Protest against them, – and against any Damage that may occur to my ship in consequence of their failure, as it is impossible to purchase more than one in lieu at this place.

The *Soolymany* had previously been an annual visitor to China from Bombay and Finey had taken it there in 1810, but it is not recorded as arriving in 1811.[23]

John Dease (Butler John), by fenestration. According to Finey, who had been acquitted of the charge of murder the previous month, Butler John had misused the £500 given to him to purchase vegetables for the ship. After slapping his face and sending for the cane Finey said he became aware that the man was in the act of falling out of the window 'by accident in going to look at the vegetables that were stowed over the cabin windows'. During the trial the serang and the seacunnies complained of ill-usage from the captain, <https://www.oldbaileyonline.org/browse.jsp?id=t18150405-166&div=t18150405-166>[Accessed 15 April 2025].

23 Van Dyke, *Whampoa*, Appendix 1.2b.

Leaks

Judging from the Protests, leaks were a common occurrence on country trading ships, but their reporting is almost always associated with storms, rough seas and bad weather and whether there was a weakness in the ship itself is difficult to discern. Sometimes, however, attention in a Protest is focused more on the leak *per se*.

On 13 October 1800 an EIC ship, the *Thames*, recorded in Dutch as *De Thims* (1,432 tons, launched in London in 1796), arrived in Malacca after a voyage from China and, unusually for an EIC ship, Captain Robert Williams registered a Protest note.[24] An extract of the ship's journal was said to be entered into the records but is not present in the *Prothocol Books*. A Protest, recorded in Dutch and signed by Henry Grant, first officer, and James Forman, carpenter, was entered, by request of the captain, on 16 October[25] and also made reference to the on-board journal. All that can be made out of this very indistinct entry is that at lat. 3°46´N there was water in the ship, suggestive of a leak. The ship had left Whampoa in August in the middle of the typhoon season when most ships remained in port. This was the second of three voyages from London to China and back made by Captain Williams in the *Thames*.[26]

Captain David Dunlop's Protest of 2 December 1805 is a straightforward account of a leak that appears to be a consequence of weaknesses of the ship though the captain blamed the sea. It described a leak developing in the brig *Alexander* (745 tons, built in Bombay) while transporting a cargo of cotton from Bengal to Canton.[27] Immediately after the vessel left the shore of India on 27 August 1805 it began to take in water, but continued sailing across the Bay of Bengal with the pumps working, to arrive at Malacca on 14 September. At this stage Captain Dunlop made a verbal report about the problem, then (presumably with his ship repaired) he continued the voyage to Canton, delaying the presentation of his written Protest until he had returned from China on 2 December. The leak, he asserted, was 'occasioned

24 *Prothocol Books*, No. 906, 13 October 1800.

25 *Prothocol Books*, No. 907, 16 October 1800.

26 Van Dyke, *Whampoa*, Appendix 1.2b; <https://en.wikipedia.org.wiki/Thames_(1796_EIC_ship)> [Accessed 15 April 2025]. A painting, 'Deck scene in an Indiaman' held at the National Maritime Museum, Greenwich, has been attributed to Captain Williams: <https://www.rmg.co.uk/collections/objects/rmgc-object-12572> [Accessed 15 April 2025]. The National Maritime Museum also holds his manuscript 'Sailing directions mainly for the Eastern Seas' *c.* 1815: <https://www.rmg.co.uk/collections/objects/rmgc-object-512750> [Accessed 15 April 2025].

27 *Prothocol Books*, No. 97, 2 December 1805; Van Dyke, *Whampoa*, Appendix 1.2b; Phipps, *Guide*, p. 84. The brig was lost in the Banda Sea in 1811: (Phipps, *Collection of Papers*, p. 140).

by causality of the sea', and not due to his or his officers' neglect, who at all times did their utmost to preserve the ship and its cargo. He arrived back in Calcutta on 26 December.[28]

The *Indian* (350 tons, built in England) was forced to call at Malacca on 20 July 1813 for repairs and to register a Protest simply because of leaks in the ship itself.[29] It was on a voyage from Batavia and Banka to China, when on 16 July in lat. 1°10′N, long. 106°00′E (east of Riau) the water in the ship exceeded 9 inches per hour and could be heard running into the vessel 'with considerable force' about 3 feet below the waterline. Captain George Dallas Barclay 'consulted with the officers', all of whom were 'unanimously of opinion with myself from the situation of the leaks that the ship could not encounter any bad weather in the China Seas in the present state'. To preserve the ship and cargo they decided to proceed to the nearest port, Malacca, for repairs, and in a brief statement, to protest against the leaks. At least one of the ship's planks appeared 'much decayed and rotten'. The Protest was signed also by the chief officer, R. K. Gibson, and Henry Burnett, the acting second officer.

There is a mystery as to why this Protest is signed by George Dallas Barclay when everything points to Andrew Barclay being the captain of the *Indian*. George Dallas Barclay RN (*c.* 1783–1834) had been promoted to lieutenant after serving as midshipman in the Battle of Trafalgar in 1805. There is nothing in his obituary[30] to suggest that he had been a country trader. Andrew Barclay on the other hand had commanded the *Indian* in 1810–11 as a convict ship on a voyage to Sydney and from there to Bengal. He had taken the ship to China in 1811 and is recorded as the captain at Whampao in the 1813 voyage discussed in the current text.[31] Is it possible that the two Barclays were one and the same person?[32]

28 *Bengal Hurkaru*, 31 December 1805. David Dunlop (*c.* 1770–1808) was an experienced captain. Beginning his career in EIC ships from about the age of twelve, as first mate he played a major role in quelling the mutiny aboard the *Belvedere* in 1787. As a country captain he made the voyage to China several times. By 1805 he had been captain of the *Alexander* for at least three years: Hardy, *Register of Ships*, pp. 94, 109, 123, 137; Van Dyke, *Whampoa*, pp.112–4, Appendix 1.2b.

29 *Ibid.*, Appendix 1.2b; <https://en.wikipedia.org/wiki_Indian_(1810)_ship> [Accessed 15 April 2025]; *Prothocol Books*, No. 911, 20 July 1813.

30 *Asiatic Journal and Monthly Register*, vol. 13, n.s., January to April 1834, p. 304.

31 Van Dyke, *Whampoa*, Appendix 1.2b.

32 Andrew Barclay was afterwards captain of the *Lucy & Maria,* which sailed between Bengal and England and in August 1817 was presented with a piece of plate by the officers of the 80th Regiment of Foot in appreciation of his professionalism and kindness during a voyage from Calcutta to Mauritius, the Cape of Good Hope and Portsmouth: *European Magazine and London Review*, vol. 72, August 1817, p. 118. There has also been some confusion between Andrew Barclay of the *Indian* and Andrew Barclay of the *Providence,* who settled in Van Dieman's Land, a muddle perhaps arising from the fact that both ships were in Port Jackson as convict transports in 1811.

One rather short Protest regarding a leak was lodged at Malacca on 5 November 1814 by Peter McLardie, captain of the brig *Eagle* (150 tons).[33] The *Eagle* was on its way to Calcutta when it sprang a leak in the Malacca Roads on 28 October after taking on supplies of firewood and water. The ship's master tendered an eight-line statement about the problem that had resulted in 18 to 20 inches of water in the hold that the crew had commenced pumping out. There was no mention of the cause of the leak. The brig was a small Calcutta vessel of only 150 tons, ten years old, with many voyages to Port Jackson undertaken, so the cause may have been the ravages of time; it foundered in 1816.[34] The Protest was also witnessed by the chief mate, Joop Dalton, and by the second (?) mate, one of those seamen who signed only with a mark.

Another Protest that was caused primarily by a leak in the ship, though there was also 'a heavy sea running', was that registered on 17 July 1816 by the captain and officers of the *Forbes* (600 tons, built in Chittagong 1812).[35] Thomas Basden wrote in the ship's journal of 15 and 16 June 1816, simply headed 'at sea', that a leak had developed on the gun deck. The carpenters were called and the leak was stopped. However, 'having reason to suppose a great quantity of the Cargo damaged We the undersigned dó protest against the above circumstances'. It was signed by the commander and three other officers.

The *Cornwallis*, already twenty-six years old, could be considered an ageing ship when it sprang a leak in August 1816 during a trip from Bombay to Canton. Captain Robert Graham protested on 6 August that 'if any of the cargo is damaged it may be from the leak above mentioned'.[36] Graham captained the ship from 1809 until 1824 and took it on regular trips to China. Notwithstanding this leak and the previously discussed bad weather problem in 1817 (Protest No. 325, 12 August), the *Cornwallis* must have been well built, as it was sailing until 1841.[37]

When water began continuously to enter the relatively youthful *Lady Flora* (705 tons, built in Calcutta 1813) on a voyage from Calcutta to Canton in 1818, the crew, as reported in a Protest of 6 August, had to take action at sea

33 *Prothocol Books*, No. 1032, 5 November 1814; *East-India Register and Directory for 1814*, p. 121.

34 Phipps, *Guide*, p. 75; Phipps, *Collection of Papers*, p. 100; Margaret J. E Steven, 'Robert Campbell, Colonial Merchant 1769–1846' (Unpublished PhD thesis, ANU, 1962), *passim*; McLardie and J. Mackay (q.v.) of the *Argo* both worked for Fairlie, Ferguson & Co., both had at various times commanded the *Eagle* and had acted to collect debts owing to the company at Port Jackson.

35 *Prothocol Books*, No. 155, 17 July 1816; Phipps, *Guide*, p. 92; *East-India Register and Directory for 1819*, p. 134.

36 *Prothocol Books*, No. 170 (?), August 1816.

37 Bulley, *Bombay Country Ships*, p. 124; Van Dyke, *Whampoa*, Appendix 1.2b; *East-India Register and Directory*, various years.

to find the source of the leak.[38] It was necessary to pump each day from 12 July until on the 29th the decision was made to lighten the ship by discarding cargo. By 1 August the crew had 'discharged a sufficiency of cargo to lighten the ship 11 or 12 inches', and then, by moving more cargo and stores from the starboard to the port side of the decks, they enabled the first and second sheets of copper sheathing on the starboard side to be visible above the water line. As Captain Balston and his officers wrote, 'on taking the copper sheathing of the Bow we found a plank very badly taken(?) extending from the Stern to 10 or 11 Feet aft, and not 4 inches any way without an opening sufficient to admit the quantity of water which the Ship have made'. They protested against the losses and damages incurred as a result of the faulty plank, having done everything they could to save the cargo. The *Flora* still managed to complete the voyage as Balston was among those who signed the testimonial to Horsburgh in October in Canton.[39]

38 Phipps, *Guide*, p. 76; *Prothocol Books*, No. 479, 6 August 1818.
39 *Asiatic Journal and Monthly Register*, January to June 1819, p. 673.

5

Pirates, Robbers and Thieves

In addition to sailing through a region of turbulent monsoonal weather and somewhat uncharted seas, the country traders operating in the Malay region and between India and China had to pass close by countries with a variety of cultures, ethnicities, languages, societies and values. Robert J. Antony has described the South China Sea, for example, as 'a maritime melting pot'.[1] Thus, when the route went through the Malacca Strait, through the Malay Archipelago and through the South China Sea and the country traders came into contact with the peoples of these regions they were often faced with social customs outside of their own European-based value systems.

One such traditional custom involving the sea was that generally described in modern studies as maritime raiding. In island Southeast Asia during the late eighteenth century there was 'an upsurge in Maritime raiding'.[2] 'Piracy' – the term formerly applied by the British to the hostile and unauthorised seizure of goods or ships by the local people in a maritime setting – covered a variety of activities intrinsic to local indigenous societies. It could, for instance, be considered a part of legitimate trading, a section of the informal economy, an extension of state power (privateering), opposition to foreign traders or simply a means of increasing labour supply by capturing slaves. It came in many forms by a variety of people, including mutiny by indigenous crews.[3]

1 Robert J. Antony (ed.), *Elusive Pirates, Pervasive Smugglers: Violence and Clandestine Trade in the Greater China Seas* (Hong Kong, 2010), p. 5.

2 Barbara Watson Andaya and Leonard Y. Andaya, *A History of Early Modern Southeast Asia, 1400–1830* (Cambridge, 2015), p. 292.

3 For a discussion of the different varieties of maritime raiding, the reasons for their increase, their nomenclature and their role in society see, among others, Nicholas Tarling, *Piracy and Politics in the Malay World: A Study of British Imperialism in Nineteenth-Century South-East Asia* (Melbourne, 1963); Anthony Reid, *Southeast Asia in the Age of Commerce 1450–1680: Volume Two, Expansion and Crisis* (New Haven CT, 1993); James Francis Warren, *Iranun and Balangingi: Globalization, Maritime Raiding and the Birth of Ethnicity* (Singapore, 2002); Michael Pearson, *Great Southern Land: the Maritime Exploration of Terra Australis* (Canberra, 2005); Ota Atsushi, 'From 'piracy' to inter-regional trade: the Sunda Straits zone, c.1750–1800', *IIAS Newsletter*, 36 (2005), 9; Stefan Eklof Amirell, *Pirates*

Descriptions of particular 'piratical' attacks on British shipping have been included in various studies of trade and traders in the Malay Archipelago.[4]

As an incentive to face such dangers sailors could be given higher pay. For example, recalling his time as a seaman aboard the country trader *Nonsuch* in about 1793, William Richardson wrote:

> She was ready for sea, and only waiting for a cargo of opium to trade among the Malays, a savage and treacherous people, who come out with their prows full of men, and, if opportunity offers, will board a ship, murder the crew, and then plunder her. Some instances of the kind had lately happened, and for this reason the Nonsuch was well armed, and, being a dangerous voyage, higher wages were given.[5]

When a ship was stuck on a reef or otherwise abandoned it could be subject to ransacking by the local 'Malays', a fate that country trader captains sometimes attempted to prevent by raising a flag on the wreck or leaving it for as short a time as possible before returning to recover the cargo. The Malacca Protests, as we have seen, afford several examples of this type of activity: the *La Paix* unable to be boarded after stranding in November 1805 as the Malays had taken possession of it; the *Triton*'s longboat attacked by six Malay prows and the wrecked ship plundered in September 1808; the theft of stores from the *New Endeavour* in January 1809 after its beaching following destruction by fire; and the ransacking of the stranded brig *Vestal* in September 1818. Captain Strut of the stranded *Caroline* feared such an outcome in November 1816 when he left the ship with the Ensign flying Union down in hopes it might deter the Malays from boarding the vessel.

These attacks, which could be described as opportunistic looting consequent upon an existing misfortune, all took place in the Malacca Strait and along the Pedir coast. There was said to be a certain regularity in escalated piratical behaviour in the Strait of Malacca when the 'pirates' wind' of August,

in Paradise: A Modern History of Southeast Asia's Maritime Marauders (Copenhagen, 2006); Adrian B Lapian, 'Violence and Armed Robbery in Indonesian Seas', in John Kleinen and Manon Osseweijer (eds), *Pirates, Ports and Coasts in Asia: Historical and Contemporary Perspectives* (Singapore, 2010), pp. 131–46; Stefan Eklof Amirell, *Pirates of Empire: Colonisation and Maritime Violence in Southeast Asia* (Cambridge, 2019). For a recent discussion of the attitudes of British and other European authorities towards 'sea nomads' see , Martin Müeller, 'Primitive, Peregrinate, Piratical: Framing Southeast Asian Sea-Nomads in Nineteenth-Century Colonial Discourse and Imperial Practice', in John Coakley, C. Nathan Kwan and David Wilson (eds), *The Problem of Piracy in the Early Modern World: Maritime Predation, Empire, and the Construction of Authority at Sea* (Amsterdam, 2024), pp. 57–92.

4 See, for example, F. Andrew Smith's articles.

5 William Richardson, *A Mariner of England: An Account of the Career of William Richardson from Cabin Boy in the Merchant Service to Warrant Officer in the Royal Navy [1780–1819] as told by himself*, ed. Colonel Spencer Childers (Greenwich, 1970), pp. 83–4.

September and October brought the dreaded Lanuns to this area.[6] The Lanuns were from the island of Mindanao with outposts around Borneo and Sulu, which area was also home to the marauding Balinini. Modern scholarship also defines three less savage groups of 'sea nomads': the Moken from the eastern coast of the Andaman Sea, the Orang Laut, native to Malacca Strait and the Sama-Bajau, from the eastern parts of the Indonesian Archipelago.[7] The Protest narratives, however, do not pinpoint particular groups. The local culprits were, more broadly, 'Malays', 'Javanese' or 'from Manila'. The most specific description was given by the captain of the American ship *Putnam,* which, he said, was captured at Riau in November 1805 by people belonging to Raja Adhrus, a Bugis.[8]

Four more incidents regarding 'pirates' have made their way into the Malacca records as British Protests: those concerning the *Admiral Troubridge* attacked in December 1807, the *Margaret* in August 1809, the *Malacca* also in 1809 and the *Argo* in December 1814, all of which misadventures took place in the Borneo-Sulu region.

The Protests (four cases in chronological order)

The only account of actual mutiny occurring in the Malacca *Prothocol Books* is that involving the brig *Admiral Troubridge*[9] in 1807. We have both a joint account by the captain and part-owner, Alexander Wallace, and another part-owner, Thomas Barnes, as a Protest on 22 December, as well as a separate account by the chief officer, William Sharp, as a Protest on the same day.[10]

6 Eklof Amirell, *Pirates in Paradise*, p. 9.

7 Müeller, 'Primitive, Peregrinate, Piratical', pp. 59–60.

8 British Library, Asia, Pacific and Africa Collections, *Malacca, General Prothocol Books (Registers of Legal Deeds) 1786–1825*, IOR: R/9/22/1–75 [referred to in this study as *Prothocol Books*], Nos 108, 26 December 1805; 109, 27 December 1805. Described in Part II – Protests: Non-British Ships.

9 The *Admiral Troubridge* was captured from the Dutch about 1806 and sold that year by auction in Penang to Thomas Jones, as revealed in a letter from Raffles to Judge John Dickins at Penang, 6 November 1806: <https://www.nas.gov.sg/citizenarchivist/Documents/Transcribe?collectionId=153&itemId=39619#collection> [Accessed 15 April 2025]. The contemporary accounts of the mutiny suggest that the *Admiral Troubridge* was never recovered, but it is possible that it is the same ship as the *Troubridge* (750 tons), which took part in the invasions of Île Bourbon and Île de France (1810) and Java (1811), this vessel said to have been originally the *Lucy Maria*, captured by the Dutch and when recaptured renamed *Troubridge*; <https://profilpelajar.com/article/Lucy_Maria_(1801_ship)> [Accessed 15 April 2025]. For the tragic events surrounding the 1803/1804 voyage of the *Lucy Maria*, see W. G. Miller, *British Traders in the East Indies 1770–1820: 'At Home in the Eastern Seas'* (Woodbridge, 2020), Chapter 4, and F. Andrew Smith, 'James Carnegy and the "Country Trade" in Penang, c.1802–1824', *JMBRAS*, 96:1 (2023), 51–80, at p. 62.

10 *Prothocol Books*, Nos 195, 22 December 1807; 196, 22 December 1807.

On 21 August of that year Wallace and Barnes went ashore at Sulu. While on land they were surprised to learn that their vessel was under way. They immediately asked the local ruler to provide them with prahus to try and get the vessel back, but it was said that none of the local craft were available.

At the time the vessel was seized, the chief officer, William Sharp, was on board and his account provides the most detail of events. Sharp was fortunate to escape with his life; the second officer, Lloyd, and the gunner were killed and their bodies thrown overboard:

> On the 21st August 1807 the brig Admiral Troubridge was laying at Sooloo all well. At 5 PM the same day Captain Wallace come on board and gave directions respecting the duty of the vessel and went on shore again at about 7 in the evening, at which time the crew were quiet and no apprehensions entertained for our safety. Mr. Loyd the Second Officer had charge of the deck from 8 to Twelve PM and a little before nine I retired to my cabin. The crew peaceable and quiet as before. To the best of my knowledge it was between Eleven and Twelve when I was alarmed with some cries and the clashing of cutlasses which made me go into the steerage and look up the hatchway where one of the people made a stab at me with a boarding pike. On seeing this I hastened to my cabin for a loaded pistol which I had scarcely time to get before two others (a Manila seacunny and a Malay lascar) rushed down with the cutlasses on whom I fired and wounded the seacunny in the arm. From the report of the pistol those on deck seemed to be frightened as no one attempted to come down till a sepoy who was stationed below as guard seized me round the waist and called for assistance, saying he had secured me, on which I forced him to the cabin with me as he would not let go his hold, and seized on another loaded pistol, when two others threw me on my cot which was a standing one in the cabin. I extricated myself so far as to regain the steerage and called to Mr. Loyd for assistance but received no answer. Those below again caught hold of me and the Seapoy seized on the pistol in my hand. I endeavoured to force myself away from them to get a sword but could not effect it. In this scuffle the ladder was displaced and three or four more jumped down who made many cuts and stabs at me by which I was severely wounded. During the tumult I discharged the pistol and wounded the seapoy in the hand and it was then wrested from me.
>
> Those below replaced the ladder and two others descended, who again made several cuts and stabs at me and cryed out he is done for, supposing they had murdered me. One of the cuts wounded me very severely on the neck, which with the other wounds I had received so weakened me by loss of blood that I was unable to support myself. They then bound my hands behind me and lashed me to the spindle of the capstan but being unable to stand they removed me in a few minutes after to my cot where I was lashed down and an armed man left to guard me. Shortly after I heard a gun discharged on deck and the noise of bending sails on which Dicky the Syrang seemes very active as I heard his voice repeatedly cheering up the people.
>
> I know nothing more of their proceedings till about eight o'clock in the morning of the 22nd when they released me from the cot, placed me in irons

> and spiked them to the deck in my cabin and left me. In the afternoon I heard several guns discharged on deck and understood they were fired at a small boat approaching the brig. At about six in the evening the Manilla Seacunny, who appeared one of the principals and named Joze, came to a resolution with the others to send me onto shore in one of the brig's boats, and I was accordingly sent away with two seacunnies who it appeared had not engaged in the mutiny, named Domingo de Cruz and Antonio Pedro, together with the Captain's servant Benjamin, a Chinese passenger and a woman, in all six persons, at which time the vessel had all convenient sail set, and standing away from the island of Sooloo.
>
> We reached the Captain's house at Sooloo between one and two o'clock in the morning of the 23rd August 1807. In witness whereof I have hereunto set my hand and seal and am ready to make oath to the truth of this declaration wherever called on.

Captain Wallace and Thomas Barnes wrote a formal Protest, dated 22 August, while at Sulu. This was also signed by G. Jones and seven crew members who did not take part in the mutiny, most of these men, with Malay and Portuguese names, signing with a cross or a sign. However, the Protest was not able to be formally presented to a legal official before 22 December 1807 when the group arrived in Malacca aboard the *Jane* (Captain E. Masquerier), which called at Sulu on 30 August and departed on 6 September. The *Jane* apparently attempted to find the *Admiral Troubridge* by heading to Manado, but the 'pirated' ship appears to have proceeded further east, under American colours, towards Ternate. The mutiny generated a great deal of interest and accounts of it were published in the *Asiatic Annual Register* for 3 January 1808, *The Naval Chronicle* for 1808 and, as a booklet, by Thomas Tegg. In all accounts the action was referred to as a 'piratical seizure'.[11]

The voyage of the mariners to Malacca on the *Jane* was itself not without misadventure. As noted above the ship ran aground on 14 December off Lingga when approaching the port and on 23 December 1807 tabled a copy of the logbook at Malacca as a Protest.

Another case of 'piracy' that resulted in a Protest, on 21 March 1809, involved the *Margaret* (perhaps the *Margaret*, 200 tons, built in Rangoon),[12] commanded by Captain Daniel Smith, which was seized off Pontianak on 25 December 1808. Daniel Smith is one country trader who suffered more than his fair share of misadventures, of which the later ones in particular have been

11 *Asiatic Annual Register*, vol. 10, January 1808 (1811), pp. 141–2; *The Naval Chronicle*, vol. 20, July to December 1808, pp. 346–8; Piratical seizure of the brig *Admiral Trowbridge* (*c.* 1808); Aaron Jaffer, *Lascars and India Ocean Seafaring, 1780–1860: Shipboard Life, Unrest and Mutiny* (Woodbridge, 2015) (various pages) compares events during the mutiny to those in other mutinies.

12 *Prothocol Books*, No. 340, 21 March 1809; *East-India Register and Directory for 1805*, p. 108.

Mr Sharp, chief of the Brig Admiral Trowbridge; barbarously wounded, put in Irons, & Spiked to the Deck by Pirates.

Fig 13. Illustration by William Eames from *Piratical seizure of the brig Admiral Trowbridge ...August 21, 1807*. London, printed for Thomas Tegg, c.1808.

discussed by F. Andrew Smith.[13] In the years 1808 and 1809 his experiences included a series of events relating to captures and attacks. First, there was the capture and release of the *Margaret* by the French in mid-1808.[14] Then there was the attempt of Smith and the *Margaret* in September of that year to assist the *Triton* after that ship had been stranded and subject to Malay attacks.[15] This was followed by the seizure of the *Margaret* in November, the subject of the current Protest, and finally in November 1809 the capture by the French of the *Mary*,[16] Smith's next command after the loss of the *Margaret*.

In respect of Smith's 1809 Malacca Protest, the *Margaret* departed Penang on a voyage to 'the Malay Islands' on 21 November 1808 with a cargo of 'sundries'. It called at Malacca, Riau and Lingga to do 'business', collecting in particular 3,300 dollars in Malacca, before arriving at Pontianak on 9 December. Smith continued to trade ashore at the port until, on 25 December, a lascar arrived with several Chinese fishermen to inform him that his ship had departed. Several Javanese who had been communicating between the ship and the shore in the longboat had also deserted into the jungle after killing the gunner.

Smith was obliged to remain at Pontianak until 28 February 1809, during which time he collected the debts owing to him, amounting to '3,560 Dollars'. He finally sailed as a passenger on the *Clyde*, commanded by Captain Samuel Stewart, reaching Malacca on 20 March. On that day he lodged a Protest: 'I Daniel Smith do solemnly Protest and declare that the loss or capture of said ship *Margaret* has not happened through any neglect or mismanagement in me but entirely owing to causes unknown to me.'[17] After this he continued on the *Clyde* back to Penang, arriving at the end of March 1809.[18]

Soon after this, on 13 May 1809, Captain Hercules Ross of the grab *Malacca*, who had been commander of a country trader out of Madras since at least 1804, recorded a note of Protest about the piratical seizure of his vessel by members of his crew. To this was appended details of the misadventure that were entered into the *Prothocol Books* on the 17th.[19] Ross explained that on the week following 23 April he had been ashore at Pontianak concluding business deals for his cargo of iron, opium and tin and was preparing to proceed to Banka to purchase more tin for sale to the Sultan at Pontianak when on Saturday the 29th at 9 p.m. 'the gunner arrived in the shore boat and informed me the brig was not in the roads'. A search conducted by the

13 F. Andrew Smith, 'Daniel Smith's last seven years: hardships in country trade in the East Indies in the early nineteenth century', *Borneo Research Bulletin*, 39 (2008), 71–90.

14 *Ibid.*, p. 72.

15 Mentioned in the Protest of Captain Patrick, *Prothocol Books*, No. 277, 4 October 1808.

16 The subject of Protest No. 517, 9 July 1810.

17 *Prothocol Books*, No. 340, 21 March 1809.

18 Smith, 'Daniel Smith's last seven years', p. 73.

19 *Prothocol Books*, No. 356, 13 May 1809.

longboat and the Sultan's boat failing to find the vessel, he purchased a large boat from the Sultan and paid 'sixteen Buggies [Bugis] men five hundred Reals to go with me with arms and three two Pounders'. When abreast of 'Linguer River' on 9 May he was informed that a brig had been sighted 'off the east end of Linger five days ago'. He recorded the details of the chase:

> Immediately made sail for Malacca, daylight Peaks of Linger East, Noon Pulo Baya, NNW, Wednesday 6P.M. Pulo Baya NEbE, daylight Pulo Baya SE, entrance of the Straits NWbN, Noon the Carrimons NE. Thursday 6PM Carrimons East. Daylight Formosa North, Noon Formosa East. Friday 6pm abreast of Padang River, midnight off the Water Island. Daylight anchored in Malacca. Found the brig in the Roads. The crew having run away with her with an intention to proceed to Java. I hereby Protest against the consequences thereof, any property that may be deficient, and also any losses incurred on the voyage.

The owner of the *Malacca*, Alexander Hare, a merchant residing at Malacca at the time, was at hand when the grab arrived in the Roads on 8 May, the vessel having been brought there by the nakhoda of a local prahu who, by a twist of circumstances, had apprehended the instigators of the seizure, Herbert Styles and Christian Kleyn. Hare submitted a Protest against the seizure of the vessel on the same day.[20] Styles and Kleyn were tried in Calcutta in December 1809 and sentenced to life imprisonment.[21]

On 25 November 1814 Captain J. Mackay and two officers from the *Argo* (250 tons, built in Pegue) tabled as a Protest a description of the day's events that they had written on 2 November 1814 while lying in the 'Road of Borneo' (most likely Brunei).[22] It related to what the officers took to be another case of attempted piracy. At 8 a.m. on that day the *Argo* was at anchor when a number of 'prows' approached the ship. The country trader was suspicious, especially when the 'prows' attempted to put themselves between the *Argo* and the open sea. Shots were fired at times, and the crew of the country trader 'thought it most prudent for the safety of the ship and our lives to cut from the anchor of fourteen hundredweight … sixty fathoms of fourteen-inch cable' and stand out to sea. Apparently, the ship had been warned the day before of a possible seizure attempt. The crew of the *Argo* had three men ashore still occupied in collecting cargo, but Mackay and his officers decided it was wiser to abandon the trading and to sail away. The

20 *Prothocol Books*, No. 355, 8 May 1809.

21 For more details of this act of piracy and its outcome and for a short biography of Ross, who was himself murdered by pirates off Banka in 1810, see F. Andrew Smith, 'Piracy off Pontianak in the early nineteenth century – and not by the Usual Villains; with an Appendix on Captain Hercules Ross, Country Trader and Native of Jamaica', *Borneo Research Bulletin*, 43 (2012), 61–71.

22 *East-India Register and Directory for 1814*, p. 120; *Prothocol Books*, No. 1045, 25 November 1814.

captain and his officers, N. Penney and Thomas Dickson, lodged the Protest against 'the behaviour of the Pirates' for any losses that occurred.

These 'piratical' incidents were serious affairs, with an officer and two gunners killed. The ships were all in good order, unlike the victims of stranding in the Malacca Strait. But they must still have been regarded as easy pickings – all anchored in the roads and, with the exception of the *Argo*, all with captains ashore. The captain of the *Argo*, aboard his ship and forewarned of possible trouble, was able to take evasive action. Furthermore, the *Argo*, *Margaret* and *Malacca*, as well as the American *Putnam*, were all small vessels. The perpetrators of the seizures were neither all locals nor all Indian lascars but a mixed bag. The *Admiral Troubridge* mutineers appear to have been a mixture of lascars, Malays and Portuguese, with some Malays and Portuguese not joining in; among the crew on the *Margaret* were mutinous Javanese who escaped ashore leaving others who, according to Smith (2012), took the commandeered vessel to Java; the two instigators of the insurrection on the *Malacca* were British (Styles) and Batavo-Malay Christian (Kleyn) with Chinese accomplices and a crew forced to acquiesce;[23] the attackers of the *Argo* were local Malays. The latter launched their attack in prahus. This was the same method employed by the 'pirates' that menaced the Dutch brig *Carolina* near the Strait of Dryon in November 1803 and whom Captain Verhaage avoided by returning to Malacca.[24] Whether prahus were involved in the capture of the *Margaret* is not known as there were no eye-witness accounts of events.

While not all lascar crews were mutinous, they were still quite likely to aid marauding parties. The recruitment of lascars by country traders followed the custom of EIC recruitment whereby the supply of local labour was controlled by Indian intermediaries known as 'ghat serangs' at Bombay and Calcutta. Another serang was employed on board to supervise and pay the men and instructions from the officers were communicated via this serang.[25] Loyalty to the ship would not therefore have been a common sentiment. In his study of lascars Aaron Jaffer also points out that a method of showing disgruntlement was a refusal to work ('a second type of mutiny'), especially in dangerous situations. Fear also propelled a propensity of the crew to save themselves rather than to work for the common good.[26] The Protests of Captain Elliott of the *Vestal*, Captain Brown of the *Abercromby* and Captain Daniels of the *Athena* all mention disobedient lascars.

23 Smith, 'Piracy off Pontianak', pp. 62–4.

24 *Prothocol Books*, No. 1298, 1 December 1803. Described in Part II – Protests: Non-British Ships.

25 Lahiri, Shompa, 'Contested Relations: The East India Company and Lascars', in H. V. Bowen, Margaret Lincoln and Nigel Rigby (eds), *The Worlds of the East India Company* (Woodbridge, 2002), pp. 169–81, at 171.

26 Jaffer, *Lascars*, pp. 83–5.

6

Coercion, Imprisonment and Detention

In addition to delays caused by storm damage, groundings, fire and ravages by pirates, country traders could also be impeded by imprisonment, detention, embargoes and other forms of harassment. Surprisingly, these interruptions to trade did not result solely from altercations with wartime enemies, such as the French, but arose also from the different agendas of the Malay States or from clashes with that ostensible defender of the country traders, the British Royal Navy. The following Protests have been divided into these different groupings where belligerence could result in loss of life, goods and time.

The Protests (nine cases)

Capture by the Malays

On a slightly different plane to the European notion of wartime capture there was also the possibility of capture by the Malays as an extension of their custom of maritime raiding. The murder of Captain Thomas Sadler at Mempawah in 1795 falls into this category.

The event has previously been described in some detail.[1] In summary, however, the Protest, in English, signed by Thomas Groube, first mate, and other officers of the country trader vessel *Transfer*, reported the murder of their captain.[2] It was presented to the Dutch notary on 5 August 1795 when the *Transfer* called at Malacca. Sadler was an experienced, highly regarded country captain who had traded around the archipelago for at least twelve years, including to Mempawah. On the particular voyage in question, the *Transfer* arrived at Mempawah on Sunday 12 July 1795 and Sadler spent the next few days ashore while cargo was being traded. When the jollyboat did

1 W. G. Miller, 'Why Did Syarif Kassim Kill Captain Sadler at Mempawah in 1795?', *JMBRAS*, 85:1 (2012), 63–84.

2 British Library, Asia, Pacific and Africa Collections, *Malacca, General Prothocol Books (Registers of Legal Deeds) 1786–1825*, IOR: R/9/22/1–75 [referred to in this study as *Prothocol Books*], No. 83, 5 August 1795.

not return to the ship on the 19th, the crew became concerned. Through the ship's Malay cabin boy who was sent to see the ruler Syarif Kassim on 21 July, the message was received that Sadler and the crew members who were with him had left the shore for the ship on the 18th. It was noted that Kassim and the residents of Mempawah were now far less friendly. The officers of the *Transfer* had no alternative but to cut their losses and sail away. At the first opportunity they lodged their Protest at Malacca.

Over the years it became evident through a number of sources that Syarif Kassim had murdered Sadler. It is reasonable to conclude that because of the current political situation Kassim was under considerable financial pressure at the time and that this was the chief reason for his action. Mempawah was a divided state and Kassim had lost control of the richest part. Furthermore, he was still a young man and relatively inexperienced at governing. He had the allegiance of the predominant European power at the time in the archipelago, the Dutch, and he might have seen the murder of Sadler and the seizure of the goods as a way of improving his financial situation without too many untoward consequences.

The Protest is a useful contribution to, among other things, our knowledge of how commercial activities were carried out by country traders in Malay states, the state of Mempawah society and politics at the time, and the character of the ruler, Syarif Kassim. The events it describes reveal how necessary it was for country traders to be aware of the fraught, even dangerous, political situation that might exist in a port into which they sailed and how difficult it was, even for an experienced captain, to grasp all the current volatilities in a Malay state.

When Captain D'Coil submitted his Protests (Nos 335, 336) on 14 March 1809 about the destruction of his ship the *New Endeavour* by fire after storm damage, he probably felt no need to report how he had arrived in Malacca, the relevant subject being the loss of the ship. However, the experiences of the ship's complement after the fire of 17 January, as reported in the *Naval Chronicle*,[3] amounted to hostile capture Malay-style by the Malays and Chuleas of Booron on the Pedir coast. After having made it to the shore in the ship's boat the company members, many of them almost naked, were surrounded by the local people and eventually marched to the town of Booron. In the meantime, the vessel was plundered for 'a great quantity of cloths'. The following day the first officer, Mr Roach, and some of the people were severely beaten after they ventured down towards the wreck that had drifted inshore. Four days later they were marched sixty miles over the beach to Tulosumoway (or Tulosamaway, now Lhokseumawe) where they had an audience with the Queen.[4] At the time, Captain John Elliot was in port

3 *Naval Chronicle*, vol. 25, January to June 1811, pp. 477–8.

4 In 1809 the young sultan of Aceh, Jauhar Alam, was trying to establish his authority over an uncle who had ruled since he had succeeded as a minor in 1790. It is not known

fitting out his vessel (name not given) and the Queen allowed the shipwrecked survivors to embark with him to Malacca where they arrived on 13 March. This was an indulgence not to be taken for granted. Horsburgh, in his entry on Tulosamaway, warned against 'the perfidy of the natives ... who have been too successful, at various times, in surprising small ships or two-masted vessels, and massacreing their crews'.[5]

Capture by foreign power

> Capture, properly so called is a taking by the enemy as prize, in time of open war, or by the way of reprisals with intent to deprive the owner of all dominion or right of property over the thing taken.[6]

Hostile capture of a British country trader by the Dutch defending their trading territory or by the French on a war footing against England was a possibility at particular times. The French, operating from their base at Île de France (Mauritius), presented a major danger to shipping in the Bay of Bengal and the Malay Archipelago during the years of the French Revolutionary and Napoleonic wars until the island was captured at the end of 1810. The British war with America during the years 1812–15 also presented a threat. Captain Daniel Smith's ship *Adele*, for example, was captured by the American *Jacob Jones* in the Pontianak roads in 1814[7] and Phipps (1840) lists three Calcutta ships captured by USS *Peacock* in 1815 in the Strait of Sunda. However, there were no Protests in Malacca arising from American hostilities.

Country ships were always armed and could be called upon to play a wartime role. Towards the end of 1793 the EIC chartered three country ships, including the *Fort William* and the *Nonsuch* to be armed as privateers cruising the Sunda Strait, and many others received letters of marque.[8] Later on two country traders captained by Frazer Sinclair, the *Forbes* in 1806 and the *Farquhar* in 1806–8, the latter referred to as a 'Private Ship of War', also acquired letters of marque and captured several Dutch vessels.[9] More typically they were recruited as transports. For example, seven of the country

---

to which camp the 'Queen' belonged.

5 James Horsburgh, *India Directory, Or, Directions for Sailing to and from the East Indies, China, New Holland, Cape of Good Hope, Brazil, and the Interjacent Ports ...*, 2nd edn (2 vols, London 1817), vol. 2, p. 153.

6 Joseph Arnould, *A Treatise on the Law of Marine Insurance and Average ...* (2 vols, London, 1848), vol. 2, p. 808.

7 F. Andrew Smith, 'Daniel Smith's last seven years: hardships in country trade in the East Indies in the early nineteenth century', *Borneo Research Bulletin*, 39 (2008), 71–90, at pp. 80–1.

8 *Bombay Courier*, 13 July, 7 December 1793, 5 April 1794, 22 December 1798.

9 Horst H. Liebner and David van Dyke, 'An account of the loss of the Country Ship Forbes and Frazer Sinclair, her late Commander', *Wacana, Journal of the Humanities of Indonesia*, 17:1 (2016), 38–67, at pp. 44, 53–56.

ships that feature in Protests at Malacca served as transport vessels for the British invasion of Bourbon (now Réunion) and Mauritius in 1810. These were the *Anna, Good Hope, Charlotte, Hamoody, Helen, Troubridge* and *Upton Castle.* Ten of the ships served in the same way for the British invasion of Java in 1811; namely, the *Asia Felix, Batavia, Charlotte, Cornwallis, Fleetwood, Fort William, James Drummond, Sullimany, Thomas Henchman* and *Troubridge.* The *Troubridge* was also taken up as a transport for the Expedition against Sambas in 1813.

Sometimes a country ship could hold its own in the face of enemy aggression either as an armed vessel or as a fast sailer, as when Robert Eastwick in the *Endeavour*, on a voyage from Calcutta to Bencoolen in 1796, was forced to outrun a Dutch cruiser, an exploit remarkable for the fact that it was his wife who took the wheel.[10] But country ships in wartime mainly featured as victims. In his 1840 list of casualties to Calcutta ships Phipps lists fifty Calcutta-built ships lost to the French between 1804 and 1810. Of these one was an EIC 'extra' ship and four were major ships of the EIC. The rest were country ships. Many country ships in operation before 1804 and built elsewhere than Calcutta were also lost. The ships were usually taken to Mauritius to be sold. The captains and officers were sometimes released to be brought home in neutral Danish or American ships as in November 1795 when two American ships delivered to Calcutta the captains of all the prizes taken by the French privateers *Cybele* and *Prudente* in the previous months.[11] Others were held at Mauritius in poor conditions. According to S. B. Singh, in 1804 more than 120 British captains and officers were 'confined in prison of the island of Mauritius, and the treatment meted out to them was extremely harsh'.[12] The situation eased after the French were defeated by the British in the Mauritius campaign of 1809–11.

The other side of the coin was the possibility of capture of foreign or neutral ships by the British. The Protests at Malacca provide examples of this. That of Captain Willem Verhaage of the private Dutch brig *Carolina* is one such, the Protests regarding the Danish ships *Charlotta Amalia* and the *Fredensborg* are others. These events receive attention in Part II of this work.

Given the circumstances, the opportunity to register a Protest at Malacca after being held at Mauritius would have been rather limited as prisoners would most likely be released to Calcutta or Madras. There was at any rate only one Protest at Malacca concerning capture by the French. On 4 June 1809, Daniel Smith, who as mentioned previously had been a victim of piracy in 1808, set sail from Penang on the *Mary*, bound for Manila with a cargo of 'sundries'. Misfortune continued to follow him. In a Protest submitted by

10 Robert William Eastwick, *A Master Mariner; Being the Life and Adventures of Captain Robert William Eastwick*, ed. Herbert Compton (London, 1891), pp. 100–4.

11 *Bombay Courier*, 14 November 1795.

12 S. B. Singh, *European Agency Houses in Bengal 1783–1833* (Calcutta, 1966), p. 201.

himself and his first mate, George Neil, at Malacca on 9 July 1810,[13] eight months later, he first described how at Manila he had sold a part of his cargo, left another part – including textiles, cooper's tools and nails – with an agent and reshipped the remainder aboard the *Mary* along with 17,568 dollars owing to Carnegy & Co from a previous sale. He then described how he had embarked from Manila on 28 October 1809 on the return trip to Penang and how on 11 November the *Mary* had been captured by a French Navy brig, *L'Entreprenant*, under the command of Captain Bouvet on the east coast of the Malay Peninsula to the west of Pulo Aur. Smith was aware of the danger of French vessels patrolling the area and had tried to sail as far west as possible before entering the Malacca Strait. At first sighting, the *Mary* tried to outrun the French but when the heavily armed ship commenced firing at the country trader, it was obliged to surrender. The French transhipped the cargo of 'spices' to the *L'Entreprenant* and the *Mary* was taken to Mauritius as a prize while the officers and crew were taken by the French and landed on Madura. They were kept there and at Java until 20 June 1810 when the Governor General of the East Indies, Herman Willem Daendels, gave them permission to leave on an Arab ketch, resulting in Smith's arrival at Malacca on 7 July 1810.[14]

Smith must have recovered well from his imprisonment and the loss of the *Margaret* and the *Mary*, for he continued to trade in other vessels for a number of years around the Archipelago and to India. He died in Malacca in June 1815.[15]

Detention and coercion by friendly power (the Royal Navy)

According to the 1848 definitions of Arnould, while capture was the forcible taking of a ship in time of war with a view to appropriating it as a prize, an arrest was 'a temporary detention of a ship with a view to ultimately releasing it, or repaying its value'. An arrest or detention could be made by the government of the country to which the ship belonged or by another friendly power. An embargo, an order of government prohibiting the departure of ships or goods from a port or ports within its dominions, was the most common form of arrest or detainment.[16]

The examples reported at Malacca of detention or harassment of British vessels by a friendly power all relate to incidents involving country ships and the British Royal Navy.

On 31 July 1808 Captain F. Patrick, in preparation for a voyage from Calcutta to China, completed loading the *Triton* at Saugor with a cargo

13 *Prothocol Books*, No. 517, 9 July 1810.

14 See also Smith, 'Daniel Smith's last seven years', pp. 73–4.

15 *Ibid.*, p. 83.

16 Arnould, *Treatise*, vol. 2, pp. 813–16.

'consisting of 5,118 bales of cotton averaging 300 pounds each, 22,739 bundles of rattans, and 270 bags of saltpetre'. The next day the ship was detained at the port by an embargo, not able to get under way until 21 August. This detention, which could by itself have warranted a Protest, depending on the consequences of the delay, was in the event included almost incidentally in the Protest of 4 October, which resulted from the complete loss of the *Triton* after a stranding near Parcelar Hill on 8 September (described above).[17] Although the circumstances of the embargo are not explained it provides an example of this type of British government action.

In May 1811 the 'private English brig' *Hope*, captained by William Robert Smith, became a victim of forcible detention. The formation by the British of a fleet of about 100 vessels for the invasion of Java in 1811 must have been a boon for many country ships, for probably more than fifty were recruited as transports.[18] However, the presence of such a large British naval expedition did not automatically prove beneficial for all country traders. The events leading to the detention of *the Hope*, which was not part of the invasion fleet, were related by Captain Smith as a Protest on 7 June 1811, found in an only partly legible document in the *Prothocol Books*.[19]

In Smith's description of the voyage, the *Hope* departed Padang on the west coast of Sumatra on 20 April 1811, calling at Bencoolen and Krui before entering the Sunda Strait. According to Smith, he and one of the owners who was on board, 'Jas' Fraser, intended to trade on the island of Java if it had fallen to the British, or alternatively, 'put ourselves under the Protection of the British Men of War cruising off Java in case that it should not have Surrendered to the British Flag'. Passing through the Sunda Strait the *Hope* had to open fire and prepare for action when several 'pirate' prahus approached.

When the country trader reached the British naval fleet standing off Java on the evening of 15 May the 'supercargo' (presumably Fraser) went on board HMS *Minden*, commanded by Captain Hoare. Smith followed at 6.00 p.m. with the brig's papers and port clearance. Unfortunately for Smith, Captain Hoare did not accept the legality of the *Hope*'s papers but 'detained the Brig and sent a Guard of Marines and a Navy Officer to take command of the Brig stating we had no pass no permission nor any clearance whatsoever to Trade in the Java Sea'. Shortly afterwards, Hoare sent three naval officers and twenty-one sailors to the *Hope* to sail it to the island of Edam (now Damar

17 *Prothocol Books*, No. 277, 4 October 1808. Although not mentioned in the Protest an account of the loss of the *Triton* in the *Asiatic Annual Register*, vol. 10, 1811, p. 89, says the ship was also carrying a valuable cargo of opium.

18 See <https://en.wikipedia.org/wiki/Transport_vessels_for_the_British_invasion_of_Java_(1811)> [Accessed 22 October 2020]. The exact number of ships varies depending on the source.

19 *Prothocol Books*, No. 679, 7 June 1811.

Besar, Pulo Seribu, off Jakarta) for the British fleet's senior officer there to decide what should be done with it. The senior officer must have agreed with Captain Hoare for after examining the ship's papers on 18 May he ordered it to be sailed to Penang. 'Wooded and Watered' at Edam, the *Hope* set out under the charge of the naval officer and sailors. The route took it via Malacca where it arrived on 6 June and where Smith took the opportunity to lodge his Protest the next day.

Smith claimed that the Navy 'took by force' control of the *Hope*, that it was a 'forcible seizure' and that the 'Heads of the Brig' were 'seized'. He further stated that Hoare had said the *Hope* was entirely outside the limits of its pass, that the port clearance from Bencoolen did not give the brig any authority to trade in the Java Sea and that Hoare 'conceived us as no more than a common smuggler'. Smith on the other hand believed that his papers were lawful and valid. He said a ship needed only a pass for twelve months from Bengal stating the areas it would be sailing to, and port clearances from English ports it called at. These he believed he possessed.[20]

Hoare must have suspected that Smith intended to trade with the enemy, for Smith stated that 'it never was my most distant Idea of having an Ilegal Communication in Trade with the Enemy or did I ever hear Mr. Fraser who had the direction of the Vessel ever hint of having any communication with the coast of Java until Such time as a part or the Whole of it came under the British Flag'. Smith said that if Java was found not to be in British hands and trade there was not possible, the intention was to proceed to Banka and Borneo, subsequently returning to Bencoolen.

There was a disdain among particular naval officers for country traders, which may partly account for Hoare's actions.[21] Nevertheless, there does appear something unusual about the *Hope*'s presence as a private vessel near the scene of action, when as many as fifty other country traders were being employed as transport vessels in the invasion fleet. Furthermore, Smith's reaction to the approach of native prahus in the Sunda Strait raises questions as to his having any previous experience in the area; the Sunda Strait was an area where European vessels often restocked with provisions from friendly villagers and while the presence of local pirates cannot be discounted, the

20 Whether the documents that Smith presented were valid is not known. Passes for ships were issued by the Master Attendant's office in Calcutta. Port Clearances are relatively basic documents and state the name of the vessel, the captain, tonnage, colours under which it was sailing, intended destination(s) and a certification that the customs had been paid. Proformas of these documents are given in John Phipps, *A Guide to the Commerce of Bengal for the Use of Merchants, Ship Owners, Commanders … Resorting to the East Indies* (Calcutta, 1823), p. 19–20.

21 W. G. Miller, *British Traders in the East Indies 1770–1820: 'At Home in the Eastern Seas'* (Woodbridge, 2020), p. 148.

month of May was somewhat early in the year for the notorious Ilanun pirates to be operating there.[22]

The arrival of the *Hope* in Madras on 10 August was recorded by the *Madras Courier*.[23] How the affair was settled in not known, but the case of the *Hope* provides an example of yet another form of misadventure that could befall a country trader during turbulent political times, that of interference or subjugation by the British Navy.

Captain George Hammett's ship, the *Charles Baillie* also fell foul of the Navy, as evidenced by his Protest of 18 June 1811. This small (200 tons) country trader was being used as a transport ship for the invasion of Java.[24] According to the extract of the ship's log the ship was 'order'd to sea' (presumably from Malacca) by Captain Peachey of HMS *Hecate*, also part of the invasion fleet, when the vessel had 'only 2 Bower anchors on board'. His Protest suggests that because of the absence of other anchors he could not manipulate the ship sufficiently when it struck a shoal in the Malacca Strait, in sight of Parcelar Hill, in conditions when 'wind blowing hard ship pitching bows under'. The crew were eventually forced to cut the small bower cable. Hammett therefore made the Protest 'against the consequences of the ship having struck on the shoals and all damages that might occur from it also the loss of the cable and the anchor which we cut from'.

The naval officers clearly had little faith in this particular country trader and acted against him, which resulted in a second Protest. The Commander of the Fleet, John Hayes, wrote to Hammett on 18 June to inform him that the services of the *Charles Baillie* (or *Charles Bailey* as it was referred to by Hayes) were no longer required as a 'consequence of the total unfitness of the Transport vessel … for the important purposes for which she was chartered'. The vessel was immediately 'discharged' from the service of the Company. Hammett received Hayes's letter on 20 June 1811 and lodged a Protest against the order the next day.[25] He tended a short and simple statement protesting against the decision to discharge the ship for and on behalf of the owners and those people 'concerned' with the ship.

In another case that denotes the lack of rapport between country traders and the British Navy, the captain of HMS *Africane*, Edward Rodney,[26]

22 James Francis Warren, *Iranun and Balangingi: Globalization, Maritime Raiding and the Birth of Ethnicity* (Singapore, 2002), p. 261.

23 August 1811, p. 1.

24 *Prothocol Books*, No. 683, 18 June 1811; <https://en.wikipedia.org/wiki/Transport_vessels_for_the_British_invasion_of_Java_(1811)> [Accessed 22 October 2020].

25 *Prothocol Books*, No. 684, 21 June 1811.

26 Captain The Hon. Edward Rodney was the youngest son of Admiral George Brydges Rodney. He had command of the *Africaine* from 1811 to 1816. The ship became notorious during the years 1811 to 1815 for multiple cases of sodomy on board. Several of the men were imprisoned and four were hanged in February 1816. See B. R. Burg, 'The HMS African Revisited; The Royal Navy and the Homosexual Community',

took control of the country trader *Mary* at Malacca, previously under the command of George Bateman, and sailed away, leaving the captain ashore. The *Mary* (216 tons, built in Chittagong)[27] had come from Manila and was sailing to Calcutta. Making apparently only a verbal Protest on 27 January 1815,[28] recorded in Dutch (there is no written statement in English), Captain Bateman said that while he was ashore in Malacca reporting to officials of his arrival and attending to some repairs, he received a message from his chief officer that Captain Rodney had sent orders on board to prepare for departure. When on the following morning Bateman prepared to return to his ship it was not there. The record states, *Dat hij Comparant dies halven kompt te Protesteeren gelijk hij doet bij deezen, tegen de gedoentens van den WelEdelen Gestrengen Heer E. Rodney, omtrent het wegvoeren in de Nagt van zijn Comparants schip Mary met dies inhebbende lading van deeze Rheede…* (The declarant herewith Protests against the actions of E. Rodney, Esq. concerning the removal during the night from this Roadstead of the Declarant's ship with its cargo). Bateman went on to declare that Rodney would henceforth be responsible for any loss or misadventures that might befall the vessel.

A fuller picture of the situation is given by a reading of the logbook of the *Africaine*.[29] According to this, HMS *Africaine*, HMS *Owen Glendower* and the 'Merchant Ship' had left Manila on 9 January 1815, the *Mary* being obliged to sail in convoy with *Owen Glendower*. The *Africaine* arrived at Malacca on 20 January. The *Owen Glendower* came in on the 21st without the *Mary* and sailed for Penang on the 26th. The next day:

> Arrived the Mary Geo Bateman Master from Manila having parted from HMS Owen Glendower through neglect sent an order on board to hold in readiness and proceed to Penang under our protection we should sail in the Evening with the Ebb-tide Midnight – called alongside the Mary – the Mate informed us the Capt had gone on shore that he had sent twice to him respecting the orders received but received no answer, and nothing prevented the ship from prosecuting her Voyage. In Consequence of which sent an officer on Board to take Charge of her to Penang.

The *Africaine* weighed and made sail in company with the *Mary* at 1.30 a.m. on 27 January.[30] While we don't know why the *Mary* was being ordered

---

Journal of Homosexuality, 56:2 (2009), 173–94.

27 *East-India Register and Directory for 1816*, p. 129.

28 *Prothocol Books*, No. 1062, 27 January 1815, attested as entered into the record 28 January 1815.

29 National Archives (London), Public Records Office. Admiralty Records, 'Logbook of the *Africaine*', ADM 51, File 2086 [Available at NLA AJCP reel no. 5712–5713].

30 An interesting aside is that Lieutenant Richard Blakeney who was serving on board the *Africaine* and who later published an account of the five-year voyage, had also been left behind at Malacca eighteen months earlier, in May 1813 when, after a brief stop in the Roads, the ship continued its journey. Blakeney and his companions were obliged to

to sail in convoy with the Navy ships, clearly Captain Bateman felt under no obligation to follow naval orders.

Later in 1815 another country trader called *Mary* (probably different from the one above) came into conflict with the Royal Navy. Captain Reano, after a voyage to the Eastwards, protested on 14 November 1815 against the actions of a Mr Van Bragt, who was acting as proxy for the owner of the vessel, Thomas Perkins of Penang.[31] The Protest in Dutch describes how Reano was commissioned in February (presumably 1815) by Perkins, the owner of a vessel called the *William*, to go on a trading voyage to Riau, Makassar, Surabaya, Gresik and Rembang. At Rembang he purchased the brig *Mary* as instructed by Perkins. The *William* returned to Penang under the officer Pedro Soriano. Reano sailed to various places in the *Mary* before arriving at Malacca on 31 October. On 7 November he undertook a voyage to Minto (the name the British gave to Muntok on Banka) to trade. He was tailed by HMS *Elk* (captain John Reynolds).[32] Shots were fired, the *Mary* was boarded and Reano was arrested. On 12 November the purser of the *Elk* at the request of Van Bragt opened the chests of cargo of the *Mary*. Reano protested against his transportation under arrest to Malacca and against any costs and interest that might occur as a consequence of Van Bragt's actions.

These examples illustrate the tensions and prejudices between the Royal Navy and the country traders. These could extend to events that prompted Protests by the country trader captains where their voyages were affected and they feared being held responsible.

---

buy a small boat from the 'natives' in which to follow the ship to Penang. See Richard Blakeney, *The Journal of an Oriental Voyage in His Majesty's Ship Africaine* (London, 1841), p. 156.

31 *Prothocol Books*, No. 37, 14 November 1815.

32 HMS *Elk*, built in 1813, was an 18 gun Cruizer-class brig-sloop captained at this time by John Reynolds: William R. O'Byrne, *A Naval Biographical Dictionary: Comprising the Life and Services of Every Living Officer in Her Majesty's Navy from the Rank of Admiral of the Fleet to that of Lieutenant* (London, 1849), p. 969; *Java Government Gazette*, 23 March 1816.

7

Accusations against Master or Crew (Commercial Problems)

The avenue of Protest was also open to other interested parties to use as a first step towards obtaining compensation or averting blame from themselves for what they perceived as commercial fraud or breaking of a commercial agreement on the part of the captain. Supercargoes, agents, owners and citizens all recorded their grievances at Malacca. While the Protests in this section consistently spring from economic roots, two of them also concern the important role of supercargoes and commanders (in this case Supercargo De Vos and Captain Allan) as carriers of official letters.[1]

The Protests (ten cases in chronological order)

On 21 April 1791 Jacob van Kal and his company protested (in Dutch) against the losses suffered through the late arrival of cargo that had been contracted by James Scott of Penang to be delivered by Captain Stewart of the *Swift*.[2] The cargo, at least 1,000 piculs of red arrack, had deteriorated, as it should have been delivered by the end of February that year. At this stage of his life, van Kal (1754–1829) was a prominent member of the Dutch burgher community in Malacca, holding the positions of secretary of police and tax collector. He was brother-in-law to Governor Abraham Couperus with whom he was in business and in 1792 was appointed Resident of Riau.[3]

1 For a discussion of the role of country traders as carriers of official letters, see W. G. Miller, *British Traders in the East Indies 1770–1820: 'At Home in the Eastern Seas'* (Woodbridge, 2020), pp. 48–9; Annabel Gallop, *The Legacy of the Malay Letter: Warisan Warkah Melayu* (London, 1994), pp. 105–6.

2 British Library, Asia, Pacific and Africa Collections, *Malacca, General Prothocol Books (Registers of Legal Deeds) 1786–1825*, IOR: R/9/22/1–75 [referred to in this study as *Prothocol Books*], No. 43, 21 April 1791.

3 Dennis De Witt, 'The Unfortunate Jacob Van Kal', *Journal of Malaysian Biographies*, 1 (2008), 57–65. Van Kal's failure in this administrative position and his subsequent relentless litigation against Couperus led to his imprisonment first in Malacca and later in Batavia.

In Protests of 10 and 11 January 1798[4] Amirzan Zachariah, a Calcutta merchant 'now residing at Mallacca', declared in an English statement that he had loaded on board the ship *Armenia* nine chests of spices, including cinnamon and nutmeg, but that the captain, John Sands, had not stood by the agreed price, had refused to sign the bill of lading and had sailed away before concluding the business. Zachariah's Protest against Sands specified 'his proceding, & to any damage (?) & prejudice [which] may arrive & occasion hereafter on the said goods'. Sands was a local country trader who had registered a Protest against storm damage in 1794, was known as a business associate of the Malaccan governor Abraham Couperus and whose ship *Armenia* had been taken up as a transport by Admiral Rainier in December 1795 for the expedition to the Moluccas.[5]

The supercargo of the small English brig *Dolphin* (120 tons, belonging to Madras), Willem Adrianus de Vos, protested on 28 May 1801 against the captain, William Dallas, and the first mate, Francis Dickson.[6] The brig had undertaken a voyage from Colombo to the Moluccas and China in February.[7] On the return trip from China it arrived at Malacca on 19 May having on board a cargo purchased with a bill drawn on Messrs Jean Martin La Vallière and Henricus Volrand van Sohsten of Colombo. Supercargo De Vos was also committed to carry letters from Lieutenant-Colonel Aldwell Taylor, commandant in Malacca 1798–1803, to the government 'on the Coast' but was still ashore waiting to receive these letters on the 28th when the *Dolphin* set sail, leaving him, the second mate and three of the crew behind. De Vos hired a boat to pursue the brig, but it was out of sight and the pursuit was futile. De Vos protested against Captain Dallas and First Mate Dickson, who had been informed of the situation, and against all associated costs and losses.

In September and October of 1803 Captain (Robert) Allan had been to Cochin China, taking the English country trader brig *Eleanor* (built in Rangoon 1802)[8] to Tourane (the port nearest the capital Hué). The Protest at Malacca on 15 December 1803 by the supercargo Charles Harvey[9] is probably to do with delays caused by decisions of the captain but the record is in too poor a condition to decipher. Other sources, however, provide interesting details of the purpose of the voyage, its implementation and the critical role in diplomacy sometimes played by country traders.

Allan met David Lance, the recently appointed Canton-based chief supercargo, off Cape St James near Saigon on 9 September and told him that he

4 *Prothocol Books*, Nos 355, 10 January 1798; 356, 11 January 1798.

5 Walter Caulfield Lennon, 'Journal of a voyage through the Straits of Malacca on an Expedition to the Molucca Islands … 1796', *JSBRAS*, 7 (1881), 51–74, at pp. 61, 72.

6 *East-India Register and Directory for 1804*, p. 214; *Prothocol Books*, No. 968, 28 May 1801.

7 Paul A. Van Dyke, *Whampoa and the Canton Trade: Life and Death in a Chinese Port* (Hong Kong, 2020), Appendix 1.2b.

8 *East-India Register and Directory for 1804*, p. 96.

9 *Prothocol Books*, No. 1304, 15 December 1803.

had on board 'a valuable cargo of opium and piece goods' that, if the season had not been so advanced, he would have tried to dispose of at Saigon. As things were, and as he believed King Nguyen Anh, without whom 'no commerce of consequence could be carried on', was at Hué, he intended to head there without delay. During this time of war with the French, Lance had been commissioned by the British Government to undertake a diplomatic mission to the king in an attempt to establish good relations between the two countries, but as he now feared a visit to Hué would prevent his reaching Canton that year he entrusted Allan with a letter to the king on his behalf.[10]

It was later established that Allan had delivered the letter to M. J. B. Chaigneau, a Frenchman in the king's employ. When the king, the following year, proved unwilling to enter into an agreement it was thought that Allan had used 'unguarded expressions' about the EIC's territorial ambitions. However, this is only conjecture, especially as the French probably needed no encouragement to jeopardise the English cause. It was also thought that the intemperate behaviour of Captain James Purefoy, another country trader in Cochin China (and Protest declarant in Malacca), had indisposed the king towards the British.[11] Purefoy himself doubted that Lance's letter would ever have been delivered to the king, as its arrival on a merchant vessel indicated that it was unsanctioned by the king of England.[12] Nevertheless, the British continued to rely on country traders in diplomatic affairs: the country trader Captain Charles Mackintosh not only carried a later emissary, John William Roberts, to Cochin China aboard his ship the *Page* in June 1804, but, because of his experience and local knowledge, actually accompanied Roberts to meet the king in Hué.[13]

Possible losses suffered because of delay were also the subject of a Dutch Protest, originally given verbally in Armenian, lodged at Malacca on 19 September 1806[14] by an Armenian trader, Petrus Carapat (Carapiet), on board the *Vulcan* (Captain Christopher Perkins). As has been discussed earlier, the *Vulcan* had had to remain in Malacca for repairs after storm damage suffered in the Bay of Bengal.

A somewhat different declaration, before the British Commandant of Malacca, William Farquhar, there being no other officials or notaries available, characterises the Protest on 5 November 1806 of Shereef Hussein (Syarif Husain), owner of the brig *Punangteen*, a Palembang vessel sailing under Arab

10 Alistair Lamb, 'British Missions to Cochin China: 1778–1822', *JMBRAS*, 34:3/4 (1961), 1–248, at pp. 101–3, 111.

11 Howard T. Fry, *Alexander Dalrymple (1737–1808) and the Expansion of British Trade* (London, 1970), p. 185; Lamb, 'British Missions', pp. 135–6.

12 James Purefoy, 'Remarques sur la Cochinchine', *Nouvelles Annales des Voyages*, ser. 2, 1 (1826), 338–53, at 351.

13 Lamb, 'British Missions', pp. 129ff.

14 *Prothocol Books*, No. 13, 19 September 1806.

colours.[15] He described the boarding of his ship and the plundering of a number of chests of cargo by the crew of another vessel while the *Punangteen* was lying in the Malacca Roads. The story is as follows: The *Punangteen* had departed Palembang on 9 September 1806, arriving in Malacca on the 27th. On 9 October the Acting Master Attendant accompanied by an English gentleman, came on board to examine the papers of the vessel. They checked several chests and sealed them, informing Hussein that they would return the next day. However, at 9 p.m. that night about twenty men, 'with a European officer' arrived and plundered the sealed chests. When Shereef Hussein reported the robbery the following morning, Farquhar ordered the Acting Master Attendant, another Englishman and a Malay Munshi to go to the ship the *General Wellesley* (400 tons), commanded by Captain (and managing owner) David Dalrymple, also lying at Malacca. Dalrymple expressed surprise and ordered the chests of his second mate 'and his people' be searched. They found a number of stolen goods. Consequently, Shereef Hussein tabled his account and, as he wrote, 'doth protest against the said commander of the said ship *General Wellesley*, David Dalrymple, and against his second mate and people, for all and every, and all manner of loss and losses, sustained by such their conduct, in plundering the said brig Punangteen'. He also presented lists in English and Malay 'of articles deficient, the property of Sherif Hussein and his People' that included gold and dollars, jewellery, clothing of various types, razors and knives. The entry of the Protest was confirmed on 6 November 1806. Dalrymple had arrived in Malacca in October and left the same month for New South Wales, so when Hussein filed his Protest the *General Wellesley* was no longer in port.

The accusation against David Dalrymple is part of a pattern surrounding the behaviour of this country trader. He appears to have been one of the most disreputable of that group of mariners. For example, his unlawful sale in 1808 of another trader's goods left his trading partner Joseph Burn to face the charge in Penang of illegally disposing of property, while his dealings in 1807 and 1808 in the Pacific, where he was described as 'a drunkard given to casual violence',[16] give the impression that Shereef Hussein may have got off lightly.[17]

Another unusual Protest is that of John Elliot, a resident of Malacca, who on 17 September 1810 lodged a Protest against the actions of John Cotton a

15 *Prothocol Books*, No. 32, 5 November 1806.

16 Anne Salmond, *Between Worlds: Early Exchanges Between Maori and Europeans 1773–1815* (Auckland, 1997), p. 363.

17 For Dalrymple's exploits, see F. Andrew Smith, 'Captain Burn and Associates: British Intelligence-gathering, Trade, and Litigation in Borneo and Beyond during the Early Nineteenth Century', *Borneo Research Bulletin*, 35 (2004), 48–69, at pp. 49–55; Greg Denning (ed.), *The Marquesan Journal of Edward Robart*, Pacific History Series No. 6 (Canberra, 1974). Dalrymple died in late 1808.

merchant of Rangoon who, according to Elliot, took Elliot's vessel, the *Helen*, on a trading voyage for Elliot to Rangoon, but failed to carry out Elliot's orders.[18] Elliot had trusted Cotton as 'an honest industrious man, though not at all experienced in book learning'. But Cotton did not obtain the cargo intended, had detained the brig in Rangoon from April until September, had 'run the said brig to the expence of three thousand six hundred rupees, without receiving any material repairs', had shipped an unauthorised cargo of timber on account of the Hon. Company and had not accounted for the passage money for himself and various passengers between Penang and Rangoon. Moreover, the master George Wales had been coerced to sign accounts that he knew to be wrong. The unusual thing about this Protest is that it refers to events that occurred four years before, in 1806. Why it took so long for Elliot to make the Protest is not known. Perhaps the fact that he had made his will in March 1810, and it was entered into the *Prothocol Books* a year later might be relevant.[19]

Goelam Ally, a Suratese resident of Bombay, and supercargo and agent for the prominent Parsi, Bombay-based trader, Hormarjee Bomanjee,[20] protested on 28 November 1811 against the captain, Gustaaf Adolph Streng, of the grab *Miracity* (600 tons, owned by the Sultan of Aceh), in a dispute over cargo.[21] Ally actually signed using the name of Hormarjee Bomanjee. The disagreement appears to have arisen in Canton, the port to which the *Miracity* had sailed from Bombay and where Streng refused to take on board any cargo until all existing accounts had been paid. This Goelam Ally said he was not authorised to do and he therefore held Streng responsible for all the losses that occurred. He arrived in Malacca on the British ship *Indien* (*Indian*) (Captain Andrew Barclay), which had departed Whampoa on 3 November and lodged his Protest. The *Miracity* had left Whampoa on the same day, bound for Bombay.[22]

In a similar vein were two Protests lodged on 16 September 1812 by two Armenian merchants residing in Malacca, Joseph Minas and Marcar Carapiet (variously Carrapet, Carrapit, Carapet), as agents for the prominent Armenian merchant, Sarkies Owen of Penang, against Captain Thomas Lambert of the *Nancy*.[23] These Protests are to do with the late delivery of a bale of linen by Lambert.

18 *Prothocol Books*, No. 553, 17 September 1810.

19 *Prothocol Books*, No. 640, 20 March 1811.

20 Anne Bulley, *The Bombay Country Ships, 1790–1833* (Richmond, 2000) includes various references to Hormarjee Bomanjee's business activities.

21 *Prothocol Books*, No. 737, 28 November 1811. Streng was an interesting captain in that he had taken a Dutch private ship *Hoop* to Canton in 1802 and before that, in 1800, a Danish private ship *Angelique*. See Van Dyke, *Whampoa*, Appendix 1.2b.

22 Van Dyke, *Whampoa*, Appendix 1.2b.

23 *Prothocol Books*, Nos 815, 816, 16 September 1812. Joseph Minas was the spokesperson for the small community of Armenian merchants in Malacca. In 1822 he and Carapiet

The first, the Protest note, includes two letters in English, signed by Lambert. In the one dated 11 April 1812 Lambert agreed to deliver a bale to Minas and Carapiet and in the event of it not being delivered to pay them 567 sicca rupees. In the second letter dated 16 September, addressed to 'J N Strecker Esq., Notary publick' and beginning 'Sir, In answer to your demand made to me this morning', Lambert said he did not feel himself obliged to pay the rupees as there was no deadline for delivery stated on the original letter. ('I do not now consider myself liable as I yesterday in presence of witnesses offered the Bale to Mssrs. Minus & Carrapit. They having refused to accept of it at this date I have to request you will protest in my name'.)

The second, longer Protest against Lambert by Minas and Carapiet is written in Dutch. The complainants stated that when the *Nancy* arrived in Malacca on 29 April they asked Lambert if there were any letters for them from Bengal or Penang. Lambert said that there were none and sailed away. Minas and Carapiet had since received a duplicate of the original letter from Sarkies Owen about the bale and insisted they should now receive the money, not the bale. They held Lambert responsible for 'costs, hurt and damages suffered by their principal'.

George Bryne, supercargo of the brig *Fair Trial* (125 tons, built in Chittagong) made a Protest before Jan Hendrik Stecher, 'Notary Public', at Malacca on 14 December 1815.[24] This was initiated by the actions of the vessel's captain William Wyatt. Bryne was acting for Messrs Lackersteen and Co. of Calcutta who had chartered the vessel. He had asked the captain to proceed further to the east to sell the property consigned to him, making the request in the presence of three other men, one of whom was Captain McLardie of the *Eagle*. Wyatt refused to do so, possibly because he believed it unsafe. The Protest suggests that Wyatt would have agreed to the request if a whole range of arms and ammunition had been provided, as well as twenty-five more crew, together with their wages and provisions. When the extended voyage was not undertaken Bryne submitted the Protest signed by him and the three gentlemen, 'against the Owners of the said Brig for all losses and damages which may sustain for the non performance of the agreement entered by the Owners of the said Brig aforesaid of Calcutta with the said Messrs Lackersteen and Co, Merchants, of the same place'. On 25 December Bryne further testified that he had delivered the Protest to Captain Wyatt at his lodgings in Malacca.[25]

---

moved to Penang where Minas died the following year. For more on the Armenians in Malacca and Penang, see Nadia H. Wright, *Respected Citizens: The History of Armenians in Singapore and Malaysia* (Middle Park, 2003).

24 John Phipps, *A Collection of Papers, Relative to Ship Building in India … also A Report, Comprehending all the Ships and Vessels Built in India to the Present Time …* (Calcutta, 1840), p. 177; *Prothocol Books*, No. 55, 14 December 1815.

25 *Prothocol Books*, No. 59½, 25 December 1815.

These complaints against owner, master or crew point to cheating, stealing and prevarication, delays and late arrival of cargo, as well as instances of early sailing or reluctance to sail. Unfortunately, the outcomes of the Protests are not known, requiring further research. However, legal proceedings concerning Captain Francis Balston and his voyage of 1820 in the *Lady Flora*, while not ensuing from a Malacca Protest are of interest and are included as Appendix D.

PART II

PROTESTS: NON-BRITISH SHIPS

Preamble

That the British Protests from the Malacca records exist at all, providing us with details of voyages, their dangers and practicalities, and the individual exploits of country traders, is indicative of an expanding British presence in the Malay world during the late eighteenth and early nineteenth centuries. Though not officially part of the EIC or the imperial bureaucracy, the country traders were nevertheless 'inadvertent imperialists', part of the growing British Empire.

However, the British did not have a monopoly on trade in the East Indies. Nor did stormy conditions differentiate between nations. It was not only British country trader vessels running into difficulties that feature in the *Prothocol Books* of Malacca, but ships of other countries as well. The officers of Danish and Portuguese private ships in particular lodged Protests at Malacca when their voyages were impacted by misadventures. This is not surprising considering that according to the 1813 British Parliamentary investigation into East India affairs the most numerous ships arriving at Calcutta in the period 1798 to 1803 after the British (and discounting Indian vessels) were the Danish, Portuguese and American.[1] Not only environmental factors and piratical menace, but British wartime action prompted protests by foreign vessels.

One of the intriguing aspects of the foreign ships was that their categorisation according to the flag they flew might not reflect the true commercial nature of their activities. Stringent EIC rules and changing political situations encouraged ruses. Thus, Dutch, or even British, interests might hide behind a Danish or Portuguese flag. More extreme possibilities are described by Paul Van Dyke in his remarks on the private trade at Canton:

> Many of these private ships randomly switched flags during their voyages to China, in order to avoid trouble along the way. They might arrive to China with a Moorish flag from India, then leave with an Armenian or Greek flag, and maybe change to a French or English flag later on, depending on what ship they encountered at sea.[2]

Whatever may have been their true nationality, the following cases are divided according to the face value of their flag. The Protests stemmed from a medley of causes.

1 UK House of Lords, *The Sessional Papers 1801–1833*, v.64 (1812–13), Paper No. 23 Papers relative to East India Affairs, p. 28.

2 Paul A. Van Dyke, *Whampoa and the Canton Trade: Life and Death in a Chinese Port* (Hong Kong, 2020), p. 23.

Preamble

8

Danish

The Danish private trade had a number of distinguishing features. It resembled the British country trade and its relationship with the EIC insofar as the Danes operated in agreement and in parallel with their EIC equivalent, the Danish Asiatic Company, during the 'boom years' between 1772 and 1807. Unlike the British country trade, however, which, apart from special dispensation cases, was limited to operating between Asian ports east of the Cape of Good Hope, the Danish private trade operated freely between Europe and Asia. It was actually larger than the trade of the Danish Company itself: 271 private Danish East Indiamen set sail for the East between 1772 and 1807 compared with 132 Company vessels.[1]

During the European wars of the late eighteenth and early nineteenth centuries Denmark adopted a policy of neutrality. British officials and trading houses, as well as British private traders themselves, took advantage of Danish neutrality in particular to circumvent the EIC monopoly and thus carry capital in the form of remittances, as well as cargo, back to Europe. Indeed, the British were involved so much through ownership in this 'neutrality' that it has even been referred to as 'camouflage'.[2] Sometimes Indian Agency Houses owned the ships but sailed them under neutral Danish colours with Danish subjects as sham owners. During the French Revolutionary and Napoleonic wars this clandestine activity meant that British trade could be carried on with enemy-held territory such as Dutch Batavia, French Mauritius and Spanish Manila.[3] The Dutch, defeated by the French in Europe and unable to trade openly in the East Indies because of the surveillance of the British, also made use of Danish neutrality, ostensibly selling many of their Batavian

1 Ole Feldbaek,'Danish East India trade 1772–1807 statistics and structure', *Scandinavian Economic History Review*, 26:2 (1978), 128–44, at p. 129, <https://doi.org/10.1080/03585522.1978.10415623> [Accessed 15 May 2025].

2 *Ibid.*, p. 131.

3 Spain, allied with France, was at war with England in 1796–1802 and 1804–8.

based ships to the Danes, but continuing to operate through them in much the same way as did the British private traders.[4]

It is most likely that all eight of the protesting Danish ships were trading with either Batavia or Manila. Two of them, the *Agatha* and the *Angelique*, also went to China. Although in 1792 the Danish Asiatic Company had been granted a renewal of its monopoly of Danish trade with China, Van Dyke lists one private Danish ship at Whampoa in 1786, seventeen between 1797 and 1806 and one in 1816.[5] This can be partly explained by Feldbaek's assertion that in 1795, with Holland now at war with England, the Dutch Company's China trade was permitted to operate under cover of the Danish flag.[6]

A singular feature of the Danish Protests at Malacca is that the submitted details of misadventure are commonly signed not by the captain, but by the mates. In comparison there are only two British country trader ship where this occurs, the *Faz Soobhany*, where in 1801 Captain Robert Shepherdson lodged the Protest note and the mates followed with the details, and the *Saigon*, again in 1801, where Captain Colvel launched the Protest and the mates followed with the details two days later. The other instances where a country captain did not sign are a result of murder (Sadler), drowning (Deans) and being accidentally left behind (Macfie). Interestingly it was the mates rather than the captains of the two 'regular' EIC ships who lodged the statements in 1795 and 1800 as recorded in the *Prothocol Books*. The instances of the British mates providing the Protest are all early in the period. Perhaps the rules changed later on?

In the case of the Danes the practice might be accounted for by Feldbaek's conclusion that, 'The [British] ships were equipped with Danish papers in Bengal, and the British houses found them not only a nominal Danish owner but also a Danish passenger who could act to outward appearances as ship's captain'.[7] In the actual Protests it is often asserted that the statement is given by the mate or mates with the full approval of the captain. In the case of the *Mijrins* (described below), for example, it was 'terrequistie van hunne Capitain den Heer Jurgen Hendrik Boijd' (at the request of their captain) that the officers, Daniel Forstell (ober Stuurman) and Fredrick Ruyer (?) (ander Stuurman) lodged the Protest.

While private British traders benefitted from Danish neutrality, the attitude of the British government towards Danish shipping was one of suspicion and hostility. The Danes insisted that neutral ships meant neutral goods, but the British claimed the right to search neutral vessels for contraband. The

4 Ole Feldbaek, 'Dutch Batavia trade via Copenhagen 1795–1807. A study of colonial trade and neutrality', *Scandinavian Economic History Review*, 21:1 (1973), 43–75, at p. 46, <https://doi.org/10.1080/03585522.1973.10407745> [Accessed 15 May 2025].

5 Paul A. Van Dyke, *Whampoa*, Appendix 1.2b.

6 Ole Feldbaek, 'The Danish Asia trade 1620–1807', *Scandinavian Economic History Review*, 39:1 (1991), 3–27, at pp. 10, 12, <https://doi.org/10.1080/03585522.1991.10408197 > [Accessed 15 May 2025].

7 Feldbaek, *Danish East India Trade*, p. 138.

British attacked and destroyed the Danish fleet at Copenhagen in April 1801, and from May 1801 until April 1802 occupied the Danish settlements of Frederiknagore (Serampore) and Tranquebar in India. Britain again moved against Denmark in September 1807. British sepoys occupied Frederiknagore in January 1808 and Admiral Pellew seized Tranquebar in February. From this time, until the peace of 1814, Denmark was aligned with France and Danish traders ceased all activity in the East Indies.

Evidence of Danish trade of one kind or another, legitimate or not, is given by several private Danish vessels registering Protests at Malacca during the years 1798 to 1806. As with British country traders, the archival sources for the study of the Danish private trade are very limited. Feldbaek has stated that 'none of the archives of East India merchants or shipowners are preserved. This fundamental bias of the sources does much to explain why scholars have concentrated mainly on the company, and why there is a lack of quite basic information about important aspects of private trade'.[8] The Malaccan Protests provide an addition to the scant resources.

The Protests (ten cases in chronological order)

The earliest example of a Protest concerning a Danish private 'bark' is very brief and there is no follow-up record, so details are scant. The ship in question was the *Charlotta Amalia* and the Protest, in Dutch, of 2 October 1796,[9] signed by Captain Francois D'Almeida, stated that the ship had arrived in the Malacca Roads on 1 October with unspecified damages sustained on a voyage to Tranquebar. As is common, the on-board journal mentioned was not included in the record.

The next Danish ship in the Malacca records, the *Agatha*, was damaged by bad weather on its way to China, via Manila. The ship had sailed from the Danish settlement at Tranquebar on 8 April 1798 carrying 331 bales of linen (perhaps a Dutch cargo). It met with strong southerly winds later in the month near the Nicobar Islands, with a storm on the 23rd, resulting in more water in the ship than the pumps could deal with. The Dutch entry in the Prothocol records of 14 May[10] is difficult to read and it is unclear how much damage was sustained. It was signed by the first and second mates, Matthias Frost and Haris Lund rather than the 'captain', Peter Hoggard. It might be an indication of clandestine practice that Frost is recorded as the captain when the *Agatha* arrived in Whampoa on 5 October. He had previously (1794) been captain of the Danish ship *Konsberg*.[11]

8 *Ibid.*, p. 129.

9 British Library, Asia, Pacific and Africa Collections, *Malacca, General Prothocol Books (Registers of Legal Deeds) 1786–1825*, IOR: R/9/22/1–75 [referred to in this study as *Prothocol Books*], No. 123½, 2 October 1796.

10 *Prothocol Books*, No. 417, 14 May 1798.

11 Van Dyke, *Whampoa*, Appendix 1.2b; Ole Feldbaek, 'The Danish trade in Bengal

The Danish private ship *Kederbox* (or *Kiederbox* or *Kederbux*) made a voyage between Tranquebar and Batavia in 1799 resulting in two Protests in June.[12] On 21 June a Protest note, signed only by Dutch officials, established that the ship, with Captain Pieter Janzen, had arrived from Madras on 17 June and that occurrences during the journey were specified in an on-board journal. On 24 June a Protest, signed by the first and second mates, Franz Wilhelm Tonder and Johan Peter Bauman, on behalf of their captain, gave details of their journey down the Strait of Malacca after leaving Madras Roads on 28 April until their arrival in the Malacca Roads. It seems that in sight of Parcelar Hill on 15 June they struck trouble and suffered substantial damage to the masts.

There is also a later submission of 29 October 1799[13] (but signed by both Captain Janzen and First Mate Tonder on 6 July 1799). Barely decipherable, the document is concerned with financial matters relating to the cargo, the owners of the ship, Tranquebar 'residents' Harrop and Stevenson,[14] and various other people including Francis Thierens, the Chief Justice and Chief Merchant of the Council of Justice in Malacca. Details of various transactions are given, the purport of which is unclear.

Another private Danish vessel, the small brig *Myrin* (or *Mijrins*) ran into heavy seas, sprang a leak and took on water after departing Manila on 20 January 1800 on a voyage to Madras. The Protest of 10 February[15] was accompanied by a long extract of the ship's journal written in idiosyncratic English and signed by the ship's two mates, though probably written by the first mate Daniel Forsfell. It described how the well-fitted ship, 'in good condition', set sail in fine weather from Manila on 20 January 1800. By the 23rd it was experiencing high winds and rough seas and shipped a great deal of water. The weather worsened, the Protest evoking heavy squalls, gales, the ship constantly under water, a monstrous heavy sea and pumps employed continuously. With a need to lighten the vessel the order was given to throw:

> all wat was on Deck Over Bord … which we Accordingly deed & truw I over bord 1 Spar Top mast 3 Spars Planks Deals [?] Water Casks Combois [cook's galley] Boy Boy ribs [buoy, buoy ropes] Boats Dragg [drogue] & a 4½ Inch Hawser Lower & Top mast Steering Siels with their booms & yards alde younks

1777–1808. An Interim Account', *Scandinavian Economic History Review*, 12:1 (1964), 26–60, at p. 58 <https://doi.org/10.1080/03585522.1964.10407633> [Accessed 15 May 2025].

12 *Prothocol Books*, Nos 603, 21 June; 604, 24 June 1799.

13 *Prothocol Books*, No. 683, 29 October 1799.

14 Harrop and Stevenson was an English agency house at Tranquebar through which the Danish private traders did most of their business. They were also agents for the King of Denmark and for the King of Cochin China, <https://www.wikitree.com/wiki/Stevenson-7473>; <https://en.wikipedia.org/wiki/Nonsuch_(1781_ship)> [Both accessed 15 April 2025].

15 *Prothocol Books*, Nos 737, 738, 10 February 1800.

> [all the junks[16]] Bording Nettings & heavy Blocks, Grein Stonne [grind stone] without whatt the sea already had carry away from the Boat & Chainge [?] such as Oars Capsten bars Bocketts Tubbs Pitch Bott Scraper with other small stores.

Given the idiosyncrasies of the language, the *Myrin* may be another case where the ship had closer ties with the Dutch rather than with the British: as is evident, the spelling was poor, the grammar unusual and on occasion Dutch words employed, not the work of a native English speaker.

The bad weather continued until 29 January when the crew were able to open one of the hatches to get some firewood and water. They found four bags of rice had been ruined and a number of bags containing sugar damaged. On 30 January they sighted land and supposed it to be Natuna Island, part of the Bunguran Group in the South China Sea. In fact, they had travelled further than calculated and the sighting was 'Ridgans' (probably Redang) Island off the Malay coast. The problems did not abate. At times 'the vessel wood not seil at all' and 'lead Dead in the water'. The vessel continued to ship water over the bow and the crew were 'almost wore out' from working the pumps.

A conference (referred to as a 'Court Martiall') was held between the captain, the supercargo and the officers and it was decided to throw some of the sugar overboard to lighten the vessel. Twelve bags of water-damaged sugar were thus discarded. By 1 February 'the vessel made mutch Lass Water with the Pomps & saild a Greath Del better as before Pomped'. Progress improved and on 9 February the ship anchored in the Malacca Roads. Forsfell and the second mate Fredrik Ruyer (?) lodged the Protest absolving themselves and the ship from responsibility for any losses. As was the case with the Danish ship *Agatha* the Captain, Jurgen Hendrik Boyd, did not sign.

All might have been well but the next fifteen months were unlucky for the *Myrin*. A report in the *Bombay Courier* of 20 June 1801 described how the ship was detained at Chittagong on 10 December 1800 on suspicion of being enemy property and held until 13 March 1801 when it was released with 2,500 rupees compensation for wrongful arrest. Having missed the winter monsoons, the captain then endeavoured to sell the ship to pay the arrears of crew wages. Finding no buyers in Chittagong he sailed for Calcutta only to run aground off the Sunderbunds (now Sundarbans), losing anchor, cable and rudder. After four weeks of 'anxiety, labour and distress' he arrived at the Hooghly where the ship was seized again by an armed military guard. The date of arrival, 8 May 1801, had unfortunately coincided with the date the EIC implemented a new law embargoing all Danish ships in British ports.

There are an unusually long series of Protests and associated documents relating to the *Kieldeweldt* in the records. This 'particuliere Dansche Snauw'

16 The name for old ropes.

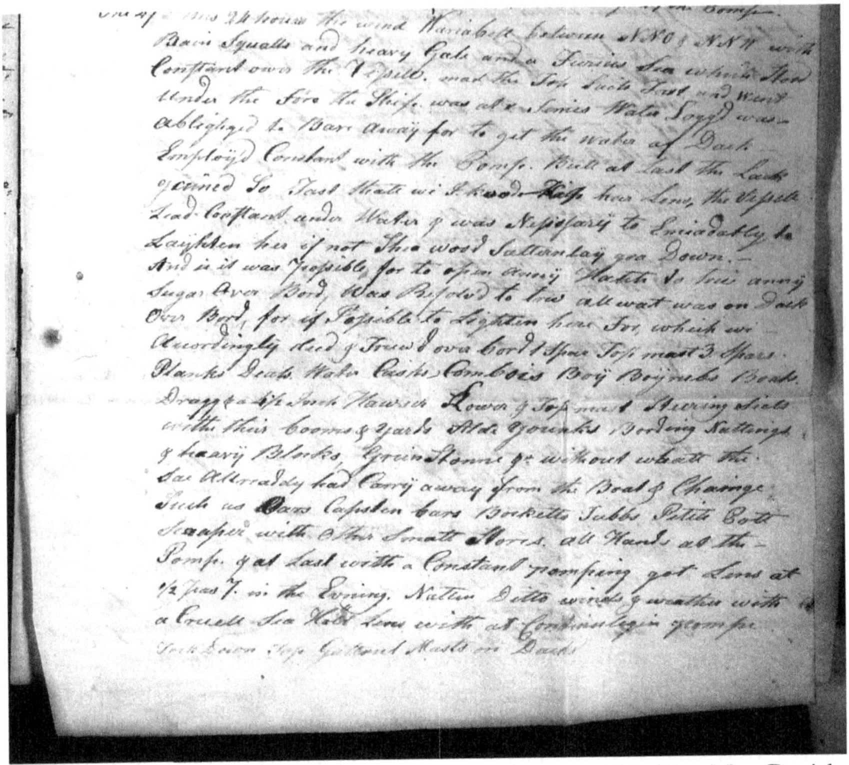

[illegible] this 24 hours the wind Variabell between NNO & NNW with [illegible] Pomp-
Rain Squalls and heavy Gale and a Furious Sea which Stood
Constant over the Vessell. and the Top Saile Fast and Went
Under the Fore the Ship was at [illegible] Water Logged was
Obliged to Bare away for to get the water of Deck
Employed Constant with the Pomp. But at Last the Leaks
gained So Fast that we [illegible] her Long, the Vessell
Lead Constant under Water & was Nessesary to Emiadatly to
Laighten her if not [illegible] would [illegible] go Down.
And is it was Impossible for to open anny Hatch to trow anny
Sugar Over Bord, Was Resolved to trow all wat was on Deck
Over Bord, for if Possible to Lighten her For, which we
Accordingly did & Trew'd over Bord 1 Spare Top mast 3 Spars
Planks Deals Water Casks Comboes Boy Boy[illegible] Boat
Dragg & a [illegible] Inch Hawser Lower & Top mast Steering Sails
with their booms & yards Old [illegible], Bording Nettings
& heavy Blocks, Grindstonne &c without what the
Sae Allready had Carry away from the Boat & Charige
Such as Oars Capsten bars Buckets Tubbs [illegible] Pots
Scraper with Other Small Stores. all Hands at the
Pomp. & at Last with a Constant pomping got Loos at
1/2 pas 7. in the Evening. Latter Ditto winds & weather with
a Cruell Sea Held Loos with at Continualy pompe
Took Down Top Gallant Masts on Deck

Fig 14. Part of the onboard statement dated 9 February 1800 by First Mate Daniel Forsell and Second Mate Fredrick Ruyer of the Danish brig *Myrin* regarding means taken to lighten the vessel.

first appears in a statement (the word 'Protest' does not appear to be used) on 30 April 1800 involving Simon Mackerton, an Armenian merchant and a passenger on the ship.[17] It appears Mackerton was asked to ascertain from the captain, Andries Neegaard (sometimes spelled as Neegaart), then residing in the house of Hendrik Kraal, why the ship, on a voyage from Tranquebar to Batavia, remained anchored in the Malacca Roads. The answer given was that, through no fault of Mackerton's, the *Kieldeweldt* was without victuals, water or firewood.

That same day the *Kieldeweldt* resumed its journey to Batavia but, having met with bad weather, was back in Malacca on 2 June when Captain Neegaard registered a Protest note against events that occurred during his 'interrupted' journey.[18] This document mentions the existence of the ship's journal, but neither the particulars of the Protest nor the journal is attached. It was not

17 *Prothocol Books*, No. 786, 30 April 1800.
18 *Prothocol Books*, No. 804, 2 June 1800.

'former' captain, protested against the seizure in Malacca on 9 January 1802 of goods and cargo belonging to the *Fredensburg* by the Malaccan commandant Lieutenant Colonel Aldwell Taylor. He asserted that the ship was arrested on 'pretence of war' and he, the officers and some of the crew had been arrested 'on their honour'. He referred to a letter of 27 January from Aldwell Taylor whereby the ship and some of the merchandise were returned, but the main part of the cargo retained and prize agents appointed. Herbst went into some detail about the number of confiscated bales and their markings. He protested not only against the actions of the commandant but against the losses incurred by the resulting inability to take advantage of the monsoons and favourable winds, the loss of interest, reduction of credit and all other disadvantages whatsoever.

The declaration was supported by another Protest by the first and second mates, Johan Maria Dayot and Conrad Tideman on 13 March 1802.[31] The principal tenor of this Protest was against the deterioration of the ship since it had been in British hands. A detailed list of the parts of the ship damaged and requiring alteration or replacement was included.

Finally, Captain Rordam of the 'Dansche Particuliere Brick *Commerce*' lodged Protests on 12 and 13 March 1806 occasioned by running aground.[32] The *Commerce* was on a voyage from Manila to Bengal when on 9 March 1806 it struck bottom in the Singapore Strait to the southwest of St John's Island and about three leagues to the northeast of Barn Island (now Pulau Senang). Rordam related the efforts he and his crew had undertaken to save the ship and its cargo. The crew discharged 'some part of the cargo' and later 'som copper from the forehold' to lighten the ship and, using the anchors, floated off on the high tide. With pumps working, the *Commerce* resumed its journey the next morning, passing the Rabbit (now Pulau Biola) and Coney (now Pulau Satuma) at 9 a.m., and reaching Malacca on 11 March.[33]

31 *Prothocol Books*, No. 1072, 13 March 1802.

32 *Prothocol Books*, Nos 155, 12 March 1806; 156, 13 March 1806.

33 Rordam was listed in August 1806 as the master of the *Hardanger* sailing from Serampore (Frederiknagore) and in 1811 as captain of the *Palmer* of Calcutta: House of Lords, *The Sessional Papers 1801–1833* v.64 (1812–1813), *Papers relative to East India Affairs*, p. 145, and *List of Trading Vessels Belonging to the Port of Calcutta*, p. 8. Earlier in its career in 1800 the *Commerce* had been reported in Canton to be trafficking with Manila under Danish colours and was recorded in Manila port entries in 1798 as Danish, but was actually registered in Madras as owned and captained by the Englishman W. N. Chapman: Cheong, 'Changing the Rules', p. 16.

9

Portuguese

The Portuguese had ruled Malacca for more than a century before the Dutch takeover in 1641 and retained a strong social presence there afterwards, as they did in the rest of the archipelago and in enclaves in India. A creole form of Portuguese remained a *lingua franca* of commerce in the East Indies throughout the eighteenth century, with English, according to Furber, not taking over as the dominant European commercial language until 1825.[1] On the west coast of India there were Portuguese settlements at Goa, Demaun and Diu until the mid-twentieth century, though for much of the period 1799 to 1815 Goa was ruled by the British for fear that it might otherwise fall into French hands. While there were no major settlements on the east coast at the time of the Malacca Protests Portuguese merchant families remained in business in various places. As an example of the continuing influence of the Indo-Portuguese community in Bengal, the Portuguese Barretto (or Barreto) family (a name that crops up in the Protests) formed one of the fifteen agency houses in Calcutta, financing a substantial part of the country trade in the early 1800s.[2]

Macao had been established as a Portuguese settlement in 1557 and continued as such during, and long after, the Dutch period of domination in the East Indies. Portuguese administration of the territory remained in place, in one form or another, until 1999. It is no surprise that many of the Portuguese ships featuring in the Malacca records belonged to the Macao privately owned merchant fleet voyaging to or from Macao, trading with Indian ports, especially Goa, ports in the archipelago and Manila. As with the British Protests the specifics of the cargo are not often listed in the Portuguese submissions at Malacca. However, opium probably formed a part. According

1 Holden Furber, *Rival Empires of Trade in the Orient 1600–1800* (Minneapolis MN, 1976), pp. 298–9.

2 Pius Malekandathil, 'Trade, Religion and Politics Portuguese Activities in the Bay of Bengal, 1632–1840', in Satish Chandra and Himanshu Prabha Ray (eds), *The Sea, Identity and History: From the Bay of Bengal to the South China Sea* (Singapore, 2013), pp. 279–301, at p. 281.

to George Bryan Souza, towards the end of the eighteenth century the Portuguese merchant fleet at Macao was supplying one half of the recorded volume of Indian opium to China.[3] Certain ships of the Macao fleet also doubled as a fighting force, particularly against the Chinese pirates in the battles that took place in the Pearl River Delta between 1805 and 1810.[4]

During the late eighteenth and early nineteenth century the special relationship of the Portuguese with Spain, enabling their entry into Spanish Manila, was of benefit to the British. Officially Manila was a closed port to British traders and, although the embargo was sometimes ignored with impunity, British trade could be conducted through the use of Portuguese ships, either by means of *bona fide* Portuguese vessels or by British ships given permission in Macao to fly the Portuguese flag and with a proxy Portuguese captain aboard – a similar set-up to the Danish arrangement.[5] Ironically, with the outbreak of war in 1796 between Britain and Spain, then an ally of France, the clandestine trade with Manila ran the risk of official British scrutiny as a case of trading with the enemy. With the French invasion of Spain in 1808, however, Spain became the friend of England and Manila a legitimate trading destination.

In spite of centuries of seafaring experience in the waters of the East Indies and the South China Sea, the Portuguese still experienced accidents. Many Protests were lodged by Portuguese vessels at Malacca, mostly written in Portuguese after the usual initial Dutch Protest note. Superficially, they appear different from the British in that the majority are very neatly written. This is because the captain could call on the services of a scribe who seems to have been a customary part of the ship's complement. To make the situation clear, Captain de Vasconcellos of the *Indiano*, in his Protest note of 25 December 1807, said he had delegated his official writer to describe events. Sometimes the captain made the Protest himself, but where a scribe was employed, this clerk wrote the report and signed it as a true account. The document was then further validated by the signatures of the captain and officers and usually by some, in certain cases many, of the crew and passengers. The signatures could number in the twenties, another feature that distinguishes these Protests from the British. Occasionally the occupations of the signatories were listed separately within the body of the Protest. Whereas the

3 George Bryan Souza, 'Macao and the Pearl River Delta Trade: The Portuguese Merchant Fleet at Macao in the 17th and 18th Centuries', <http://www.icm.gov.mo/rc/viewer/40013/2320> [Accessed 15 April 2025], pp. 20–1.

4 Luis Gonzaga Gomes, *Páginas da História de Macau*, Colecçao Notícias de Macau, XXIII (Macau, 1966). An English translation of parts of the book dealing with the Delta River pirates is available at <https://www.icm.gov.mo/rc/viewer/20003/797> [Accessed 15 April 2025].

5 Weng Eang Cheong, 'Changing the Rules of the Game (The India-Manila Trade: 1785–1809)', *Journal of Southeast Asian Studies*, 1:2 (September 1970), 1–19, at pp. 2, 6, 18.

terms 'officer' and 'mate' seem to be interchangeable in the British Protests, the Portuguese made careful distinction between officers, masters and pilots. The formal attestation of truth also incorporated a religious element missing from the British examples. Similarly, the Portuguese ships themselves mostly have religious names, whereas the British names range from the heroic to the homely, but are not religious.

We include a large selection of the numerous Portuguese Protests here, but not all. Many were registered after 1808 and were concerned not with seizure or intimidation by the British Navy with regard to the Manila trade, but with misadventures of the sea or other trading disputes. Of the twenty Portuguese ships found to be reporting at Malacca several made more than one Protest.

The Protests (twenty-eight cases in chronological order)

An early Protest in the records is that concerning the private Portuguese vessel *St Simao*, the Dutch-language Protest note being entered on 16 October 1792.[6] The text of the Protest itself has not been retained. Captain Joaquim Rodrigues Lima appears to have had a dispute about a matter of trade on a voyage to China that also involved the English country trader *Philippe*.

The Portuguese country ship *Dories* arrived in Malacca on 14 May 1798 when the commander, Manuel Fernandus Lobo, lodged a Protest note concerning a lost voyage to Macao ('van een verlooren reijs naar Macao'), perhaps pertaining to storm damage.[7] No further details are available as, once again, the text of the Portuguese Protest was not included in the records. However, Captain Frost of the Danish ship *Agatha* had the same day reported storm damage suffered near the Nicobar Islands.

Captain Joze Ramos of the Portuguese private schooner *Mercurio* lodged a Protest note in Dutch on 1 September 1800 after his ship's arrival in Malacca from Madras the day before.[8] This was followed on 6 September by a Protest in Dutch[9] submitted (probably verbally) at the request of the captain by the first and second mates, Manuel Ignatio de Mathos and William Jones, concerning events of the 28th of August. A statement written in Portuguese by Captain Ramos himself on 28 August also formed part of the Protest. It appears that at that time the ship was struggling with a bad leak which had overwhelmed the pumps, causing the crew to attempt to bail out the water with buckets in four-hourly shifts. A decision was made, in order to save lives, to navigate through the Colong Strait to Malacca. They anchored in calm

6 British Library, Asia, Pacific and Africa Collections, *Malacca, General Prothocol Books (Registers of Legal Deeds) 1786–1825*, IOR: R/9/22/1–75 [referred to in this study as *Prothocol Books*], No. 129, 16 October 1792.

7 *Prothocol Books*, No. 418, 14 May 1798.

8 *Prothocol Books*, No. 879, 1 September 1800.

9 *Prothocol Books*, No. 883, 6 September 1800.

Fig 15. *Macao*. Artist unknown, Chinese, early 19th century.

seas against the tide in 13 fathoms of mud near Cape Caran,[10] but the leak persisted. Ramos's Protest, neatly written, is signed by six other officers and crew members, including the first and second mates. Later, in both January and April 1801, the captain requested copies of the Protest.

Another Portuguese Protest, on 30 December 1800, was that by the first and second mates (names illegible) at the request of Captain Joze Joaquim Barroz of the galley *St Antonio Luzitania*.[11] Only the first two pages of the Protest note, in Dutch, are in the records; the actual Portuguese language Protest is not present. The *St Antonio Luzitania* departed Malacca for Penang on 25 December. It must have made slow progress for it had only reached the vicinity of Cape Rachado when, on the 28th, it was struck by a heavy storm with strong winds from the east and northeast and huge seas. Visibility was poor and on the next day it was determined that the vessel would return to Malacca.

Captain Manoel Antonio da Silva Rangel of the Macao-based ship *Santo Antonio* lodged a Protest on 24 December 1806 against the captain and officers of the ship *Angelica de Senhor de Joaõ de Deos de Castro*.[12] Rangel had arrived the previous day from Macao. Appended to the Dutch Protest note was a Portuguese-language Protest written by the scribe Jose Rodriguez Costa. In neat clerical handwriting this document describes the events of 16 December, seemingly a collision, involving the *Santo Antonio* and the *Angelica*, which occurred within sight of Pulo Pisao[13] and that resulted in the destruction of the longboat and damage to the rigging of the *Santo Antonio*. It was signed by the scribe and twenty-two other officers (including the captain) and crew.

Captain Bernardo Gomes de Lemos protested on 25 December 1806 about events that took place on his Macao ship *Palla N.S.* (*Nossa Senhora*) *da Conceiçao*.[14] This ship was originally the British ship *Nancy* that had been operating as an opium warehouse at Whampoa when it was sold to the Portuguese in Macao in March 1804.[15] In 1806 the ship was travelling between Macao and Manila. While the Portuguese language Protest is included in the records

10 North of the Colong Strait, also called Mud Point or Tanjong Awat.

11 *Prothocol Books*, No. 938, 30 December 1800.

12 *Prothocol Books*, No. 60, 24 December 1806.

13 It is not clear which island this is. Perhaps it is Pulo Pisang 'in lat. 2°37′N., distant about 5 leagues N.W. by W. from Pulo Aur': James Horsburgh, *India Directory, Or, Directions for Sailing to and from the East Indies, China, New Holland, Cape of Good Hope, Brazil, and the Interjacent Ports …*, 2nd edn (2 vols, London 1817), vol. 2, p. 217.

14 *Prothocol Books*, No. 62, 25 December 1806. It is not clear whether the Portuguese word 'Palla' forms part of the ship's name or whether it refers to the type of ship. At the time one of the meanings of 'palla' was 'a sort of Indian man-of-war': Vieyra, Anthony (transtagano), *Dictionary of the Portuguese and English Languages, in Two Parts … Part I – Portuguese and English*, new edn by J. Dias Do Canto (London, 1827).

15 Paul A. Van Dyke, *Whampoa and the Canton Trade: Life and Death in a Chinese Port* (Hong Kong, 2020), p. 129.

and the writing is neat, the document is smudged and unclear, the date it was written illegible; but it appears to be a protest against great seas and winds. The statement is attested to by nine signatories. It was confirmed as entered in the records the following day, 26 December 1806.

A Protest was lodged on 25 December 1807 by Antonio Joze de Vasconcellos, captain of another Macao vessel, the *Indiano*, which was also *en route* from Macao to Manila when it was blown off course.[16] According to the account of the scribe, Simaõ Nimes, written aboard the ship on 11 December, the *Indiano* met with furious winds and high seas in lat. 17°32′N and long. 117°26′E on 8 December. By the next day it was realised that they were powerless in the grip of a hurricane or typhoon (furação ó tufão). They lost masts, sails and other equipment and the seams gave way, with the ship in danger of being completely submerged. The next position given was lat. 14°36′N and long. 115°(?)′E. It was decided to sail to Malacca as the only feasible place for shelter and repair. In very neat, attractive handwriting, the document is a more dramatic description of events than one finds in the British Protests, with thanks to God for salvation. The Protest, in duplicate, was made against the wind, seas, wholesale breakdown, shippers, insurers and all who had an interest in the property and goods of the ship. It was signed by the scribe and four officers, including the captain, and five passengers. From a note added to the Protest note, a copy of the Protest was requested and provided on 12 April 1808.

Captain Faustino Coelho dos Santos of the Macao ship *N.S. de Luz* (also called *Admiral Drury*) submitted a Protest on 31 January 1809.[17] This took the form of a one-and-a-half-page document written in Portuguese by the scribe Joaquim dos Remedios on 21 January on board the ship during a voyage from Macao to Malacca. At lat. 15°N the *Luz* and four other ships, including the *Carmo*, the *Jullia* and the *Palla Conceiçao* were waiting for an armed convoy when the *Carmo* set sail and the others followed. With no designated leader there seems to have been confusion about the signalling and the course set. On 20 January the *Jullia* was lost sight of. It appears the *Luz* had already suffered sail damage and after communication between the *Luz* and the 'senhorio' aboard the *Carmo* it was decided on 21 January not to wait. The Protest was signed by the scribe, the captain and seven others. One of the two passengers who signed was Caetano Joze Cabral, later captain of the *Palla Conceiçao*.

There were two Protests in Portuguese lodged on 23 April 1809 by Captain Francisco Joze da Vitoria Ry (?) Vianna, commander of the Macao ship *Ulysses* (also *Ulyses*, *Ulices*), which had arrived that morning from Macao.[18] Written by the scribe Joze Joaquim Pereira, the first, on 9 April at lat. 16′N,

16 *Prothocol Books*, No. 198, 25 December 1807.

17 *Prothocol Books*, No. 315, 31 January 1809.

18 *Prothocol Books*, Nos 351, 352, 23 April 1809.

described the problem of water in the bilge and damage to the deck, with a unanimous decision to go to the Island of Santa Barbara.[19] The second written on 15 April described how, having left Santa Barbara on the 10th with winds from the southeast, in consultation with the second and third pilots, it was decided to head for the Malacca Strait rather than the Sunda Strait, for example, as the best way of avoiding the (unspecified) enemy. The ultimate destination of the *Ulysses* is not given, but perhaps it was Goa. The two Dutch notes confirming entry in the records were signed by the captain and seven other people, one with a cross, on 24 April. The occupations of the signatories (although not everyone listed actually signed) were given by the scribe as commander, scribe, second officer, third officer and master, boatswain, guard, second guard, carpenter, caulker, and steward, to which were added in the second Protest three supercargoes.

The Captain of the Macao 'gallera' (three-masted ship) *Julia Felix do Senhor Joaõ de Castro*, Antonio Fez da Silva, tabled a Protest note on 13 July 1809, having arrived in Malacca from Goa via Penang. This was followed on the 14th by a Protest in Portuguese written on 12 July by the scribe Bonaventura Lourenço Pereira.[20] He wrote that after the captain was informed by the first officer that the ship was making 12 inches of water an hour and was unfit to navigate the South China Sea, it was agreed by all officers that it was necessary to unload the ship in Malacca and heave down[21] in order to have the vessel repaired. On 15 July Captain da Silva submitted another document stating that his people, now having examined the ship and having found substantial damage, advised the unloading to continue to facilitate repairs. The same day J. M. B. Alms, master attendant at Malacca, and two Portuguese shipwrights, Gregorie d'Souza and Stavo de Souza, submitted their report after having examined the hull.[22] These men made a joint statement regarding the vessel of 'two hundred tons or thereabouts', declaring that parts of the bottom were badly decayed and the ship unfit to proceed to sea. They also stated that it was impracticable to undertake the repairs at Malacca because of the exposure to the southwest monsoon that 'might utterly destroy her'. The case surrounding the ship must have continued for some years because in December 1811 an annotation to the master attendant's report indicated that a copy had been requested by Captain da Silva.

Protests were lodged when the Macao ship *Activo*, captained by Joze Caetano Pedro, travelling from Macao to Goa had a collision with the British country trader *Anna*, captained by Francis Smith, off Point Romania, on 29 or 30 November 1809 (as mentioned above). Captain Smith who blamed Pedro

19 Horsburgh, *India Directory* (1817), vol. 2, p. 212 gives this as the Island of St Barbe, or Pulo Paneeky Bassar (now Pengiki Besar).

20 *Prothocol Books*, Nos 378, 13 July 1809; 380, 14 July 1809.

21 To careen or turn the ship on its side.

22 *Prothocol Books*, Nos 381, 382, 15 July 1809.

for veering across the *Anna*'s bow tendered a log entry of 30 November in evidence.[23] Pedro in his Protest of 7 December against Smith[24] recorded the events as taking place on 29 November. The scribe, Antonio Vincente de Norenha, described the entanglement of masts and the cutting of cables and addressed the question of losses and payments. Again, in addition to the captain and scribe there are a large number of signatories (eighteen), with three signing with a cross.

The *N.S. de Luz* and the *Indiano* feature again within two days of each other in December 1810. Captain Faustino Coelho dos Santos of the Macao ship *N.S. de Luz*, with the same scribe (Joaquim dos Remedios) as in the previous year, made a multi-page Protest followed by a large number of signatures when he arrived from Macao on 15 December 1810.[25] Regrettably the condition of the document makes it impossible to read.

Captain Antonio Joze de Vasconcellos, still captain of the now 'veronge-lukte' (unfortunate) Macao ship *Indiano*, with the same scribe (Simao Nunez) as when he submitted a Protest in December 1807, arrived in Malacca on the Macao warship *Sn. Joaõ Baptista de Capital de Goa* on 16 December 1810 and submitted two Protests that day.[26] In the first, written on 4 December, the scribe described the *Indiano* as sailing in convoy and taking in a large quantity of water. In the second, written on 6 December aboard the 'brig of war', also referred to as the 'frigate', he relates the circumstances leading up to the decision to abandon ship near Pulo Aur. The first Protest was signed by the captain, scribe, and three others, one signing with a cross. The second carried the additional signature of the captain of the frigate, Raimundo de Assa Castelbranco (?).

The *N.S. de Luz* ran into trouble again a year later, for on 4 December 1811 Captain Dos Santos, through his scribe Joaquim dos Remedios, lodged another Protest outlining the events that occurred in the previous month.[27] Having left Macao on 16 November they ran into bad weather on the 18th in the South China Sea at lat. 17°2′N, long. 111°10′E. Citing damage to the ship and cargo, the captain protested against the wind and sea.

The following day, 5 December 1811, the *Palla N.S. da Conceiçao*, now commanded by Captain Caetano Joze Cabral, also arrived from Macao to make another Protest.[28] According to the account the *Palla* had been forced to anchor near the mouth of the Strait of Malacca on 27 November because of contrary tides and lack of wind. Then, after losing an anchor, the ship had to contend throughout the night with a fierce Sumatra blowing from

23 *Prothocol Books*, No. 427, 7 December 1809.
24 *Prothocol Books*, No. 428, 7 December 1809.
25 *Prothocol Books*, No. 607, 15 December 1810.
26 *Prothocol Books*, Nos 608, 609, 16 December 1810.
27 *Prothocol Books*, No. 744, 4 December 1811.
28 *Prothocol Books*, No. 745, 5 December 1811.

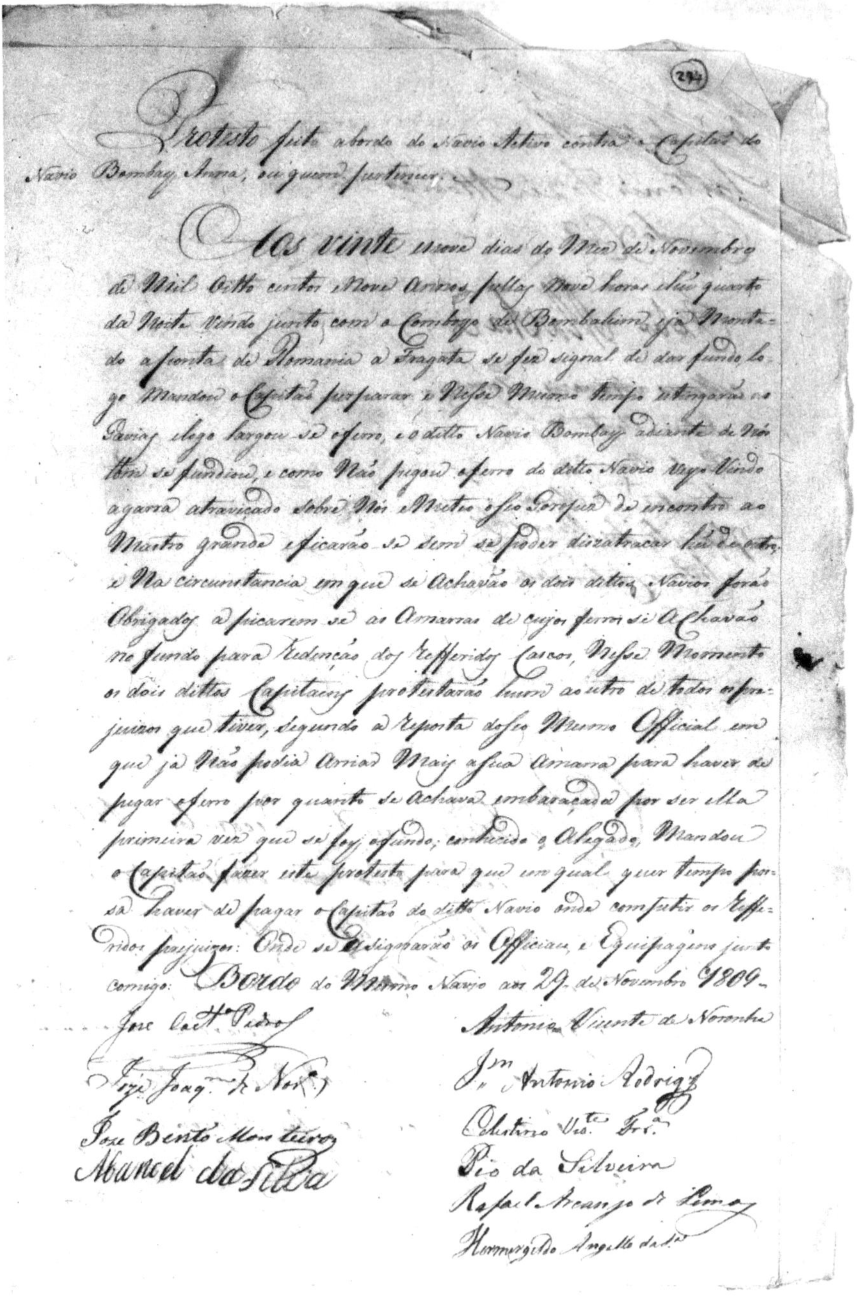
(274)

Protesto feito abordo do Navio Activo contra o Capitão do Navio Bombay Anna, ou quem pertencer.

Aos vinte e nove dias do Mes de Novembro de Mil Oitto centos e Nove Annos, pellas nove horas e hum quarto da Noite Vindo junto com a Comboye de Bombahim, ja Montado a ponta de Romania a Fragata se fez signal de dar fundo logo Mandou o Capitão preparar e Nesse Mesmo tempo atingarão os Navios e logo largou se o ferro, e o ditto Navio Bombay adiante de Nós tem se fundiou, e como Não pegou o ferro do ditto Navio veyo Vindo agarra atravicado sobre Nós Mettendo o seo Gorupes de incontro ao Mastro grande e ficarão se sem se poder dizatracar hum do outro e Na circunstancia em que se Achavão os dois dittos Navios forão Obrigados a picarem se as Amarras de cujos ferros se Achavão no fundo para Redenção dos Refferidos Cascos, Nesse Momento os dois dittos Capitaens protestarão hum ao outro de todos os prejuizos que tiver, segundo a reporta do seo Mesmo Official em que já Não podia Arriar Mais a sua Amarra para haver de pegar o ferro por quanto se Achava embaraçado por ser ella primeira vez que se foy a fundo; conhecido e Alegado, Mandou o Capitão fazer este protesto para que em qual quer tempo possa haver de pagar o Capitão do ditto Navio onde competir os Refferidos prejuizos: Onde se Assignarão os Officiaes, e Equipagens junto Comigo: Bordo do Mesmo Navio aos 29 de Novembro 1809.

Joze Caet.o Pedro
Antonio Vicente de Noronha
Jozé Joaq.m [illegible]
J.m Antonio Rodrig.s
Joze Bento Monteiro
Celestino Vic.te Fr.e
Manoel da Silva
Pio da Silveira
Rafael Arcanjo de Lima
Hermenegildo Angello da S.a

Fig 16. The Portuguese Protest dated 29 November 1809 of Captain Joze Caetano Pedro of the Macao vessel *Activo* against the captain of the *Bombay Anna* before the notary Jan Hendrik Stecher.

the southwest and west. The Protest, concerning in broad terms 'whatsoever pertains', was signed by the captain and seven others.

Unusually, the *N.S. do Carmo* was on a voyage from Lisbon to Macao when Captain Jacinto Lopes Cardoza lodged a Protest at Malacca on 22 November 1812.[29] Several pages long, the account is unfortunately badly smudged and for practical purposes unreadable, though references to Sumatras suggest bad weather. The Protest is noteworthy for carrying one-and-a-half pages of signatures.

On 28 December 1812 the captain of the Macao ship *Mariana Feliz*, Joze Alves da Costa, submitted two Protests both relating to the same voyage.[30] The initial embarkation port is not given but the first Protest is written by the scribe André Gomes Torros on 16 December at the port of Bassiq[31] in Cambodia. The crew were having trouble loading the cargo, there was a war on in the country and the ship was suffering the 'impertinances' of the Cochin China mandarins. Unable to continue the voyage to Macao because of the contrary monsoons and unwilling to overwinter in the hostile conditions of Bassiq, the captain decided, after consultation with the ship's people, to go back the way they had come. The second Protest, written at Riau on 25 December, is much harder to decipher because of ink bleeding through from the other side of the page, but appears to be an account of attempts to sell the cargo at various ports, starting with Pontianak in Borneo after they left the 'Reino de Camboja' and before the ship reached Malacca. The Protests were signed into the record on 29 January 1813 by the captain, the first officer Joaquim Joze da Silva and the master (called 'bootsman' by the Dutch) Joaquim Roos de Pinto.

On 3 April 1813 Captain Jose Alves da Costa lodged a third Protest about the payment owing on certain goods,[32] presumably related to the 1812 voyage. Apart from the 'Fiscio', the problem involved the merchant Henrique Christiano Sebastao Donnenberg and the Malaccan burgher Hubertus Van Bragt, the latter probably the same man who ordered a search of the cargo of the *Mary* in 1815.[33]

29 *Prothocol Books*, No. 845, 22 November 1812.

30 *Prothocol Books*, Nos 856, 857, 28 December 1812.

31 According to Alistair Lamb, 'British Missions to Cochin China: 1778–1822', *JMBRAS*, 34:3/4 (1961), 1–248, at pp. 30, 31, 195, 212–13, this is Bassac or Ba Tac situated about two miles up the Bassac River, the most westerly arm of the Mekong Delta. In the late eighteenth century this area formed the boundary between the southern parts of Cambodia and Cochin China. Although between 1812 and 1814 Cambodia was 'more or less partitioned between Vietnam and Siam', with the larger part of the country deemed a protectorate of Vietnam, the term 'Cambodia' was still used by Europeans to denote the Mekong Delta area.

32 *Prothocol Books*, No. 886, 3 April 1813.

33 *Prothocol Books*, No. 37, 14 November 1815.

Captain Luis Carlos de Miranda[34] of the Macao ship *Carmo*[35] registered a Protest note on 16 July 1814, followed by a Protest in Portuguese on the 18th.[36] This latter was an account by the scribe Joze Vincente Lopez of how the *Carmo*, a new ship, in lat. 14°30′, long. 93°30′ in the Bay of Bengal, with strong winds and big seas, began to take on water on 30 June, pumping 12 inches in twenty-four hours. On 4 July, with better weather, it was found that everything inside was wet and a certain amount of the cargo of cloth had to be jettisoned. The Protest, against whatever may arise from the damage, was signed by the scribe, captain and two others to whom the Dutch ascribed the term 'stuurman' or mate, Constantino Joze Lopez and Joze Bento Monteiro.

A series of documents in Dutch and Portuguese concerning the brig *Ulysses* (or *Ulicis*) were lodged on 28 and 29 August 1814.[37] The first, a Protest written in Portuguese on 27 August and signed by the captain José Ribeiro and the second pilot Luis Villanos (?), described the series of mishaps that had taken place in the voyage from Bengal. On 5 June, in difficult wind conditions, they had passed the Island of Narcondam (lat. 13°.45′N, long. 94°27′E). Around this time the first pilot fell sick and was left prostrate. For the following month and ten days the *Ulysses* was pushed towards the coast of Barama (Burma, now Myanmar) and it was not until 1 August that the winds allowed them to reach Penang. Here they carried the ill pilot to the Penang surgeon who pronounced the man unfit to proceed to sea. After remonstration from the captain, the police commissioner (juiz da policia) declared that the law of the nation would not allow the invalid to rejoin the ship.

For a further eleven days the captain searched in vain for a replacement pilot until, on the advice of the Penang merchants, he proceeded to Malacca to continue the search there, arriving on 22 August. With no more success in Malacca Ribeiro determined to proceed to Manila making do with only the second pilot, but the boatswain (contra mestre) refused to take part in such a risky voyage. It was then determined to unload the cargo to protect it

34 As captain of the armed *Conceiçao* in 1809 de Miranda had fought heroically against the Chinese pirates in the Pearl River Delta: Gomes, *Páginas*, p. 164. Making the most of the opportunity, the *Conceiçao* and the *Belezario*, in their raids against the pirates, also took with them a shipment of opium to sell to the merchants of Canton: Paul A. Van Dyke, *The Canton Trade: Life and Enterprise on the China Coast, 1700–1845* (Hong Kong, repr. 2012, orig, 2005), p. 131.

35 This is probably the *New Carmo*, a ship of 400 tons launched in May 1814, and that left Kedgeree, on the Hooghly, for Macao on 20 June 1814. It was built as a successor to the *Carmo*, 'long employed in the Opium trade between Calcutta and Macao': *Calcutta Monthly Journal*, 23 May 1814, 351; 27 June 1814, 433. The old *Carmo*, listed in the *East-India Register and Directory for 1816* as of 540 tons and owned by J. Barretto & Sons, was still in business, sailing from Saugor for Macao on 22 July. There was also the *N.S. do Carmo*, Captain Cardoza (q.v.).

36 *Prothocol Books*, Nos 994, 16 July 1814; 995, 18 July 1814.

37 *Prothocol Books*, Nos 1002, 28 August 1814; 1003, 1004, 29 August 1814.

from continuing bad weather. The Protest was made against the unfavourable weather and whatsoever other misfortunes.

Another document written on 29 August, in Dutch, at Malacca registered the sale of the *Ulysses*.[38] Franscisco José da Vitoria Pereira Barretto, the brig's owner, and a Thomas Cooper are named in the transaction. Attached to this document is another in Portuguese headed 'Senhor Capitaõ José Ribeiro'. This, issued on 14 January 1814 at Binondoc (Binondo, Manila) by Pereira Barretto, contains the sailing instructions as well as instructions as to the conduct of the brig and, leaving the details to Ribeiro's discretion, the disposal of both brig and its cargo of timber and copper at Bengal. At the time Pereira Barretto had command of the *Conceiçao*, which he was taking to Macao where he hoped later on to meet with Ribeiro if they did not meet earlier at Manila.[39]

A second Protest signed by Ribeiro and Second Pilot Villanos was written on the same day (29 August).[40] Introduced by a note in Dutch about selling the ship to provide liquidity, Ribeiro in his Protest represented himself as both captain and owner of the brig (perhaps he had bought the brig in Bengal?) and protested against its urgent sale occasioned by his failure to obtain requisite officers, the dangers of continual exposure to bad weather, and the expenses associated with the original crew of twenty-five men exacerbated by some of the cargo having lost 50% of its value. He regretted the low price reached by the sale, which was explained as in some way (unclear) associated with papers in Bengal.

Three Portuguese Protests lodged in 1816 all relate to the same storm near Pulo Aur and the Singapore Strait in the last week of December 1815. The first Protest note, presented by Captain Urbano do Rozario of the *N.S. da Portaria* on 3 January 1816,[41] was accompanied by a Portuguese account headed 'Protesto' written by the scribe Francisco Antonio da Silva on 26 December 1815. This document protested against the extraordinarily strong winds and seas which the ship, having left Macao for Bengal on 17 December, endured from the 24th to 26th within sight of Pulo Aur. It includes details of problems with the anchors and sails that beset the ship in conditions which

38 *Prothocol Books*, No. 1003, 29 August 1814.

39 Pereira Barretto, known to his compatriots in Macao as 'Tiger of the Sea', had found fame by defeating the Chinese pirates in the Pearl River Delta in 1807: Gomes, *Páginas*, p. 144. In 1816 he recorded a Protest (No. 94, 27 February 1816) at Malacca as captain of the *Theresa*; in 1819 as sea captain of the Goa Navy he requested appointment to the government of Demaun or Timor: <https://digitarq.ahu.arquivos.pt/details?id=1404154> [Accessed 15 April 2025]. On 2 September 1822 he was appointed first captain of the port (Mercantile Navy) in Macao: <https://www.macaumemory.mo/entries_c411810c02564cb5b3a3bce8f8984ad1?token=S98IkQs27+ATd1DCr8rceA==&lgType=pt> [Accessed 15 April 2025].

40 *Prothocol Books*, No. 1004, 29 August 1814.

41 *Prothocol Books*, No. 62, 3 January 1816.

made it too dangerous to 'take the Strait'. The Protest is signed, along with the captain and the scribe, by the second mate and the 'contre mestre'.

The Protest of the captain of the Macao ship *Belezario*, Florencio Joze Marcal, lodged on 4 January 1816[42] was similar. The scribe, Joze Rodrigues da Costa, writing aboard the ship on 29 December 1815, described the worsening conditions with strong winds and seas from the night of 26 December until the night of the 28th with the ship failing to maintain anchorage and taking on water. He protested against the wind and seas and the insurers. The Protest was signed by the scribe who also described himself as the second pilot, by the captain and by eight other officers, crew and passengers among whom was the ship's owner Caetano Antonio de Campos.[43]

On 27 February 1816 a Protest note was lodged at Malacca by the third victim of the December 1815 storm, the captain of the Portuguese private ship *Theresa* (*Thereza* in the Dutch), Francisco da Vitoria Vasconcellos Pereira Barretto, who had arrived from Macao via Minto. The note was accompanied by a Protest in English,[44] written on 4 January at Minto probably by the first officer, Peter Isaac Foster, as a translation of the Portuguese Protest which is referred to but which is not present in the records. On a voyage from Macao to Bengal that began in December 1815 the ship ran into tempestuous weather that lasted from the 26th until the 29th. Two anchors were lost in the vicinity of Pulo Aur. On 3 January the decision was made, with the agreement of the officers, to head for the Banka Strait and, at the nearest port, refit the *Theresa* with the anchors 'necessary to her safety'. The Portuguese Protest was signed by all officers and passengers. In the English version, which does not carry all these signatures but which is witnessed by a resident of Minto (signature indecipherable), Captain Pereira Barretto did 'duly protest before the Competent Magistrate against the Winds, Seas and Currents for all and every Damages, Losses, Demurrages, Deviation of Voyage, etc. etc. which by the act of the aforesaid has resulted, results and may result thereafter'.

On 31 December 1817 the *Belezario* appears once more in Malacca, again following a voyage from Macao but this time with Caetano Antonio de Campos, the ship's owner, as captain.[45] The Protest note refers to 'what befell on the voyage'[46] but the details from the mentioned on-board journal are not present in the records.

A Protest note of 1 August 1818 described the captain of the brig *Hero*, André de Santa Maria, as a native Christian and resident of Malacca. A second Protest note on 3 August was accompanied by a document written by the captain, signed by him alone, and declared as a copy from the ship's

42 *Prothocol Books*, No. 63, 4 January 1816.
43 Gomes, *Páginas*, p. 143.
44 *Prothocol Books*, No. 94, 27 February 1816.
45 Gomes, *Páginas*, p. 143.
46 *Prothocol Books*, No. 380, 31 December 1817.

journal.[47] The vessel had departed from Lingga for Minto on 25 July but on the 27th encountered strong Sumatras that damaged the foremast and caused the brig to ship more water than the pumps could handle. In consultation with the officers it was decided to return to Lingga, but when it was found impossible to effect repairs there they sailed on 31 July for Malacca, arriving in the roads the next day.

Portuguese Protests continued to be lodged at Malacca after the resumption of Dutch authority in September 1818. The two examples for 1819 include a reference in the preliminary Protest note to the Dutch legal regulation of 16 October 1817 allowing the Protests to be received at Malacca. On 25 April 1819 Captain Joaõ Joze de Souza lodged a smudgy, difficult-to-read Protest in Portuguese concerning the loss of an anchor from his private Portuguese brig *Eliza*.[48] This was signed by the scribe Sebastiaõ Antonio Tigueira and thirteen other officers and mariners, three signing with a cross.

Captain Joze Joaquim de Noronha of the Macao brig *Caçador* protested against the events suffered on a voyage from Bombay when he landed in Malacca on 5 June 1819.[49] The scribe Francisco Xavier Homem Rebello Freire wrote of the bad weather of 27 May beginning at lat. 5°06′N, long. 79°(?)21′E, around Ceylon and in the Bay of Bengal, the continuing Sumatras bringing rain, strong winds and rough seas that made the brig roll day and night from portside to starboard with water entering through the scuttles and flooding the cabins. The Protest was made against the bad weather and any breakdown, damages, losses and injuries to the hull. The signatories were the scribe, captain and seven others, three of whom signed with a cross or mark. Probably the cargo was opium as the *Caçador* is recorded elsewhere as carrying between 334 and 390 chests of opium from Goa to Macao that year.[50]

In summary, one may conclude that although the Portuguese Protests vary from the British in their ecriture and layout, and although they evince a consultation with a wider selection of the ship's company, their essence of

47 *Prothocol Books*, No. 476, 1 August 1818; 477, 3 August 1818. The captain signed himself as A. D. Sta. Maria. Some information about the Santa Maria family in Malacca is given in Bernard Sta Maria, *My People, My Country: the story of the Malacca Portuguese Community* (Malacca, 1982).

48 *Prothocol Books*, No. 628, 25 April 1819. In 1780 the English country ship *Eliza* was sold, presumably at Macao, by 'a private Englishman' to a Portuguese supercargo, Mr Miranda. On the list of English private ships at Whampoa in September 1780 the *Eliza* is also given the name *Marquez de Anjeja*, a title associated with the Noronha family: Van Dyke, *Whampoa*, p. 186; Appendix 1.2b. Perhaps the 1819 *Eliza* is the same vessel.

49 *Prothocol Books*, No. 651, 5 June 1819.

50 Celsa Pinto, *Trade and Finance in Portuguese India: A Study of the Portuguese Country Trade 1770–1840* (New Delhi, 1994), Appendix 8, p. 274. Other Portuguese ships that feature in the Protests, the *N.S. da Luz*, the *Activo*, *Angelica*, *Carmo* and *Santo Antonio*, are also on this list of opium ships.

complaint and excuse remains the same as that of their British counterparts. There is one notable difference. Although, like the British ships, many of the Portuguese suffered storm damage, there was only one ship lost – the *Indiano* abandoned near Pulo Aur. There were no groundings or strandings reported. This would support the hypothesis that the Portuguese were more experienced sailors in local conditions or had better charts. Certainly, there was a great emphasis on having qualified pilots as part of the ship's company.

Half of the twenty-eight noted voyages that engendered a Protest had commenced in Macao and the mishaps suffered by these ships, apart from the misadventure of the *Ulysses* in April, invariably took place in December or January. They avoided the worst typhoon months of July to September and took advantage of the northeast monsoons to make their run in the same months as did the British when they departed Whampoa, risking the accompanying rough seas. The weather-related incidents reported by Portuguese ships on their way to Macao were experienced in the Bay of Bengal or the Malacca Straits and, apart from the *N.S. Carmo* from Lisbon, took place in the months of May to July, the same as the British experience. These Portuguese Protests often mention the Sumatras as winds prevailing more widely than in the more localised British usage.

It is interesting that copies of a number of the Portuguese Protests were requested at later dates (as indicated by remarks in the margins of the records), presumably because cases surrounding the misadventures were still proceeding.

10

Dutch, American, Hamburg, Malay

The Protests (five cases)

On 1 December 1803 Captain Willem Verhaage of the private Dutch brig *Carolina* protested at Malacca against the seizure of his vessel by HMS *Rattlesnake.*[1] The events leading up to the arrest illustrate the political circumstances operating in the area at the time.

The British had occupied Dutch Amboina in 1796 under the same conditions as they occupied Malacca, that is to forestall a French occupation. Under the Treaty of Amiens of 1802 the British-held Dutch possessions in the East Indies were to be returned to the Dutch and, in spite of an unofficial British policy of procrastination, Amboina was restored to Dutch rule on 28 February 1803 by the Resident, Colonel James Oliver. Under Oliver's authorisation (on behalf of the EIC) the *Carolina* sailed for Madras on 6 May as a cartel ship carrying British troops. Captain Verhaage was also authorised to purchase goods at Madras (which he accordingly did, taking on board a load of cotton and copper) and to return to Amboina under the protection of a 'Cartel Pass'[2] dated 2 September 1803. The *Carolina* embarked for Batavia on 5 September intending to travel via the Sunda Strait, but bad weather around Aceh dictated a route down the Malacca Strait. The brig arrived at Malacca to take on provisions on 30 October. It departed again on 3 November only to meet with a number of pirates around the Carimons and the Strait of Dryon on the 10th, which convinced the captain to return to Malacca, where he anchored in the Roads on the 16th.

1 British Library, Asia, Pacific and Africa Collections, *Malacca, General Prothocol Books (Registers of Legal Deeds) 1786–1825*, IOR: R/9/22/1–75 [referred to in this study as *Prothocol Books*], No. 1298, 1 December 1803.

2 A cartel ship is one employed in the exchange of prisoners or in carrying proposals from one side to another. Such a ship flew a special flag. A cartel pass was also needed in this case as cartel ships did not usually engage in trade: Francis H. Upton, *The Law of Nations Affecting Commerce During War: With a Review of the Jurisdiction, Practice and Proceedings of Prize Courts* (New York, 1863), pp. 20–7.

In the meantime, hostilities between England and France had resumed in Europe and orders had been received in India by 25 September 1803[3] to once again detain all French and Dutch ships.

On 31 November HMS *Rattlesnake* commanded by Josiah John Cramer[4] arrived at Malacca. An officer immediately boarded the *Carolina*, ran down the Dutch flag and pennant as well as the cartel flag and took possession of the brig, removing a number of the crew. Captain Verhaage, on shore at the time of the arrest, returned to show Cramer the cartel pass, apparently to no avail. He registered his Protest not only against the actions of Cramer but against the EIC whom he held responsible for all damage and losses.

A second Protest concerning the *Carolina* was registered at Malacca on 1 December 1803.[5] The declarant, Johan Anthon Neubronner,[6] was representing David Ruhde, a former president of the Malacca Orphan Chamber, whose chest containing valuable goods had been despatched aboard the *Carolina* to Carel Hendrik Specht, vice president of the College of Magistrates at Batavia. The goods had been despatched on the understanding that the ship was protected by its cartel pass. The Protest was made against the seizure of the chest and contents by the *Rattlesnake* as well as against all other disadvantages connected with the event now and in the future.

In this Protest Neubronner describes Verhaage as 'the old Captain of the sea' suggestive of an experienced and venerated seafarer. He was described in exactly the same terms by another declarant, the surgeon Arij van der Baan, in an earlier statement relating to the *Carolina* on 26 November 1803.[7]

The seizure of the *Carolina* and condemnation of the property as belonging to the enemy was contested in the High Court of Admiralty in London jointly by the EIC and the Dutch owner of the vessel (the Protest against the EIC by Verhaage had therefore been wrongly directed). The argument of the captors, upholding the actions of the *Rattlesnake*, was that the cartel had been granted in a time of peace and the EIC had no power to grant the privilege. Moreover, if the cartel were valid, the master had forfeited the benefit of the protection by taking goods on board, as trading by cartel ships was prohibited.

3 British Library, 'Papers of Richard Wellesley, 1st Marquess, Wellesley to Hobart, 25 September 1803', Add MS 13469/item f32 [Available at NLA AJCP Mfm M1888–1889].

4 Cramer was the son of a baronet and on succeeding to the title in 1817 he assumed the name of Sir Josiah Coghill Coghill. He was promoted to vice-admiral in 1841: William R O'Byrne, *A Naval Biographical Dictionary: Comprising the Life and Services of Every Living Officer in Her Majesty's Navy from the Rank of Admiral of the Fleet to that of Lieutenant* (London, 1849), pp. 209–10.

5 *Prothocol Books*, No. 1299, 1 December 1803.

6 Neubronner had originally come to Batavia as a gunner on the ship *Doggersbank*: <https://www.openarch.nl/ghn:c2bd06e3-a156-43c8-80ca-62c8109e3e8b/en> [Accessed 15 April 2025].

7 *Prothocol Books*, No. 1064, 26 November 1803.

The judgement handed down by Sir William Scott on 27 February 1807, more than three years after the protested event, consisted of several parts. First, the cartel was valid both in the time of peace and in the time of the ensuing war; second, the right of the EIC to issue the cartel devolved from the Crown; and third, the freight taken on board at Madras was in accordance with the terms of the particular cartel pass. The ship, cargo and personal belongings of the captain were ordered to be returned to the owners. However, the goods that had been taken on at Malacca were in contravention of the terms of the cartel pass and were forfeit. These goods amounted to nineteen packages containing writing desks, a sealed chest, earthen pots, barrels, a small box, two cinnamon sticks and three small parcels, consigned to different persons at Batavia.[8]

While the Dutch ship *Carolina* avoided an attack by pirates in the southern end of the Malacca Strait in November 1803 by turning back to Malacca, the American Salem ship *Putnam* (266 tons, built Danvers 1802),[9] attacked and seized by Malays at Riau in November 1805, was caught unawares. The captain, John Carlton, submitted a Protest note at Malacca on 26 December 1805. His Protest, dated the same day, was confirmed as written into the records before the Dutch notary Francois Adam Lefevre on the 27th.[10] He stated that while he and the third officer were ashore trading for tin on 28 November, people belonging to Raja Adhrus, a Bugis, went on board the *Putnam* and killed the second officer, Samuel Puson (Pierson), and five more of the ship's company, 'forcibly taking the ship from my command'.

There have been several published accounts of the *Putnam* incident based on the testimony of the ship's carpenter William Brown after he reached Calcutta, as well as on Captain Carlton's papers and his recounting of the events, news that did not reach Salem until almost a year later.[11] The *Transfer* (Captain Matthews) and the *Malcolm* (Captain Fenwick), two English brigs at anchor in the Riau Roads, gave chase to the 'Malays' but were outgunned by the well-armed *Putnam*. The ship was never recovered. Captain Carlton with his remaining officers and crew sailed to Penang on the *Malcolm*, stopping to protest at Malacca *en route*.

8 Christopher Robinson, *Reports of Cases Argued and Determined in the High Court of Admiralty commencing with The Judgement of the Right Hon. Sir William Scott. Michelmas Term, 1798*, vol. 6, ed. George Minot (Boston MA, 1853), pp. 336–40.

9 *Ships Registers of the District of Salem and Beverly, Massachusetts*, copied by A. Frank Hitchinson with annotations by Stephen Willard Phillips (Salem MA, 1906) pp. 151–2.

10 *Prothocol Books*, Nos 108, 26 December 1805; 109, 27 December 1805.

11 For example, James Francis Warren, *Iranun and Balangingi: Globalization, Maritime Raiding and the Birth of Ethnicity* (Singapore, 2002), p. 280; James Duncan Phillips, *Pepper and Pirates: Adventures in the Sumatra Pepper Trade of Sale* (Boston MA, 1949), chapter 4; George Grenville Putnam, *Salem Vessels and their Voyages: A History of the Pepper Trade with the Island Of Sumatra*, ser. 1 (Salem MA, 1924), pp. 23–5.

Like the Danish, Portuguese and American ships, vessels registered in Hamburg were 'neutral' during the wars between European powers of the period and therefore subject to suspicion of carrying out clandestine activities. However, there was no suggestion that seizure was involved when a private Hamburg ship, the *Charlotte*, made a Protest at Malacca on 19 January 1803 after a voyage from Manila during a temporary period of peace.[12] As an indication of the close ties Hamburg ships had with the Danish agencies in Bengal,[13] the *Charlotte* had left Manila for 'Fredericksburg' (probably Frederiknagore, now Serampore) on 6 January. At lat. 13°7′N it had encountered high seas, which it battled until the 17th, consequently springing a bad leak. The Dutch Protest was signed by the two supercargoes, William Miller and Carl Kirkkberger on behalf of the captain, Johan Christof Schleiden. There was also a statement by Alexion Constapol and John Jacob (surname indecipherable) who signed with crosses.[14]

The extensive Protest lodged by the first mate and Portuguese citizen Jean Anthony on 21 March 1809[15] is unique in the records because of its intertwining European and Malay overtones and its confusion as to where loyalties lay. At its most basic level, as far as it can be ascertained, it is an example of an officer protecting himself against charges that might be brought by the owner or supercargo as a consequence of certain maritime misadventures. It is also revealing, however, of the suspicions surrounding the real identity of a ship, as well as the inherent difficulties of the prevailing pass system that could arise because of a complicated political situation. The case involved Portuguese, English and French citizens, local residents of Malacca and Riau, as well as the ruler of Riau.

In the long Protest recorded in Dutch, Anthony describes how he was hired, on 4 December 1808, as first mate, to take command of the brig *Tiriwinaga Cany* on a voyage from Malacca to Java. The vessel belonged to a local Hindu of Malacca, Ferewinade Plee, but was sailing under the flag of the Sultan of Riau. Anthony was hired at a rate of Sp. $60 per month and this was confirmed in writing with the supercargo whom he referred to as Na'da (probably an abbreviation of nakhoda) and who ordered him to sail to Riau. The vessel was seized by the French Privateer *Le Curieux* (Captain Jean Piros) near Pulo Pisang and it looked as though Anthony would be sent to Mauritius with his brig as a prize. Anthony pleaded that he had a family in Bengal and was only a mate, and he suggested to the French they could send the captain of another ship, the *Coemarapa* (also spelt *Comoerapa*) to Mauritius.

12 *Prothocol Books*, No. 1180, 19 January 1803.

13 For more on Hamburg private traders in India see Hermann Kellenbenz, 'German Trade Relations with the Indian Ocean from the End of the Eighteenth Century to 1870', *Journal of Southeast Asian Studies*, 13:1 (1982), 133–52.

14 *Prothocol Books*, No. 1181, 24 January 1803.

15 *Prothocol Books*, No. 338, 21 March 1809.

Piros showed him the English pass from Malacca, asserting that the vessel had been under Portuguese command, a dangerous situation for Anthony as France was then at war with Portugal. Eventually, however, on 13 December 1808 the French captain, after a discussion with the second mate of the brig, Louis Pareira (who said the vessel was in no fit state to sail all the way to Mauritius), gave Anthony a French pass to sail back to Malacca. The next day, the French sailed away.

The nakhoda of the *Coemarapa* insisted that Anthony should not go to Malacca, despite possessing the French pass, but should go to Riau. Anthony then requested a pass from the nakhoda in case he should meet the French again and be asked by them why he was not sailing to Malacca. This received, he sailed to Riau, having to take along two passengers. Anthony remained so long at Riau that the owner of the *Tiriwinaga Cany*, Ferewinade Plee, arrived there from Malacca on 13 January. Anthony handed over to Na'da the papers received from the French that Na'da later informed him he had torn up. It was then that Anthony realised he was in a 'Malay place' and had no rights. There were discussions as to whether Anthony could sail as mate on one of Na'da's vessels, but Na'da believed this would not be permitted by the Sultan of Riau. Anthony escaped from Riau on one of a certain Achmat Sap's vessels back to Malacca. There, on 21 March 1809, he protested against the behaviour of the owner of the *Tiriwinaga Cany*, Ferewinade Plee, and against any claims by Na'da against him, the ship and its cargo.

CONCLUSION

The evidence presented by the Protests recorded in the Malacca *Prothocol Books* provides a distinctive perspective on British and other European activities in the East Indies in the last decade of the eighteenth and first decades of the nineteenth centuries. This was an era when sail was a vital means of travel for people, of transportation for goods and of communication, both personal and official. The country traders participated in all these undertakings but their *raison d'être* was trade, where disruption by misadventure meant delay, and every delay a potential loss of profit.

The misadventures described in the Protests highlight at first hand the ever-present dangers faced by country traders sailing in the Bay of Bengal, the Malay Archipelago and the South China Sea. In addition to the normal hazards that mariners everywhere encountered, it can be argued that sailors in this part of the world had to deal with additional and more intense hazards: they had to sail through the monsoon storms of the Bay of Bengal, navigate the narrow channels of the Malacca Strait and Western Malay Archipelago and they had to prevail against the typhoons of the South China Sea. Not only that, the European sailors had to safely guide their vessels through an alien region far from home where hostility to foreign intervention often prevailed and the norms of some societies encouraged the seizure of foreign vessels. They also had to deal with the political fallout in the East Indies engendered by European wars.

The calamities were mostly met with on voyages between India and Canton or within the seas of the Malay Archipelago itself and were recorded at Malacca because it was a traditional staging post with the appropriate facilities. The years 1815–18 following the Tambora volcanic eruption were especially busy in the Malacca notarial office. The frequency of the reporting of the misadventures is indicative of the risks that the traders were prepared to take to complete their voyages, which in turn suggests the rewards of the trade – namely, the profits – that were achievable with perseverance and luck.

Some of the captains of British country traders were owners, but most were not, commanding a variety of vessels for others who had to accord them a high level of trust, relying upon them to navigate the often-unchartered waters safely and protect the cargo. These men sometimes belonged to distinguished English or Scottish families, but for the most part little is known about them. Nevertheless, the names of those unsung identities who feature in the Protests are not necessarily unrecorded elsewhere. Many appear in the annual listing of merchant vessels in the *East-India Register and Directory*; in John Phipps' lists of mainly Calcutta shipping published in 1823 and 1840; in contemporary newspaper notices of shipping departures and arrivals; and in the Canton records so usefully tabulated by Paul A. Van Dyke. Many would have known each other, some commanding the same vessel at different times, others meeting annually in Whampoa.

The more dramatic of the reported adventures, or misadventures, feature in the contemporary press, usually a repetition of the Protest, embellished with further detail. However, most of the mishaps recorded at Malacca were not sensational enough to attract public interest and therefore, in the absence of ships' logs, it is the Protests alone that throw a distinctive light on the management, resourcefulness and decision-making of the captain in the face of challenging situations.

It is hard to know for sure, without a more specific understanding of the Malaccan administrative procedures, whether the English-language Protests are the physical handiwork of the captains themselves or of a Malaccan official. Certainly there are common phrases, 'every reason to believe the cargo must be damaged', 'a protest against the insurers', but from the variations in the handwriting, the spelling, punctuation and turn of phrase it is likely that as it is the captain who signs, it is also the captain himself, or an officer, who pens the accounts. Some are extracts from the ship's log, others not. Some are lengthy, some are brief; some poorly written, others formally expressed. By contrast, in the case of the Portuguese, the Protests are usually the work of the scribe who was a normal part of the ship's company. These documents are often filed as an appendage to the captain's Protest note rather than as a separate Protest with a unique number.

The target of the Protest, regardless of nationality, sometimes seems rather nebulous. Storm damage, for example, could elicit a Protest 'against' the winds, weather, sea, losses, underwriters or insurers, or, vaguely, any person concerning any loss or damage. Nevertheless, the Protests often show evidence of every endeavour on the part of the captain to do things by the rule book, particularly consulting with officers before making a decision to turn back the ship or throw part of the cargo overboard. This is especially the case with the Portuguese Protests, where any decision is always cited as unanimously that of the captain and all the officers.

The Protests lift at least a corner of the veil of obscurity with which the mates (or officers) on a country ship are usually shrouded. As well as being consulted on difficult decisions, they are there as signatories to the captain's submission, sometimes signing with a firm hand, sometimes with a suggestion of unfamiliarity with writing and sometimes, in the cases of second and third mates, with a cross signifying illiteracy. On British ships they are usually British, occasionally Portuguese. One hopes that the altercating mates aboard the *City of Goa* are not typical. In the absence of the captain the first mate, having command of the ship, had the responsibility of submitting a Protest. Where this situation occurred at Malacca the reasons for the absence of the captain ranged from death to detention by an enemy, to being accidentally stranded ashore. In the earlier of the British Protests the first mates sometimes took responsibility for the detailed Protest, regardless of the whereabouts of the captain, but that practice appears to have ceased after 1802. The Danish Protests, mostly written in Dutch, are much more likely to be signed by the first and second mates without the signature of the captain.

The 'mate' does not seem to have had an exact equivalent on the Portuguese ships. Sometimes the English term 'mate' or the Dutch 'stuurman' is used by the non-Portuguese to refer to a seaman on a Portuguese ship, but the Portuguese Protests themselves, rather than using a general term, make a distinction between officers, masters and pilots, where an officer could also be a master with a navigational role within the hierarchy. Other roles sometimes specified include carpenter and caulker, boatswain, guard and steward.

Lascar crews, usually Indians or Malays, formed the majority of the British country ship's people, the complement typically being composed of the captain, two or three European officers and the rest lascars with their leader, the serang. As an example of the numbers we can cite four ships that made Protests at Malacca and that are also included, with a record of their number of men, in Phipps' 1823 list of shipping belonging to Calcutta in 1822.[1] The largest, the *Fort William*, 1,236 tons, was manned by fifty-two Europeans and 116 natives; the *Earl Kellie*, 520 tons, by three Europeans and sixty-seven natives; the *Good Hope*, 388 tons, by four Europeans and fifty-nine natives; and the *Matilda*, 250 tons, by three Europeans and thirty natives. In his Protest of November 1815 Captain Kidd describes the crew of the 600-ton *Duchess of Wellington* as comprising eighty men and boys. Bulley describes another of the Protest ships, the *Travancore* of 1,000 tons, as having a crew of 150 men.

From the Protests as a whole we obtain descriptions of the actions taken by the crew to overcome various dangerous situations: adjusting sails, manning the pumps, deploying the anchors, shifting cargo or throwing it overboard, replacing rotten planks etcetera. Although there is an occasional mention of the effect of disaster on the sailors themselves, 'our crew so exhausted with fatigue and several with wounds' (Captain Ramsey of the *Experiment*) and 'the greatest part of our crew being sick' (Captain Deans of the *Christina*), a feature of the majority of the Protests is the lack of mention of injuries or illness suffered by either officers or crew. Nevertheless, injuries to or death of crew members would have had an impact on the efficient conclusion of a

1 John Phipps, *A Guide to the Commerce of Bengal for the Use of Merchants, Ship Owners, Commanders … Resorting to the East Indies* (Calcutta, 1823), pp. 91–5.

voyage. This is clearly shown in the case of the Portuguese brig *Ulysses* where the failure of Captain Ribeiro to find a replacement for the sick first pilot eventually led to the sale of the ship.

The focus of the Protests on the 'men' more often occurs when they are found wanting – participating in mutiny or piracy, refusing to work in times of danger, or endeavouring to save their own skins instead of contributing to the common effort. Even the number of those lost when a ship went down is not reported. This is perhaps understandable given that the Protests are essentially business documents relating to damages to cargo and vessel, a financial matter, with an adverse situation always presented as unavoidable and the human cost irrelevant or understated. Even the death of the captain's wife when the *Christina* was lost was not mentioned in the resulting Protest.

There are only two instances in the Protests where a woman is referred to: one, the case of Mrs Yeats aboard the *New Endeavour*, an older woman who gave the alarm when the ship caught fire; and second, an anonymous woman who was among those spared by the mutineers aboard the *Admiral Troubridge*.

As well as the considerable range in the size of vessels lodging Protests at Malacca, the type of vessel, where it is specified, varies from the occasional snow, grab, bark or schooner to the majority designated as 'ships' (three masted, square rigged) and 'brigs' (two masted, square rigged). While all those vessels known to be 600 tons and over were voyaging to or from China, the residue were not necessarily confined, as might be expected, to the archipelago 'local trade'. The smallest plying to China, the *Tweed*, was only 150 tons.

Apart from Whampoa (and Portuguese Macao), the ports of call mentioned in the Protests encompassed not only the main Indian ports of Bombay, Calcutta and Madras, the Danish settlements of Tranquebar and Frederiknagore, the Portuguese ports on the west coast of India and the British-held Malacca, Penang and Bencoolen in the archipelago, but myriad islands and coastal settlements in the Bay of Bengal, the Malacca and Singapore straits, places along the north and west coasts of Sumatra, and a host of settlements, including Batavia, along the north coast of Java. Some of the ships sailed through the Moluccas as far east as the Marianas. Others traded along the coast of Borneo, at Manila and at ports little-visited by Europeans in Siam, Cambodia and Cochin China.

No ship was completely alone in the ocean, and some were in close proximity at crucial times. A ship rendering aid to another could mean the difference between life and death. A Dutch gunboat came to the rescue of the British *Christina*, but it was generally country traders that came to the rescue of fellow country traders. Many anonymous ships failed to acknowledge a distress signal, or didn't see it. Captains Elliott, Strut and Patrick all included instances of this in their Protests, Patrick reporting ten ships that had failed to come to his aid when wrecked on Bambek Shoal.

On the other hand, some Protests mention travelling in convoy, a safety precaution particularly during wartime, and a ready means of mutual help, though also carrying a risk of collision. We also find reports of British country traders being bullied by their Royal Navy convoy leaders.

As trade 'to the Eastward' increased, mariners, including country traders, had to come to terms with the environmental dangers and try to minimise them. While there is little evidence in the Protests of the use of new navigational tools such as chronometers, many of those British country traders who had recourse to Malacca relayed their experiences to Horsburgh for publication in his directories in order to disseminate their increasing knowledge of the East Indies routes. This continuation of an established tradition helped both protect individuals and contributed to the ongoing advancement of trade (and ultimately empire). In the case of the Portuguese, it is arguable that they had a better knowledge of the shipping hazards, based on a longer acquaintance of the area.

Apart from when it is thrown overboard, the cargo carried by the protesting ships is rarely specified. We know from other sources that cotton was the main commodity carried from India to China. As well, we occasionally read in the Protests of cargoes of rice, wheat, sugar, spices, copper, iron, coopers' tools and nails, tin, rattans, saltpetre, gunpowder, arrack, letters, textiles and supplies for the British troops. Only once, by Captain Ross of the *Malacca*, is opium listed, but several ships carried the all-encompassing 'Sundries'. The Protest concerning the loss of the cotton ship *Triton* made no mention of opium, but a public account included opium as part of 'a valuable cargo', and similarly with the *Caroline*.[2] Homeward-bound exotic goods included the silverware, fans and boxes of tea from China saved at the time from the wreck of the *Diana*, the elephants' teeth being loaded aboard the *Hammudy* in Siam and the embroidered clothing and boxes of jewellery that were victims of the overturning of the *Hammudy*'s cargo boat. The *Diana*'s 1818 inventory is the only time tea is mentioned as cargo in a Protest. Even though the EIC retained a monopoly on the tea trade with China after 1813, country ships could still participate in the trade under special licence such as that under which Francis Balston operated in 1820[3] and they perhaps also carried tea illicitly. We know the *La Paix* traded in tea as its 1804 cargo of tea was advertised in the Bengal *Hurkaru*,[4] but when the ship sank in 1805 the cargo, which may have included another load of tea, was not specified in the Protest. Textiles are sometimes mentioned in the Portuguese Protests, but there is no mention of the opium of which the Portuguese were reputed to be major carriers.

2 *Asiatic Annual Register*, vol. 10, 1811, p. 89; *Asiatic Journal and Monthly Register*, January to June 1817, pp. 509, 615.

3 See Appendix D.

4 January 8, 1805, p. 1.

In keeping with the understanding that the EIC handled insurance matters and reporting of failures within the company itself, Protests lodged at Malacca by EIC regular ships were not the expected thing, but there were two; a statement by the *Surprize* in 1795 and in 1800 a Protest by the *Thames*. As well, one EIC 'extra' ship, the *Batavia*, lodged a Protest when acting as a transport and the Protests of the captains of three country ships hired by the EIC as transports, the *Thomas Henchman* (a total loss), the *Fleetwood* and the *Fort William* are also recorded at Malacca, all relating to the 1811 invasion of Java.

The incidents that arose when the fleet for the invasion of Java was assembled at Malacca are indicative of how crowded conditions can multiply the effect of a mishap, the fire on the *Henchman*, for example, being the direct cause of damage to the *Fleetwood* and *Fort William*. Harassment of country ships by the Royal Navy was also a feature of the invasion preparations, generating two of the five Protests against the British Navy. The collisions reported at Malacca, however, which one might expect to be a feature of a crowded port, took place on the open seas, although they were related to travelling in convoy.

The Protests of the country traders at Malacca show evidence of their running foul of Malay maritime raiders ('pirates'), as well as of having to manage disgruntled crew aboard ship. The country traders might not have understood the complicated motives behind the piracy and mutiny to which they were sometimes subjected but these examples of attacks on four British ships and one American show that the onslaughts could not only leave the captain and his officers in a perilous situation but were in fact deadly – to the tune of two officers, two gunners and five others, not to mention the murder of Captain Sadler at the hands of a Malay ruler. Although these numbers are minor compared to the scores of lascars lost in storms and strandings, from the point of view of captain and officers the risk from hostile encounters was considerable.

We have only one testimony of a British ship falling victim to the French as the long arm of the European wars reached the East Indies. It is the Protests of the non-British traders that illustrate more clearly aspects of European belligerence. The EIC was always suspicious of foreign vessels that could be used as a front by British private interests to flout EIC restrictive trading rules, wartime or not; but as the Napoleonic Wars expanded to align more countries against Britain, the complaints of the Danish and Dutch against seizures by the British Navy started to arise, with the validity of the 'pass' system a particular point of contention. Thus, in small ways we see participation in large historical events.

Nevertheless, while the battle against pirates, the trading restrictions and disputes and the political transformation of friend into foe are an intriguing aspect of the Malacca submissions, it is the struggle against the tempestuous and fickle weather and the physical dangers hidden beneath the waves that inform the majority of the Protests, all taking place at a time when sophisticated navigational tools were not routinely used and when charts were incomplete and sometimes misleading. Tales of help rendered or not rendered, of broken masts, spars and rudders, damaged sails, loss of anchors and cables, overwhelming seas requiring pumping to beyond exhaustion provide the grist of the accounts.

A reading of the Protests highlights the enormous dangers faced by country traders in the East Indies and the risk-taking they engaged in, facts easily lost sight of in discussions of trade, profit and loss and the expansion of empire.

APPENDIX A
LIST OF CAPTAINS OF THE PROTEST SHIPS

Vessel Key: A=American, B=British, D=Danish, Dch=Dutch, H=Hamburg, M=Malay, P=Portuguese

Captain	Vessel
Allan, (Robert)	*Eleanor* (B)
Anderson, James Thomas	*Mary Ann* (B)
Anthony, Jean (acting as captain)	*Tiriwinaga Cany* (M)
Atkinson, (Thomas Jasper)	*Hibernia* (B)
Ballard, Richard	*Asia Felix* (B)
Balston, Francis	*James Drummond* (B)
Balston, Francis	*Lady Flora* (B)
Barclay, George Dallas (Barclay, Andrew?)	*Indian* (B)
Barretto, Francisco da Vitoria Vasconcellos Pereira	*Theresa* (P)
Barroz, Joze Joaquim	*St Antonio Luzitania* (P)
Basden, Thomas	*Forbes* (B)
Bateman, George	*Mary* (B)
Beyts, Henry W.	*Upton Castle* (B)
Boyd, Jurgen Hendrik	*Myrin* (D)
Brace, John	*Thainstone* (B)
Briggs, (F. D.?)	*Ruparell* (B)
Brown, David	*Abercromby* (B)
Cabral, Caetano Joze	*Palla N.S. da Conceiçao* (P)
Campbell, Patrick	*Surprize* (EIC)
Cardoza, Jacinto Lopes	*N.S. do Carmo* (P)
Carlton, John	*Putnam* (A)
Carter, Robert	*Sulimany* (B)

Cleland, Walter	*Bombay Castle* (B)
Collie, John	*City of Goa* (B)
Colvel, William	*Saigon* (B)
Crockett, John C.	*Shah Byramgore* (B)
D'Almeida, Francois	*Charlotta Amalia* (D)
D'Coil Joze Antonio	*New Endeavour* (B)
Da Costa, Joze Alves	*Mariana Feliz* (P)
Da Silva, Antonio Fez	*Julia Felix* (P)
Dallas, William	*Dolphin* (B)
Dalrymple, David	*General Wellesley* (B)
Daniels, John	*Athena* (B)
De Campos, Caetano Antonio	*Belezario* (P)
De Lemos, Bernardo Gomes	*Palla N.S. da Conceiçao* (P)
De Miranda, Luis Carlos	*Carmo* (P)
De Noronha, Joze Joaquim	*Caçador* (P)
De Santa Maria, André	*Hero* (P)
De Souza, Joaõ Joze	*Eliza* (P)
De Vasconcellos, Antonio Joze	*Indiano* (P)
Deans, Robert	*Christina* (B)
Dew, William	*Hope* (B)
Do Rozario, Urbano	*N.S. da Portaria* (P)
Dos Santos, Faustino Coelho	*N.S. de Luz* (P)
Drysdale, Hugh	*Nancy* (B)
Duncan, John Gray	*Lady Sophia* (B)
Dunlop, David	*Alexander* (B)
Elliott, Henry	*Vestal* (B)
Finey, Thomas Dixie	*Soolymany* (B)
Frost, Henry	*Travancore* (B)
Fulcher, W. P.	*Asia* (B)
Graham, Robert	*Cornwallis* (B)
Green, James	*Fleetwood* (B)
Hamilton, Forrest	*Earl Kellie* (B)
Hammett, George	*Charles Baillie* (B)
Hammett, George	*Shah Byramgore* (B)
Hammond, William	*Lady*(?) *Flora* (B)
Harford, John	*General Baird* (B)
Henning, Alexander	*Hammudy* (B)

Herbst, Michael	*Fredensborg* (D)
Hoggard, Peter	*Agatha* (D)
Horn, John	*Anna* (B)
Janzen, Pieter	*Kederbox* (D)
Kidd, David	*Duchess of Wellington* (B)
Laird, John	*United Kingdom* (B)
Lambert, Thomas	*Nancy* (B)
Lima, Joaquim Rodrigues	*St Simao* (P)
Lobo, Manuel Fernandus	*Dories* (P)
Lyell, Alexander	*Diana* (B)
Macfie, James	*Cartier* (B)
Mackay, J	*Argo* (B)
Mann, George	*Providence* (B)
Marcal, Florencio Joze	*Belezario* (P)
Marchant, John	*Matilda* (B)
Masquerier, Edward	*Jane* (B)
Maurel, Joseph	*Fictum Eyzac* (B)
Mayne, John	*Batavia* (B)
McLardie, Peter	*Eagle* (B)
Neegaard, Andries	*Kieldeweldt* (D)
Nicholls, George	*Thomas Henchman* (B)
Parrish, John Ross	*Fort William* (B)
Patrick, F	*Triton* (B)
Pedro, Joze Caetano	*Activo* (P)
Perkins, Christopher	*Vulcan* (B)
Peters, Joseph	*Ganges* (B)
Peters, Joseph	*Penang* (B)
Peterson, Simon	*Expedition* (B)
Purefoy, James	*Pelican* (B)
Ramos, Joze	*Mercurio* (P)
Ramsay, (Sylvester)	*Good Hope* (B)
Ramsey, Silv	*Experiment* (B)
Rangel, Manoel Antonio da Silva	*Santo Antonio* (P)
Reano	*Mary* (B)
Reid, John	*Indian* (B)
Ribeiro, José	*Ulysses* (P)
Rordam	*Commerce* (D)

Ross, Hercules	*Malacca* (B)
Sadler, Thomas	*Transfer* (B)
Sands, John	*Armenia* (B)
Schleiden, Johan Christof	*Charlotte* (H)
Scott, Robert	*Experiment* (B)
Shepherdson, Robert	*Faz Soobhany* (B)
Smith, Daniel	*Margaret* (B)
Smith, Daniel	*Mary* (B)
Smith, Francis	*Anna* (B)
Smith, William Robert	*Hope* (B)
Spiers, William	*Tweed* (B)
Stevenson, C. James	*Charlotte* (B)
Stewart	*Swift* (B)
Streng, Gustaaf Adolf	*Angelique* (D)
Streng, Gustaaf Adolf	*Miracity* (B)
Strut, George	*Caroline* (B)
Verhaage, Willem	*Carolina* (Dch)
Vianna, Francisco Joze da Vitoria Ry (?)	*Ulysses* (P)
Wales, George	*Helen* (B)
Wallace, Alexander	*Admiral Troubridge* (B)
Warren	*Jane* (B)
Williams, Robert	*Thames* (EIC)
Woods, Edward	*Little Mary* (B)
Wright, John	*La Paix* (B)
Wyatt, William	*Fair Trial* (B)

APPENDIX B – LIST OF PROTESTS ORDERED BY PROTEST DATE

Vessel Key: A=American, B=British, D=Danish, Dch=Dutch, H=Hamburg, M=Malay, P=Portuguese
Tonnage and date of mishap are approximate.

Protest Date/ Protest No.	Principal Declarant	Declarant's Position	Vessel	Tons	Protest Reason	China/Macao Voyage: Y/N	Date of mishap	Where
21 April 1791 *43*	Van Kal, Jacob	Merchant	*Swift* (B)		Commercial problem	N	Feb. 1791	Malacca
16 Oct. 1792 *129*	Lima, Joaquin Rodrigues	Captain	*St Simao* (P)		Commercial problem			
9 July 1793 *93*	Maurel, Joseph	Captain	*Fictum Eyzac* (B)		Storm		June 1793	Bay of Bengal
11 Sept. 1794 *181*	Collie, John	Captain	*City of Goa* (B)	600	Storm	Y To China	August 1794	West coast of India
7 Nov. 1794 *224*	Collie, John	Captain	*City of Goa* (B)	600	Storm	Y To China	Oct. 1794	Near the Marianas
8 Nov. 1794 11 Nov. 1794 *225, 228*	Sands, John	Captain	*Armenia* (B)	300	Storm	N	Nov. 1794	South China Sea
16 Dec. 1794 17 Dec. 1794 *241, 243*	Frost, Henry	Captain	*Travancore* (B)	1000	Storm	Y From China	Dec. 1794	Near Marianas

Protest Date/ Protest No.	Principal Declarant	Declarant's Position	Vessel	Tons	Protest Reason	China/Macao Voyage: Y/N	Date of mishap	Where
16 Dec. 1794 17 Dec. 1794 *242, 244*	Horn, John	Captain	*Anna* (B)	749	Storm	Y From China	Dec. 1794	Near Marianas
8 July 1795 *60*	Burnet, John	1st Mate	*Surprize* (EIC)	395	Storm	N	Dec. 1794	Coral Sea
5 August 1795 *83*	Groube, Thomas	1st Mate	*Transfer* (B)		Coercion: Malays	N	July 1795	Mempawah
2 Oct. 1796 *123½*	D'Almeida, Francois	Captain	*Charlotta Amalia* (D)		Storm	N	Sept. (?) 1796	
10 Jan. 1798 11 Jan. 1798 *355, 356*	Zachariah, Amirzan	Merchant	*Armenia* (B)		Commercial problem		Jan. 1798	Malacca
14 May 1798 *417*	Frost, Matthias	1st Officer	*Agatha* (D)		Storm	Y To China	April 1798	Bay of Bengal
14 May 1798 *418*	Lobo, Manuel Fernandus	Captain	*Dories* (P)		Storm? ('lost voyage')	Y To Macao		
6 June 1798 *430*	Drysdale, Hugh	Captain	*Nancy* (B)		Grounding	N	May 1798	South China Sea
21 June 1799 24 June 1799 *603, 604*	Tonder, Franz Wilhelm	1st Officer	*Kederbox* (D)		Storm		June 1799	Malacca Strait
10 Feb. 1800 *737, 738*	Forsfell, Daniel	1st Mate	*Myrin* (D)		Storm	N	Jan. 1800	South China Sea

2 June 1800 *804*	Neegaard, Andries	Captain	*Kieldeweldt* (D)		Storm	N	May 1800	Java Sea?
10 July 1800 *838*	Neegaard, Andries	Captain	*Kieldeweldt* (D)		Dilapidation	N	May 1800	Malacca
14 July 1800 *849*	Petersen, John	1st Mate	*Kieldeweldt* (D)		Storm	N	May 1800	Java Sea?
1 Sept. 1800 *879*	Ramos, Joze	Captain	*Mercurio* (P)		Storm	N	August 1800	Malacca Strait
6 Sept. 1800 *883*	De Mathos, Manuel Ignatio	1st Mate	*Mercurio* (P)		Storm	N	August 1800	Malacca Strait
13 Oct. 1800 *906*	Williams, Robert	Captain	*Thames* (EIC)	1432	Leak	Y From China	Sept. (?) 1800	South China Sea
16 Oct. 1800 *907*	Grant, Henry	1st Officer	*Thames* (EIC)	1432	Leak	Y From China	Sept. (?) 1800	South China Sea
30 Dec. 1800 *938*		1st Mate	*St Antonio Luzitania* (P)		Storm	N	Dec. 1800	Malacca Strait
10 Jan. 1801 *942*	Streng, Gustaaf Adolf	Captain	*Angelique* (D)	288	Storm	Y From China	Dec. 1800	South China Sea
14 Jan. 1801 *945*	De Kater, Christian	1st Mate	*Angelique* (D)	288	Storm	Y From China	Dec. 800	South China Sea
28 May 1801 *968*	De Vos, Willem Adrianus	Supercargo	*Dolphin* (B)		Commercial problem	Y From China	May 1801	Malacca
7 June 1801 *973*	Herbst, Michael	Captain	*Fredensborg* (D)		Storm		May 1801	Bay of Bengal

Protest Date/ Protest No.	Principal Declarant	Declarant's Position	Vessel	Tons	Protest Reason	China/Macao Voyage: Y/N	Date of mishap	Where
9 June 1801 *974*	Dayot, Johan Maria	1st Mate	*Fredensborg* (D)		Storm		May 1801	Bay of Bengal
26 August 1801 *1,006*	Colvel, William	Captain	*Saigon* (B)		Collision		July 1801	Bay of Bengal
28 August 1801 *1,007*	Barry, Edmond	1st Mate	*Saigon* (B)		Collision		July 1801	Bay of Bengal
1 Dec. 1801 *1,036*	Shepherdson, Robert	Captain	*Faz Soobhany* (B)	600	Storm	Y From China	Nov. 1801	South China Sea
1 Dec. 1801 *1,037*	Merriman, Thomas	1st Mate	*Faz Soobhany* (B)	600	Storm	Y From China	Nov. 1801	South China Sea
19 Feb. 1802 *1,064*	Purefoy, James	Captain	*Pelican* (B)		Storm	N From Cochin China	Feb. 1802	South China Sea
24 Feb. 1802 *1,068*	Peterson, Simon	Captain	*Expedition* (B)	70?	Storm?	N	Feb. 1802	Malacca Strait
27 Feb. 1802 *1,070*	Morgan, Jorge	1st Mate	*Pelican* (B)		Storm	N From Cochin China	Feb. 1802	South China Sea
8 March 1802 *1,071*	Herbst, Michael	Captain	*Fredensborg* (D)		Coercion: foreign power		Jan. 1802	Malacca
13 March 1802 *1,072*	Dayot, Johan Maria	1st Mate	*Fredensborg* (D)		Coercion: foreign power		Jan. 1802	Malacca
19 Jan. 1803 *1,180*	Miller, William	Supercargo	*Charlotte* (H)		Leak	N	Jan. 1803	South China Sea

24 Jan. 1803 *1,181*	Constapol, Alexion	1st Mate?	*Charlotte* (H)		Leak	N		Jan. 1803	South China Sea
1 Dec. 1803 *1,298*	Verhaage, Willem	Captain	*Carolina* (Dch)		Coercion: foreign power	N		Nov. 1803	Malacca
1 Dec. 1803 *1,299*	Neubronner, Johan Anthon	Citizen of Malacca	*Carolina* (Dch)		Coercion: foreign power	N		Nov. 1803	Malacca
15 Dec. 1803 *1,304*	Harvey, Charles	Supercargo	*Eleanor* (B)		Commercial problem	N	From Cochin China	Sept. 1803	South China Sea
14 Sept. 1805 2 Dec. 1805 *41, 97*	Dunlop, David	Captain	*Alexander* (B)	745	Leak	Y	To China	August 1805	Bay of Bengal
4 Dec. 1805 *98, 99*	Wright, John	Captain	*La Paix* (B)	500	Grounding	Y	From China	Nov. 1805	Malacca Strait
26 Dec. 1805 27 Dec. 1805 *108, 109*	Carlton, John	Captain	*Putnam* (A)	266	Pirates	N		Nov. 1805	Riau Roads
12 March 1806 13 March 1806 *155, 156*	Rordam	Captain	*Commerce* (D)		Grounding	N		March 1806	Singapore Strait
19 Sept. 1806 *12*	Perkins, Christo-pher	Captain	*Vulcan* (B)	391	Storm	Y	To China	August 1806	Bay of Bengal
19 Sept. 1806 *13*	Carapiet, Petrus	Trader	*Vulcan* (B)	391	Commercial problem	Y	To China	August 1806	Bay of Bengal
5 Oct. 1806 *21*	Scott, Robert	Captain	*Experiment* (B)	500	Storm	Y	To China	Sept. 1806	Bay of Bengal

Protest Date/ Protest No.	Principal Declarant	Declarant's Position	Vessel	Tons	Protest Reason	China/Macao Voyage: Y/N	Date of mishap	Where
5 Nov. 1806 *32*	Hussein, Shereef	Owner of ship *Punangteen*	*General Wellesley* (B)	400	Commercial problem	N	Oct. 1806	Malacca
10 Dec. 1806 *53*	Hart, Jonas James	1st Officer	*Cartier* (B)	400	Storm	Y From China	Nov. 1806	South China Sea
24 Dec. 1806 *60*	Rangel, Manoel Antonio da Silva	Captain	*Santo Antonio* (P)		Collision?	Y From Macao	16 Dec. 1806	South China Sea
25 Dec. 1806 *62*	De Lemos, Bernardo Gomes	Captain	*Palla N.S. da Conceiçao* (P)		Storm	Y From Macao	Dec. (?) 1806	South China Sea
8 Jan. 1807 *67½*	Harford, John	Captain	*General Baird* (B)	600	Storm	Y To China	Oct. 1806	South China Sea
22 Dec. 1807 *195*	Wallace, Alex-ander	Captain	*Admiral Troubridge* (B)	750?	Pirates	N	Dec. 1807	Sulu
22 Dec. 1807 *196*	Sharp, William	1st Officer	*Admiral Troubridge* (B)	750?	Pirates	N	Dec. 1807	Sulu
23 Dec.1807 *197*	Masquerier, Edward	Captain	*Jane* (B)	300	Grounding	N	Dec. 1807	Near Lingga
25 Dec. 1807 *198*	De Vasconcellos, Antonio Joze	Captain	*Indiano* (P)		Storm	Y From Macao	Dec. 1807	South China Sea
4 Oct. 1808 *277*	Patrick, F.	Captain	*Triton* (B)	800	Coercion: friendly power	Y To China	August 1808	Saugor
4 Oct. 1808 *277*	Patrick, F.	Captain	*Triton* (B)	800	Grounding	Y To China	Sept. 1808	Malacca Strait

31 Jan. 1809 *315*	Dos Santos, Faustino Coelho	Captain	*N.S. de Luz* (P)		Convoy problem	Y From Macao	Jan. 1809	South China Sea
14 March 1809 *335, 336*	D'Coil Joze Antonio	Captain	*New Endeavour* (B)	140	Fire	N	Jan. 1809	Pedir coast
14 March 1809 *335, 336*	D'Coil Joze Antonio	Captain	*New Endeavour* (B)	140	Collision	N	Dec. 1808	Bay of Bengal
21 March 1809 *338*	Anthony, Jean	Captain (acting)	*Tiriwinaga Cany* (M)		Coercion: French and Malays	N	Dec. 1808–March 1809	Malacca Strait
21 March 1809 *340*	Smith, Daniel	Captain	*Margaret* (B)	200?	Pirates	N	Dec. 1808	Pontianak
23 April 1809 *351, 352*	Vianna, Francisco Joze da Vitoria Ry (?)	Captain	*Ulysses* (P)		Storm?	Y From Macao	April 1809	South China Sea
8 May 1809 *355*	Hare, Alexander	Owner of *Malacca*	*Malacca* (B)		Pirates	N	May 1809	Malacca
13 May 1809 17 May 1809 *356*	Ross, Hercules	Captain	*Malacca* (B)		Pirates	N	May 1809	Pontianak
13 July 1809 14 July 1809 *378, 380*	Da Silva, Antonio Fez	Captain	*Julia Felix* (P)	200	Dilapidation	Y To Macao	July 1809	Malacca
7 Dec. 1809 *427*	Smith, Francis	Captain	*Anna* (B)	899	Collision	Y From China	Nov. 1809	Singapore Strait

Protest Date/ Protest No.	Principal Declarant	Declarant's Position	Vessel	Tons	Protest Reason	China/Macao Voyage: Y/N	Date of mishap	Where
7 Dec. 1809 *428*	Pedro, Joze Caetano	Captain	*Activo* (P)		Collision	Y From Macao	Nov. 1809	Singapore Strait
9 July 1810 *517*	Smith, Daniel	Captain	*Mary* (B)		Coercion: foreign power	N	Nov. 1809	South China Sea
17 Sept. 1810 *553*	Elliot, John	Resident of Malacca and owner of *Helen*	*Helen* (B)		Commercial problem		1806	Malacca
15 Dec. 1810 *607*	Dos Santos, Faustino Coelho	Captain	*N.S. de Luz* (P)		Unknown	Y From Macao	Dec. 1810	South China Sea?
16 Dec. 1810 *608, 609*	De Vasconcellos, Antonio Joze	Captain	*Indiano* (P)		Abandoned ship	Y From Macao	Dec. 1810	Near Pulo Aur
16 May 1811 *648*	Mayne, John	Captain	*Batavia* (B)	555	Grounding	N	May 1811	Malacca Strait
28 May 1811 *666*	Parrish, John Ross	Captain	*Fort William* (B)	1,236	Fire	N	May 1811	Malacca
28 May 1811 *667*	Green, James	Captain	*Fleetwood* (B)	380	Fire	N	May 1811	Malacca
3 June 1811 *672*	Nicholls, George	Captain	*Thomas Henchman* (B)	500	Fire	N	May 1811	Malacca
7 June 1811 *679*	Smith, William Robert	Captain	*Hope* (B)		Coercion: friendly power	N	May 1811	Java Sea
10 June 1811 *680*	Finey, Thomas Dixie	Captain	*Soolymany* (B)	679	Loss of anchor and cable		June 1811	Malacca Strait

18 June 1811 *683*	Hammett, George	Captain	*Charles Baillie* (B)	200	Coercion: friendly power	N	June 1811	Malacca Strait
21 June 1811 *684*	Hammett, George	Captain	*Charles Baillie* (B)	200	Coercion: friendly power	N	June 1811	Malacca Strait
28 Nov. 1811 *737*	Ally, Goelam	Resident of Bombay, supercargo	*Miracity* (B)	600	Commercial problem	Y From Macao	Oct. (?) 1811	Canton
4 Dec. 1811 *744*	Dos Santos, Faustino Coelho	Captain	*N.S. de Luz* (P)		Storm	Y From Macao	Nov. 1811	South China Sea
5 Dec. 1811 *745*	Cabral, Caetano Joze	Captain	*Palla N.S. da Conceiçao* (P)		Storm	Y From Macao	Nov. 1811	Malacca Strait
13 Jan. 1812 *757*	Mann, George	Captain	*Providence* (B)		Storm	N From Manila	Jan. 1812	South China Sea
9 March 1812 *784*	Peters, Joseph	Captain	*Ganges* (B)	140	Storm	N	Feb. 1812	Java Sea
5 August 1812 6 August 1812 *808, 809*	Brown, David	Captain	*Abercromby* (B)	1,280	Grounding	Y To China	July 1812	Java Sea
16 Sept. 1812 *815, 816*	Minas, Joseph and Marcar Carapiet	Merchants	*Nancy* (B)		Commercial problem		April 1812	Malacca
23 Oct. 1812 *840*	Parrish, John Ross	Captain	*Fort William* (B)	1,137	Loss of anchor and cable	Y From China	Oct. 1812	Singapore Strait
22 Nov. 1812 *845*	Cardoza, Jacinto Lopes	Captain	*N.S. do Carmo* (P)		Storm?	Y To Macao	Nov. (?) 1812	Bay of Bengal?

Protest Date/ Protest No.	Principal Declarant	Declarant's Position	Vessel	Tons	Protest Reason	China/Macao Voyage: Y/N	Date of mishap	Where
28 Dec. 1812 *856*	Da Costa, Joze Alves	Captain	*Mariana Feliz* (P)		Commercial problem	Y To Macao	Dec. 1812	Bassiq, Cambodia
28 Dec. 1812 *857*	Da Costa, Joze Alves	Captain	*Mariana Feliz* (P)		Commercial problem	N	Dec. 1812	Pontianak and other ports
3 April 1813 *886*	Da Costa, Joze Alves	Captain	*Mariana Feliz* (P)		Commercial problem	N		Malacca
25 April 1813 26 April 1813 *888, 889*	Peters, Joseph	Captain	*Penang* (B)		Storm	N	April 1813	Malacca Strait
20 July 1813 *911*	Barclay, George Dallas (Barclay, Andrew?)	Captain	*Indian* (B)	350	Leak	Y To China	July 1813	East of Riau
16 August 1813 *919*	Woods, Edward	Captain	*Little Mary* (B)		Storm	N	July 1813	Near Bintang Island
30 June 1814 *991, 992*	Laird, John	Captain	*United Kingdom* (B)	850	Storm	Y To China	June 1814	Bay of Bengal
16 July 1814 18 July 1814 *994, 995*	De Miranda, Luis Carlos	Captain	*Carmo* (P)	400	Storm	Y To Macao	June 1814	Bay of Bengal
1 August 1814 *999*	Dew, William	Captain	*Hope* (B)	650	Storm	Y To China	July 1814	Bay of Bengal

28 August 1814 *1,002*	Ribeiro, José	Captain	*Ulysses* (P)		Storm	N To Manila	June 1814–August 1814	Bay of Bengal, Malacca Strait
29 August 1814 *1,003, 1,004*	Ribeiro, José	Captain	*Ulysses* (P)		Commercial problem	N	August 1814	Malacca
5 Nov. 1814 *1,032*	McLardie, Peter M	Captain	*Eagle* (B)	150	Leak		Oct. 1814	Malacca Roads
25 Nov. 1814 *1,045*	Mackay, J.	Captain	*Argo* (B)	250	Pirates	N	Nov. 1814	Brunei Roads
27 Jan. 1815 *1,062*	Bateman, George	Captain	*Mary* (B)	216	Coercion: friendly power	N	Jan. 1815	Malacca
18 July 1815 *1,101*	Ballard, Richard	Captain	*Asia Felix* (B)	374	Storm	Y To China	June 1815	Bay of Bengal
4 Sept. 1815 *1,105*	Balston, Francis	Captain	*James Drummond* (B)	680	Storm	Y To China	August 1815	Bay of Bengal
4 Sept. 1815 *1,106*	Daniels, John	Captain	*Athena* (B)		Grounding	N	August 1815	Bay of Bengal
14 Nov. 1815 *37*	Reano	Captain	*Mary* (B)		Coercion: friendly power	N	Nov. 1815	Malacca Strait
22 Nov. 1815 *39*	Kidd, David	Captain	*Duchess of Wellington* (B)	600	Storm	Y From China	Nov. 1815	South China Sea
14 Dec. 1815 25 Dec. 1815 *55, 59½*	Bryne, George	Supercargo	*Fair Trial* (B)	125	Commercial problem		Dec. 1815	Malacca

Protest Date/ Protest No.	Principal Declarant	Declarant's Position	Vessel	Tons	Protest Reason	China/Macao Voyage: Y/N	Date of mishap	Where
15 Dec. 1815 *56*	Ramsey, Silv	Captain	*Experiment* (B)	300	Storm	N From Guam	Sept. 1815	Near Marianas
3 Jan. 1816 *62*	Do Rozario, Urbano	Captain	*N.S. da Portaria* (P)		Storm	Y From Macao	Dec. 1815	Near Pulo Aur
4 Jan. 1816 *63*	Marcal, Florencio Joze	Captain	*Belezario* (P)		Storm	Y From Macao	Dec. 1815	Near Pulo Aur
11 Feb. 1816 *87, 88*	Brace, John	Captain	*Thainstone* (B)		Grounding	N	Dec. 1815	Java Sea
27 Feb. 1816 *94*	Barretto, Francisco da Victoria Vasconcellos Pereira	Captain	*Theresa* (P)		Storm	Y From Macao	Dec. 1815	Near Pulo Aur
21 June 1816 *144*	Warren	Captain	*Jane* (B)		Storm	N	May 1816	Malacca Strait
24 June 1816 *149*	Hamilton, Forrest	Captain	*Earl Kellie* (B)	520	Storm?	Y To China	June 1816	Bay of Bengal?
5 July 1816 *152*	Beyts, Henry W.	Captain	*Upton Castle* (B)	675	Storm	Y To China	June (?) 1816	Malabar Coast
17 July 1816 *155*	Basden, Thomas	Captain	*Forbes* (B)	600	Leak		June 1816	
6 August 1816 *170?*	Graham, Robert	Captain	*Cornwallis* (B)	784	Leak	Y To China	August 1816	

23 August 1816 *174?*	Cleland, Walter	Captain	*Bombay Castle* (B)	602	Storm	Y To China	July 1816	Bay of Bengal
2 Sept. 1816 *178*	Strut, George	Captain	*Caroline* (B)	456	Grounding	Y To China	August 1816	Malacca Strait
23 Nov. 1816 *213*	Briggs, (F. D.?)	Captain	*Ruparell* (B)	318	Storm	Y From China	Nov. 1816	South China Sea
8 March 1817 *252*	Crichton, James	1st Officer	*Diana* (B)	300	Grounding	Y From China	March 1817	Malacca Strait
28 May 1817 *290*	Stevenson, C. James	Captain	*Charlotte* (B)	650	Storm	Y To China	May 1817	Malabar coast?
13 June 1817 14 June 1817 *301, 302*	Deans, Robert	Captain	*Christina* (B)		Grounding	N	May 1817	Marawang River, Banka
18 June 1817 *303*	Hammond, William	Captain	*Lady (?) Flora* (B)	705	Grounding	N	June 1817	Malacca Strait
12 Dec. 1817 *325*	Graham, Robert	Captain	*Cornwallis* (B)	650	Storm	Y To China	July 1817	Malabar coast
16 August 1817 *327*	Atkinson, (Thomas Jasper)	Captain	*Hibernia* (B)	156	Storm		July 1817	Malabar coast?
26 August 1817 *334*	Ramsay, (Sylvester)	Captain	*Good Hope* (B)	388	Storm		July 1817	Bay of Bengal
24 Oct. 1817 *355*	Galway, James	1st Officer	*Christina* (B)		Storm	N	Oct. 1817	Malacca Strait
31 Dec. 1817 *380*	De Campos, Caetano Antonio	Captain	*Belezario* (P)		Unknown	Y From Macao		

Protest Date/ Protest No.	Principal Declarant	Declarant's Position	Vessel	Tons	Protest Reason	China/Macao Voyage: Y/N	Date of mishap	Where
7 March 1818 *255*	Crichton, James	1st Officer	*Diana* (B)	300	Grounding	Y From China	March 1817	Malacca Strait
1 August 1818 3 August 1818 *476, 477*	De Santa Maria, André	Captain	*Hero* (P)		Storm	N	July 1818	Malacca Strait
5 August 1818 *478*	Spiers, William	Captain	*Tweed* (B)	180	Grounding	Y To China	July 1818	Malacca Strait
6 August 1818 *479*	Balston, Francis	Captain	*Lady Flora* (B)	705	Leak	Y To China	July 1818	Bay of Bengal
12 August 1818 *484*	Hammett, George	Captain	*Shah Byramgore* (B)	550	Storm	Y To China	August (?) 1818	Bay of Bengal?
10 Sept. 1818 *499*	Duncan, John Gray	Captain	*Lady Sophia* (B)	319	Storm	Y To China	Sept. (?) 1818	Bay of Bengal?
15 Sept. 1818 *503*	Elliott, Henry	Captain	*Vestal* (B)	140	Grounding	N	Sept. 1818	Malacca Strait
15 Feb. 1819 *587, 588*	Anderson, James Thomas	Captain	*Mary Ann* (B)		Storm	N From Manila	Jan. 1819	South China Sea
12 April 1819 *624*	Henning, Alexander	Captain	*Hammudy* (B)		Overturning	N From Siam	Feb. 1819	Siam River
25 April 1819 *628*	De Souza, Joaõ Joze	Captain	*Eliza* (P)		Loss of anchor and cable			
5 June 1819 *651*	De Noronha, Joze Joaquim	Captain	*Caçador* (P)		Storm	Y To Macao	May 1819	Bay of Bengal

12 Nov. 1819 13 Nov. 1819 *944, 945*	Reid, John	Captain	*Indian* (B)		Storm	N	Oct. 1818	Pacific Ocean
22 Nov. 1819 *1,298, 1,299*	Fulcher, W. P.	Captain	*Asia* (B)	492	Storm	Y From China	Nov. (?) 1819	South China Sea
23 May 1820 *85*	Crockett, John C.	Captain	*Shah Byramgore* (B)	791	Storm	Y To China	May 1820	Indian Ocean
19 July 1820 *138*	Carter, Robert	Captain	*Sulimany* (B)	679	Storm	Y To China	June 1820	Bay of Bengal
27 June 1821 *97*	Marchant, John	Captain	*Matilda* (B)	250	Storm	Y From China	May 1821	South China Sea

APPENDIX C
THE *FANNY*: A CASE OF A MISSING PROTEST?

In mid-February 1804, at Malacca, Thomas Page, second mate of the *Fanny* (600 tons, belonging to Calcutta),[1] wrote an 'affidavit' detailing the stranding of the ship on 26 November 1803 in the South China Sea, lat. 9°44′N, long. 115°51′E, 250 miles from Cochin China. The document was produced at the request of the captain, William Robertson. One would expect the account to be filed as a Protest in the *Prothocol Books*, but it is not there; nor are any other Protests for 1804, suggesting that for this year they must be located elsewhere, or lost. The following account is taken from the pamphlet published by Thomas Tegg in 1808.[2] It provides evidence that not all maritime misadventures where the next port of call was Malacca were recorded in the Malaccan *Prothocol Books* as a Protest, even where there is proof that an account was actually written.

The *Fanny* had left Bombay for China on 8 August 1803, the late departure, with its risk of meeting severe weather, probably explained by the fact that the ship had not left Whampoa for its previous return to Bombay until 20 January that year.[3] The voyage towards China comprised a long series of mishaps, with the loss of rudder a frequent occurrence. First, the ship ran aground in the Malacca Strait, temporarily losing the rudder. Then, on 21 September, it was hit by a typhoon, losing the rudder and foremast. Reaching Hainan on 13 October the crew were able to effect repairs, but the first mate and some of the men became stranded on the island, the ship lost an anchor and cable, and the local inhabitants refused to provide supplies.

On 4 November, with a view to taking action against the Hainanese, the *Fanny* got under way but was blown out to sea by an unfavourable wind, lost the new rudder and, notwithstanding another new rudder shipped on 21

1 John Phipps, *A Collection of Papers, Relative to Ship Building in India … also A Report, Comprehending all the Ships and Vessels Built in India to the Present Time …* (Calcutta, 1840), p. 137.

2 *Wreck and loss of the ship Fanny, Capt. Robertson, on her Passage from Bombay to China, November 29, 1803: Including Particulars of the Tremendous Hurricanes Called Typhons, and the Wonderful Preservation of the Greater Part of the Crew …* (London, 1808).

3 Paul A. Van Dyke, *Whampoa and the Canton Trade: Life and Death in a Chinese Port* (Hong Kong, 2020), Appendix 2.1b.

Fig 17. Illustration from *Wreck and loss of the ship Fanny, Capt. Robertson, on her passage from Bombay to China, November 29*, 1803. London, Printed for Thomas Tegg, 1808.

November, was driven upon a reef. The captain refused help from a passing American brig, *Pensylvania*, though four Portuguese were taken aboard, and on 4 January 1804 left the wreck with the ship's company in two 'floats' constructed from the ship's poop. The lascar occupants of one of the floats were, all but one, massacred by Malays on an island near the entrance to Malacca Strait. The other float reached Malacca on 4 February 1804, the occupants much debilitated.

The report gives an insight into the way an affidavit or Protest was written. It took Second Mate Page two-and-a-half days to write, revise, correct and make out a fair copy. On the third day the captain said that Page was too slow and that he intended to hire a Portuguese clerk instead, a choice that perhaps reflected the important role a scribe played aboard a Portuguese ship.

APPENDIX D
THE *LADY FLORA* AND THE BALSTON CASE

Legal proceedings concerning Captain Francis Balston and his voyage of 1820 in the *Lady Flora* are of interest as an illustration of the restrictions under which private trade took place and the sort of legal argument that could be advanced.[1] Although this matter does not involve a Protest at Malacca, Balston had in the past availed himself of the facility, once in 1816 as captain of the *James Drummond* and again in 1818 when he commanded the *Lady Flora*.

In 1820 Balston took the *Lady Flora*, owned by John Palmer, in ballast from Calcutta to Canton under special licence from the EIC to take on a cargo of tea there and bring it back to Calcutta or 'any intermediate port'. Instead, the ship took on not tea but other goods at Canton, then proceeded to Batavia to take on more cargo and then to the Cape of Good Hope, arriving on 20 January 1821. Here the Comptroller of Customs, Mr Bird, after taking advice and in conjunction with Mr Luson, the EIC Resident, arrested the ship and refused permission to land the cargo, alleging an infringement of the terms of the ship's licence. However, the suit brought by the Fiscal General in the Court of Justice for condemnation of the ship and cargo was lost; the ship was returned to Balston and the cargo unloaded on 27 February.

Not content with this outcome, later described as 'an indulgence to which …

1 *Francis Balston v William Wilberforce Bird*, 31 May, 14 and 21 June 1828: <https://www.bailii.org/uk/cases/UKPC/1828/1828_4.html> [Accessed 15 April 2025]; EIC correspondence relating to the *Lady Flora* is listed under the heading 'D Minutes and Memoranda of East India Company General Committees and Offices 84B/B', in Jill Louise Geber, 'The East India Company and Southern Africa: A Guide to the East India Company and the Board of Control 1500–1858, Appendix vol. 2 Catalogue of Archival Descriptions' (Unpublished Doctoral Thesis, University of London, 1998), <https://discovery.ucl.ac.uk/id/eprint/1349288/> (1998) [Accessed 15 April 2025]. For a discussion of the Privy Council case see Rukmini Chakraborty, '"Fraudsters", "Tricksters" and "Registers": Inter-Asia trading an British Registry Acts in the eastern Indian Ocean littoral (1813–1850)', <https://www.academia.edu/44616990/Writing_Sample_Fraudsters_Tricksters_and_Registers_Inter_Asia_trading_and_British_Registry_Acts_in_the_eastern_Indian_Ocean_littoral_1813_1850:10-11> [Accessed 15 April 2025] (n.d.), pp. 10–11.

[he] was not entitled', Balston brought actions against both Bird and Luson for damages resulting from the delay in unloading the cargo. The cases were lost first in the Cape of Good Hope Court of Justice, subsequently in the Court of Appeals and finally in mid-1828 in the Privy Council. The first argument brought to bear, that the Cape of Good Hope was a legitimate intermediary port between India and China, was dismissed in the Privy Council as manifestly untrue. The second argument was that as John Palmer was a British resident of Calcutta and had not traded in tea, he had no need of a special licence. This was deemed irrelevant as a special licence had in fact been granted; moreover, it was deemed that, unless visited as part of the circuitous country trade, the Cape of Good Hope was not within the EIC's charter.

An additional, but not necessary, finding was that, notwithstanding that private trade had been legitimised by the British government in 1813, the requirements for a manifest remained unchanged. Balston's ship's manifest was deficient in that it had not been signed by the EIC supercargo in Canton and did not include the build and tonnage of the ship or the name of the port to which it belonged. This it itself was enough to make the voyage illegal.

BIBLIOGRAPHY

Manuscripts

Aberdeen University Library, Museums and Special Collections, 'Letter of William Anderson, Madras, 30 September 1798', Papers of Seton Family of Mounie. MS2787/5/2/4/18.

British Library, Asia, Pacific and Africa Collections, *Correspondence between Charles Wallace Young and Captain Anders Neegaard, Jun – Jul 1800*, IOR: R/9/38/6.

British Library, Asia, Pacific and Africa Collections, *Malacca, General Prothocol Books (Registers of Legal Deeds) 1786–1825*, IOR: R/9/22/1–75 [Available at ANU Library, microfilm DS 591.P76 1786].

British Library, 'Papers of Richard Wellesley, 1st Marquess, Wellesley to Hobart, 25 September 1803', Add MS 13469/item f32 [Available at NLA AJCP Mfm M1888–1889].

National Archives (London), Public Records Office, Admiralty Records, 'Captain Henning's Log of the ship *Hammudy*', ADM 55, File 144 item A [Available at NLA AJCP reel no. 1,600].

National Archives (London), Public Records Office. Admiralty Records, 'Logbook of the *Africaine*', ADM 51, File 2086 [Available at NLA AJCP reel no. 5712–5713].

National Library of Australia, Bowes Smyth, Arthur, 'Journal 1787 March 22–1789 August', MS 4568.

Secondary Sources

Abdullah, Munshi, 'The Hikayat Abdullah, an annotated translation by A. H. Hill', *JMBRAS*, 28:3 (1955), 1–355.

Andaya, Barbara Watson, 'Melaka under the Dutch, 1641–1795', in K. S. Sandhu and P. Wheatley (eds), *Melaka: The Transformation of a Malay Capital c.1400–1980*, vol. 1 (Kuala Lumpur, 1983), pp. 195–241.

—and Leonard Y. Andaya, *A History of Early Modern Southeast Asia, 1400–1830* (Cambridge, 2015).

Antony, Robert J. (ed.), *Elusive Pirates, Pervasive Smugglers: Violence and Clandestine Trade in the Greater China Seas* (Hong Kong, 2010).

Arnould, Joseph, *A Treatise on the Law of Marine Insurance and Average …* (2 vols, London, 1848), vol. 2. <https://www.google.com.au/books/edition/A_Treatise_

on_the_Law_of_Marine_Insuranc/x7gDAAAAQAAJ?hl=en> [Accessed 15 April 2025].

—*A Treatise on the Law of Marine Insurance and Average* …, ed. David Maclachan (2 vols, London, 1877), vol. 1.

Atsushi, Ota, 'From 'piracy' to inter-regional trade: the Sunda Straits zone, c.1750–1800', *IIAS Newsletter*, 36 (2005), 9.

Ball, Dorian, *The Diana Adventure* (Kuala Lumpur/Groningen, 1995).

Bassett, D. K., *British Trade and Policy in Indonesia and Malaysia in the Late Eighteenth Century* (Zug, 1971).

Bastin, John, 'Raffles and British policy in the Indian Archipelago, 1811–1816', *JMBRAS*, 27:1 (1954), 84–119.

Baxter, Ian, 'Records of Dutch Malacca: India Office Library and Records, London', *BISEA Newsletter*, 9 (1982), 5–6.

—'Dutch Records from Malacca in the India Office Records', *JMBRAS*, 56:2 (1983), 105–33.

Blakeney, Richard, *The Journal of an Oriental Voyage in His Majesty's Ship Africaine* (London, 1841).

Boxer, C. R., *The Dutch Seaborne Empire 1600–1800* (Harmondsworth, 1965).

Bowen, H. V., Margaret Lincoln and Nigel Rigby (eds), *The Worlds of the East India Company* (Woodbridge, 2002).

Bulley, Anne, *The Bombay Country Ships, 1790–1833* (Richmond, 2000).

—Free Mariner; *John Adolphus Pope in the East Indies 1786–1821* (Putney, 1992).

Burg, B. R., 'The HMS African Revisited; The Royal Navy and the Homosexual Community', *Journal of Homosexuality*, 56:2 (2009), 173–94.

Burke, John, and John Bernard Burke, *A Genealogical and Heraldic Dictionary of the Landed Gentry of Great Britain and Ireland*, vol. 3 (London, 1850).

Chakraborty, Rukmini, '"Fraudsters", "Tricksters" and "Registers": Inter-Asia trading and British Registry Acts in the eastern Indian Ocean littoral (1813–1850)', <https://www.academia.edu/44616990/Writing_Sample_Fraudsters_Tricksters_and_Registers_Inter_Asia_trading_and_British_Registry_Acts_in_the_eastern_Indian_Ocean_littoral_1813_1850:10-11> [Accessed 15 April 2025].

Cheong, Weng Eang, 'Changing the Rules of the Game (The India-Manila Trade: 1785–1809)', *Journal of Southeast Asian Studies*, 1:2 (September 1970), 1–19.

Clodd, H. P., *Malaya's First British Pioneer: the Life of Francis Light* (London, 1948).

Cook, Andrew S., 'Establishing the Sea Routes to India and China: Stages in the Development of Hydrographical Knowledge', in H. V. Bowen, Margaret Lincoln and Nigel Rigby (eds), *The Worlds of the East India Company* (Woodbridge, 2002), pp. 119–36.

—'Surveying the Seas: establishing the sea routes to the East Indies', in James R. Akerman (ed.), *Cartographies of Travel and Navigation* (Chicago IL, 2006), pp. 69–96.

Cotton, Evan, *East Indiamen: The East India Company's Maritime Service* (London, 1949).

Cumming, Ed (ed.), *A Compendium of Incidents Incurred by the Major Ships used by the English (later British) East India Company c.1600–c.1834* (MIBEC Publications, 2016), <https://www.nauticalarchaeologysociety.org/east-india-company-incidents> [Accessed 15 April 2025].

Dalrymple, Alexander, *Collection of Plans of Ports in the East Indies 1779 and 1780*, 2nd edn (London, 1787).

De Witt, Dennis, 'The Unfortunate Jacob Van Kal', *Journal of Malaysian Biographies*, 1 (2008), 57–65.

Denning, Greg (ed), *The Marquesan Journal of Edward Robart*, Pacific History Series No. 6 (Canberra, 1974).

Eastwick, Robert William, *A Master Mariner; Being the Life and Adventures of Captain Robert William Eastwick*, ed. Herbert Compton (London, 1891).

Eklof Amirell, Stefan, *Pirates in Paradise: A Modern History of Southeast Asia's Maritime Marauders* (Copenhagen, 2006).

—*Pirates of Empire: Colonisation and Maritime Violence in Southeast Asia* (Cambridge, 2019).

Elmore, H. M., *The British Mariner's Directory and Guide to the Trade and Navigation of the Indian and China Seas. Containing Instructions for Navigation from Europe to India and China, and from Port to Port in those Regions, and parts adjacent: with an Account of the Trade, Mercantile Habits, Manners and Customs of the Natives* (London, 1802).

Fayle, C. Ernest, 'Shipowning and Marine Insurance', in C. Northcote Parkinson (ed.), *The Trade Winds: A Study of British Overseas Trade During the French Wars 1793–1815* (London, 1948), pp. 25–48.

Feldbaek, Ole, 'The Danish trade in Bengal 1777–1808. An Interim Account', *Scandinavian Economic History Review*, 12:1 (1964), 26–60, <https://doi.org/10.1080/03585522.1964.10407633> [Accessed 15 May 2025].

—'Dutch Batavia trade via Copenhagen 1795–1807. A study of colonial trade and neutrality', *Scandinavian Economic History Review*, 21:1 (1973), 43–75, <https://doi.org/10.1080/03585522.1973.10407745> [Accessed 15 May 2025].

—'Danish East India trade 1772–1807 statistics and structure', *Scandinavian Economic History Review*, 26:2 (1978), 128–44, <https://doi.org/10.1080/03585522.1978.10415623> [Accessed 15 May 2025].

—'The Danish Asia trade 1620–1807', *Scandinavian Economic History Review*, 39:1 (1991), 3–27, <https://doi.org/10.1080/03585522.1991.10408197> [Accessed 15 May 2025].

Fernando, M. R., 'The Lost Archives of Melaka: Are They Really Lost?', *JMBRAS*, 78:1 (2005), 1–36.

Fisher, Michael H., 'Finding Lascar "Wilful Incendiarism": British Ship-Burning Panic and Indian Maritime Labour in the Indian Ocean', *South Asia*, 35:3 (2012), 596–623.

Forrest, Thomas, *A Treatise on the Monsoons in East-India* (London, 1783).

Frey, James W., 'Getting Away with Murder: The Wrongful Deaths of Lascars Aboard the *Union* in 1802', *International Review of Social History*, 59 Special Issue 22 (2014), 45–88.

Fry, Howard T., *Alexander Dalrymple (1737–1808) and the Expansion of British Trade* (London, 1970).

Furber, Holden, *Rival Empires of Trade in the Orient 1600–1800* (Minneapolis MN, 1976).

Gallop, Annabel, *The Legacy of the Malay Letter: Warisan Warkah Melayu* (London, 1994).

—'Malay Documents in the Melaka Records in the British Library', *Itinario*, 30:2 (2006), 54–77.

Geber, Jill Louise, 'The East India Company and Southern Africa: A Guide to the East India Company and the Board of Control 1500–1858, Appendix vol. 2 Catalogue of Archival Descriptions' (Unpublished Doctoral Thesis, University of London, 1998), <https://discovery.ucl.ac.uk/id/eprint/1349288/> [Accessed 15 April 2025].

Go, Sabine C. P. J., 'Shared burdens: The General Average adjustment of the Jan Maria', *International Journal of Maritime History*, 33:2 (2021), 322–43.

Goltenboth, Friedhelm, *et al.* (eds), *Ecology of Insular Southeast Asia: The Indonesian Archipelago* (Amsterdam, 2006).

Gomes, Luis Gonzaga, *Páginas da História de Macau, Colecçao Notícias de Macau, XXIII (Macau, 1966).* An English translation of parts of the book dealing with the Delta River pirates is available at <https://www.icm.gov.mo/rc/viewer/20003/797> [Accessed 15 April 2025].

'Goodbye Burma', <https://www.goodbyeburma-book.com/more-about-hazlewoods> [Accessed 21 August 2021].

Greenberg, Michael, *British Trade and the Opening of China 1800–42* (Cambridge, 1951).

Hanson, Neil, *The Custom of the Sea* (London, 1999).

Hardy, Charles, *A Register of Ships, Employed in the Service of the Honorable the United East India Company, From the Year 1760 to 1819, with an Appendix … revised by Horatio Charles A. Hardy*, 3rd edn (London, 1820).

Harrison, Brian, *Holding the Fort: Melaka Under Two Flags, 1795–1845*, Malaysian Branch of the Royal Asiatic Society Monograph No. 14 (Kuala Lumpur, 1985).

Hayles, Sally, 'Charles Atkinson', <htpps://siberiansteppes.files.wordpress.com>.

Herivel, Jan-maree, '"A Perfect Malay": James Scott, East Indies Country Trader' (Unpublished PhD thesis, Charles Darwin University, 2020), <https://ris.cdu.edu.au/ws/portalfiles/portal/44135311/Thesis_CDU_Herivel_J.pdf> [Accessed 15 April 2025].

Hobson Jobson: A Glossary of Colloquial Anglo-Indian Words and Phrases, and Kindred Terms, Etymological, Historical, Geographical and Discursive by Henry Yule and A. C. Burnell, new edn. by William Crooke (London, 1903).

Holmes and Co. (Calcutta), *Bengal Obituary or a Record to Perpetuate the Memory of Departed Worth* … (London, 1851), <https://wellcomecollection.org/works/u973e2dw> [Accessed 15 April 2025].

Horsburgh, James, *India Directory, Or, Directions for Sailing to and from the East Indies, China, New Holland, Cape of Good Hope, Brazil, and the Interjacent Ports* …, 2nd edn (2 vols, London 1817).

—*India Directory, Or, Directions for Sailing to and from the East Indies, China, New Holland, Cape of Good Hope, Brazil, and the Interjacent Ports* …, 3rd edn (2 vols, London, 1827).

Huddart, Joseph, *The Oriental Navigator; or, New Directions for Sailing to and from the East Indies. Also for the use of the Country Ships, Trading in the Indian and China Seas, to New Holland, etc. etc. Collected from the Manuscripts, Journals, Memoirs, and Observations, of the most experienced Officers in the Hon. East India Company's Service; and from the last Edition of the French Neptune Oriental, by Mons. D'Apres de Mannevillette. Being a Companion to the East India Pilot, in two large Volumes of Charts and Plans, originally published by the late Mr. Robert Sayer* … (London, 1794).

Hussin, Nordin, *Trade and Society in the Straits of Melaka: Dutch Melaka and English Penang, 1790–1830* (Singapore, 2007).

—'Trading Networks of Malay Merchants and Traders in the Straits of Malacca from 1780 to 1830', *Asian Journal of Social Sciences*, 40:1 (2012), 51–82.

Jaffer, Aaron, *Lascars and India Ocean Seafaring, 1780–1860: Shipboard Life, Unrest and Mutiny* (Woodbridge, 2015).

Kellenbenz, Hermann, 'German Trade Relations with the Indian Ocean from the End of the Eighteenth Century to 1870', *Journal of Southeast Asian Studies*, 13:1 (1982), 133–52.

La Touanne, E. B. de, *Vicomte, Album pittoresque de la frégate La Thétis et de la corvette L'Espérance: collection de dessins relatifs à leur voyage autour du monde en 1824, 1825 et 1826, sous les ordres de M. le baron de Bougainville, … / receuillis et publiés par M. le vicomte de La Touanne* (Paris, 1828).

Lahiri, Shompa, 'Contested Relations: The East India Company and Lascars', in H. V. Bowen, Margaret Lincoln and Nigel Rigby (eds), *The Worlds of the East India Company* (Woodbridge, 2002), pp. 169–81.

Lamb, Alistair, 'British Missions to Cochin China: 1778–1822', *JMBRAS*, 34:3/4 (1961), 1–248.

Lapian, Adrian B, 'Violence and Armed Robbery in Indonesian Seas', in John Kleinen and Manon Osseweijer (eds), *Pirates, Ports and Coasts in Asia: Historical and Contemporary Perspectives* (Singapore, 2010), pp. 131–46.

Lennon, Walter Caulfield, 'Journal of a voyage through the Straits of Malacca on an Expedition to the Molucca Islands … 1796', *JSBRAS*, 7 (1881), 51–74.

Leonard, A. B., 'Underwriting British Trade to India and China, 1780–1835', *The Historical Journal*, 55:4 (2012), 983–1006.

Lewis, Dianne, 'The Growth of the Country Trade in the Straits of Malacca 1760–1777', *JMBRAS*, 43:2 (1970), 114–30.

—*Jan Compagnie in the Straits of Malacca 1641–1795* (Athens OH, 1995).

Liebner, Horst H., and David van Dyke, 'An account of the loss of the Country Ship Forbes and Frazer Sinclair, her late Commander', *Wacana, Journal of the Humanities of Indonesia*, 17:1 (2016), 38–67.

Lubbock, Basil, 'Ships of the Period and Developments in Rig', in C. Northcote Parkinson (ed.), The Trade Winds: A Study of British Overseas Trade During the French Wars 1793–1815 (London, 1948), pp. 87–101.

McNally, Louis K., K. A. Maasch and K. A. Zuill, 'The Use of Ships' Protests for Reconstruction of Synoptic-Scale Weather and Tropical Storm Identification in the Late Eighteenth Century', *Weather*, 63:7 (2008), 208–13, <https://digitalcommons.library.umaine.edu/ers_facpub/105> [Accessed 15 May 2025].

Magens, Nicolaus, *An Essay on Insurances* (2 vols, London, 1755).

Malekandathil, Pius, 'Trade, Religion and Politics Portuguese Activities in the Bay of Bengal, 1632–1840', in Satish Chandra and Himanshu Prabha Ray (eds), *The Sea, Identity and History: From the Bay of Bengal to the South China Sea* (Singapore, 2013), pp. 279–301.

Miller, W. G., 'Why Did Syarif Kassim Kill Captain Sadler at Mempawah in 1795?', *JMBRAS*, 85:1 (2012), 63–84.

—*British Traders in the East Indies 1770–1820: 'At Home in the Eastern Seas'* (Woodbridge, 2020).

—and Ann G. Smith, 'European wives and local concubines: Women on board

English country trader vessels in the Malay Archipelago and beyond, from the 1770s to the 1830s, with some reference to life on board other contemporary sailing vessels', *International Journal of Maritime History*, 32:3 (2020), 596–615.

Mills, J. V., and J. V. G. Mills, 'Arab and Chinese Navigators in Malaysian Waters in about A.D. 1500', *JMBRAS*, 47:2 (1974), 1–82.

Mills, L. A., *British Malaya 1824–1867* (Singapore, 1925).

Morse, H. B., *The Chronicles of the East India Company Trading to China 1635–1834* (5 vols, Oxford, 1926–9).

Müeller, Martin, 'Primitive, Peregrinate, Piratical: Framing Southeast Asian Sea-Nomads in Nineteenth-Century Colonial Discourse and Imperial Practice', in John Coakley, C. Nathan Kwan and David Wilson (eds), *The Problem of Piracy in the Early Modern World: Maritime Predation, Empire, and the Construction of Authority at Sea* (Amsterdam, 2024), pp. 57–92.

Navy List (London, 1860).

O'Byrne, William R., *A Naval Biographical Dictionary: Comprising the Life and Services of Every Living Officer in Her Majesty's Navy from the Rank of Admiral of the Fleet to that of Lieutenant* (London, 1849).

Ooi, Keat Gin, 'Maritime Treasures off Peninsular Malaysia', *Journal of Indo-Pacific Archaeology*, 36 (2015), 5–15.

Oxford English Dictionary ([8 vols, Oxford, 1933]; repr. Oxford, 1961).

Parkinson, C. Northcote, *Trade in the Eastern Seas 1793–1813* (Cambridge, 1937).

Pearson, Michael, *Great Southern Land: The Maritime Exploration of Terra Australis* (Canberra, 2005).

'Philippine Historical Documents in the National Archives of Mexico', *Asian Studies*, 4:1 (1966), 149–97.

Philips, C. H., and B. B. Misra (eds), *Fort William-India House Correspondence and other Contemporary Papers Relating Thereto, Vol. XV Foreign and Secret 1782–1786* (Delhi, 1963).

Phillips, James Duncan, *Pepper and Pirates: Adventures in the Sumatra Pepper Trade of Sale* (Boston MA, 1949).

Phipps, John, *A Guide to the Commerce of Bengal for the Use of Merchants, Ship Owners, Commanders … Resorting to the East Indies* (Calcutta, 1823).

—*A Collection of Papers, Relative to Ship Building in India … also A Report, Comprehending all the Ships and Vessels Built in India to the Present Time …* (Calcutta, 1840).

Pinto, Celsa, *Trade and Finance in Portuguese India: A Study of the Portuguese Country Trade 1770–1840* (New Delhi, 1994).

Piratical Seizure of the Brig Admiral Trowbridge by Part of her Crew, While Lying at Anchor off the Island of Sooloo, August 21, 1807 Communicated by Capt. Alexander Wallace: Including the Murder of Mr. C. B. Lloyd and the Narrow Escape of Mr. William Sharpe (London, *c.*1808).

Pizzoni, Giada, 'British Power in the Mediterranean: Sea Protests and Notarial Practice in Nineteenth-century Malta', *The Journal of Imperial and Commonwealth History*, 50:2 (2022), 829–59.

Purdy, John, *Tables of the Positions, or of the Latitudes and Longitudes of Places, Composed to Accompany the 'Oriental Navigator', or Sailing Directions for the East Indies, China, Australia Etc …* (London, 1816).

Purefoy, James, 'Remarques sur la Cochinchine', *Nouvelles Annales des Voyages*, 2:1 (1826), 338–53.

Putnam, George Grenville, *Salem Vessels and their Voyages: A History of the Pepper Trade with the Island Of Sumatra*, ser. 1 (Salem MA, 1924).

Raffles, Sophie, Lady, *Memoir of the Life and Public Services of Sir Thomas Stamford Raffles* … (London, 1830).

Reid, Anthony, *Southeast Asia in the Age of Commerce 1450–1680: Volume One, The Lands Below the Winds* (New Haven CT, 1988).

—*Southeast Asia in the Age of Commerce 1450–1680: Volume Two, Expansion and Crisis* (New Haven CT, 1993).

—and Radin Fernando, 'Shipping on Melaka and Singapore as an Index of Growth, 1760–1840', *South Asia: Journal of South Asian Studies*, 19 (1996), 59–84.

Richardson, J. D., *Narrative of the Transactions on Board the Ship Calcutta of Bengal, and Commanded by Captain Hugh Drysdale, who was Unfortunately Cut Off by the Malays at Slackhow on the Island of Borneo, on the 8th of July 1803: Principally Extracted from the Journal of Mr John Burgh* … (Bombay, 1805).

Richardson, William, *A Mariner of England: An Account of the Career of William Richardson from Cabin Boy in the Merchant Service to Warrant Officer in the Royal Navy [1780–1819] as told by himself*, ed. Colonel Spencer Childers (Greenwich, 1970).

Rivers P. J., 'Monsoon Rhythms and Trade Patterns: Ancient Times East of Suez', *JMBRAS*, 77:2 (2004), 59–93.

Robinson, Christopher, *Reports of Cases Argued and Determined in the High Court of Admiralty commencing with The Judgement of the Right Hon. Sir William Scott. Michelmas Term, 1798*, vol. 6, ed. George Minot (Boston MA, 1853).

Royle, J. Forbes, *The Fibrous Plants of India fitted for Cordage, Clothing, and Paper. With an Account of the Cultivation and Preparation of Flax, Hemp, and their Substitutes* (London, 1855).

Salmond, Anne, *Between Worlds: Early Exchanges Between Maori and Europeans 1773–1815* (Auckland, 1997).

Shardlow, Ross, 'The Byramgou Cup and the Extermination of Pirates', *Maritime Heritage Association Journal*, 19:3 (2008), 12–19.

Shepherdson, P. J., and K. L. Shepherdson, *Journey to the Straits: The Shepherdson Story* (Singapore, 2003).

Ships Registers of the District of Salem and Beverly, Massachusetts, copied by A. Frank Hitchinson with annotations by Stephen Willard Phillips (Salem MA, 1906).

Singh, S. B., *European Agency Houses in Bengal 1783–1833* (Calcutta, 1966).

Smith, F. Andrew, 'Missionaries, Mariners, and Merchants: Overlooked British travellers to West Borneo in the early Nineteenth century', *Borneo Research Bulletin*, 33 (2002), 45–61.

—'Captain Burn and Associates: British Intelligence-gathering, Trade, and Litigation in Borneo and Beyond during the Early Nineteenth Century', *Borneo Research Bulletin*, 35 (2004), 48–69.

—'Daniel Smith's last seven years: hardships in country trade in the East Indies in the early nineteenth century', *Borneo Research Bulletin*, 39 (2008), 71–90.

—'Piracy against the Sambas "Pirates"? The case of Captain Burnside – and What Happened to him Afterwards in the Antipodes', *Borneo Research Bulletin*, 40 (2009), 67–80.

—'Piracy off Pontianak in the early nineteenth century – and not by the Usual Villains; with an Appendix on Captain Hercules Ross, Country Trader and Native of Jamaica', *Borneo Research Bulletin*, 43 (2012), 61–71.

—'William Scott in Penang: Missing Material, Maritime Matters and More', *JMBRAS*, 94:2 (2021), 185–97.

—'James Carnegy and the "Country Trade" in Penang, c.1802–1824', *JMBRAS*, 96:1 (2023), 51–80.

—'Mercantile Life in Early 19th Century Asia: the Ross Brothers', *JMBRAS*, 96:2 (2023), 49–75.

Smollett, Tobias, *Roderick Random* (London, 1927, orig. 1748).

Sobel, Dava, and William J. H. Andrewes, *The Illustrated Longitude* (London, 1998).

Souza, George Bryan, 'Macao and the Pearl River Delta Trade: The Portuguese Merchant Fleet at Macao in the 17th and 18th Centuries', <http://www.icm.gov.mo/rc/viewer/40013/2320> [Accessed 15 April 2025].

Sta Maria, Bernard, *My People, My Country: the story of the Malacca Portuguese Community* (Malacca, 1982).

Sternstein, Larry, 'The London Company's Envoys Plot Siam', *The Journal of the Siam Society*, 81:2 (1993), 11–95.

Steven, Margaret J. E., 'Robert Campbell, Colonial Merchant 1769–1846' (Unpublished PhD thesis, ANU, 1962).

Suarez, Thomas, *Early Mapping of Southeast Asia; The Epic Story of Seafarers, Adventurers, and Cartographers Who first Mapped the Regions between China and India* (Singapore, 1999).

Subramanian, Lakshmi, 'Seths and sahibs: negotiated relationships between indigenous capital and the East India Company', in H. V. Bowen, Elizabeth Mancke and John Reid (eds), *Britain's Oceanic Empire: Atlantic and Indian Ocean Worlds, c. 1550–1850* (Cambridge, 2012), pp. 311–39.

Tagliacozzo, Eric, *In Asian Waters: Oceanic Worlds from Yemen to Yokohama* (Princeton NJ, 2022).

Tarling, Nicholas, *Piracy and Politics in the Malay World: A Study of British Imperialism in Nineteenth-Century South-East Asia* (Melbourne, 1963).

Tenterden, Charles, Lord, *Treatise of the Law Relative to Merchant Ships and Seamen*, ed. James Perronet Aspinall *et al.*, 14th edn (London, 1901).

The Extraordinary Trial of Capt. Harrower, at the Old Bailey, Feb. 17, 1816, on an indictment for marrying the daughter of Mr Giblet, the Celebrated Butcher, his former wife being alive, A Lunatic in India …, 2nd edn (London, 1816).

Turnbull, C. M., 'Melaka under British Colonial Rule', in K. S. Sandhu and P. Wheatley (eds), *Melaka: The Transformation of a Malay Capital c.1400–1980*, vol. 1 (Kuala Lumpur, 1983), pp. 242–96.

U.K. House of Lords, The Sessional Papers 1801–1833, vol. 64 (1812–13), Paper No. 23, Papers Relative [Relating] to East India Affairs.

Upton, Francis H., *The Law of Nations Affecting Commerce During War: With a Review of the Jurisdiction, Practice and Proceedings of Prize Courts* (New York, 1863).

Van Dyke, Paul A., *The Canton Trade: Life and Enterprise on the China Coast, 1700–1845* (Hong Kong, repr. 2012, orig, 2005).

—*Whampoa and the Canton Trade: Life and Death in a Chinese Port* (Hong Kong, 2020).

Verhoeven, F. R. J., 'The Lost Archives of Malacca 1641–1824', *JMBRAS*, 37:2 (1964), 11–27.

Vieyra, Anthony (transtagano), *Dictionary of the Portuguese and English Languages, in Two Parts … Part I – Portuguese and English*, new edn by J. Dias Do Canto (London, 1827).

Vos, Reinout, *Gentle Janus, Merchant Prince: The VOC and the Tightrope of Diplomacy in the Malay World, 1740–1800* (Leiden, 1993).

Wade, Geoff, 'Some Sources for the Economic History of the Chinese in the Malay Archipelago – 1780s–1820s', Paper presented to the 15th Biennial Conference of the Asian Studies Association of Australia, Canberra 29 June–2 July 2004 (Canberra, 2004).

—'The Pre-Modern East Asian Maritime Realm: An Overview of European-Language Studies', in Satish Chandra and Himanshu Prabha Ray (eds), *The Sea, Identity and History: From the Bay of Bengal to the South China Sea* (Singapore, 2013), pp. 93–136.

Warren, James Francis, *Iranun and Balangingi: Globalization, Maritime Raiding and the Birth of Ethnicity* (Singapore, 2002).

Wathen, James, *Journal of a Voyage in 1811 and 1812, to Madras and China: Returning by the Cape of Good Hope; In the H.C.S. The Hope, Capt. James Pendergrass* (London, 1814).

Webster, Anthony, 'British Expansion in South-East Asia and the Role of Robert Farquhar, Lieutenant-Governor of Penang, 1804–5', *Journal of Imperial and Commonwealth History*, 23:1 (1995), 1–25.

—*Gentlemen Capitalists: British Imperialism in South East Asia 1770–1890* (London, 1998).

Wilson, James, 'The Anglo-Dutch Imperial Meridian in the Indian Ocean World, 1795–1820' (Unpublished PhD thesis, University of Cambridge, 2019), <https://doi.org/10.17863/CAM.38350> [Accessed 15 May 2025].

Wood, Gillen D'Arcy, *Tambora: The Eruption That Changed the World (Princeton NJ, 2014).*

Wreck and loss of the ship Fanny, Capt. Robertson, on her Passage from Bombay to China, November 29, 1803: Including Particulars of the Tremendous Hurricanes Called Typhons, and the Wonderful Preservation of the Greater Part of the Crew … (London, 1808).

Wright, G. N., *New and Comprehensive Gazetteer; being a Delineation of the Present State of the World …*, vol. 1 (London, 1834).

Wright, Nadia H., *Respected Citizens: The History of Armenians in Singapore and Malaysia* (Middle Park, 2003).

—*William Farquhar and Singapore: Stepping out from Raffles' Shadow* (Penang, 2017).

Wurtzburg, C. E, 'Who Planned the Sea Route of the Java Expedition in 1811?', *The Mariner's Mirror: The Journal of the Society for Nautical Research*, 37 (1951), 104–8.

—*Raffles of the Eastern Isles* (London, 1954).

Yule, Henry, see Hobson Jobson.

Zandvliet, Kees, *Mapping for Money: Maps, plans and topographic paintings and their role in Dutch overseas expansion during the 16th and 17th centuries* (Amsterdam, 1998).

Newspapers and Journals

Allen's Indian Mail

Asiatic Annual Register

Asiatic Journal and Monthly Register (*Asiatic Journal*)

Bombay Calendar and Almanac

Bombay Courier. Accessed online through Roger Houghton, *A People's History 1793–1844 from the Newspapers*, <https://houghton.hk/china-1793-1844-part-1> and <https://houghton.hk/prizetaking> [Both accessed 15 April 2025].

Calcutta Monthly Journal

Caledonian Mercury

East-India Register and Directory

European Magazine and London Review. London

Historical Records of Australia (1916), edited by Frederick Watson. Series 1: 7. Sydney: Government Printer.

India Gazette

Indian News and Chronicle of Eastern Affairs

Java Government Gazette

Java half-yearly almanac and directory

London Morning Post

Madras Courier

Nautical Magazine and Naval Chronicle

Naval Chronicle

New Scots Magazine

Oriental Magazine and Calcutta Review

Penang Government Gazette

INDEX

Ships names and the official rank and position of individuals are in italics. Names in Appendices A and B are not indexed.

WORLDS OF THE EAST INDIA COMPANY

ISSN 1752-5667

Series Editor
John McAleer (University of Southampton)

This series offers high-quality studies of the East India Company, drawn from across a broad chronological, geographical and thematic range. The rich history of the Company has long been of interest to those who engage in the study of Britain's commercial, imperial, maritime and military past, but in recent years it has also attracted considerable attention from those who explore art, cultural and social themes within a historical context. The series will thus provide a forum for scholars from different disciplinary backgrounds, and for those whose have interests in the history of Britain (London and the regions), India, China, Indonesia, as well as the seas and oceans.

The series welcome submissions from both established scholars and those beginning their career; monographs are particularly encouraged, but volumes of essays will also be considered. All submissions will receive rapid, informed attention. They should be sent in the first instance to:

Dr John McAleer, Department of History, University of Southampton, j.mcaleer@soton.ac.uk

Other books in the series can be viewed on our website at https://boydellandbrewer.com

WORLDS OF THE EAST INDIA COMPANY

The Richest East India Merchant: The Life and Business of John Palmer of Calcutta, 1767–1836, Anthony Webster

The Great Uprising in India, 1857–58: Untold Stories, Indian and British, Rosie Llewellyn-Jones

The Twilight of the East India Company: The Evolution of Anglo-Asian Commerce and Politics, 1790–1860, Anthony Webster

Scottish Orientalists and India: The Muir Brothers, Religion, Education and Empire, Avril A. Powell

The East India Company's London Workers: Management of the Warehouse Labourers, 1800–1858, Margaret Makepeace

The East India Company's Maritime Service, 1746–1834: Masters of the Eastern Seas, Jean Sutton

The East India Company and Religion, 1698–1858, Penelope Carson

British Naval Power in the East, 1794–1805: The Command of Admiral Peter Rainier, Peter A. Ward

The Emergence of British Power in India, 1600–1784: A Grand Strategic Interpretation, G. J. Bryant

Naval Resistance to Britain's Growing Power in India, 1660–1800: The Saffron Banner and the Tiger of Mysore, Philip MacDougall

Trade and Empire in Early Nineteenth-Century Southeast Asia: Gillian Maclaine and his Business Network, G. Roger Knight

Lascars and Indian Ocean Seafaring, 1780–1860: Shipboard Life, Unrest and Mutiny, Aaron Jaffer

Defending British India against Napoleon: The Foreign Policy of Governor-General Lord Minto, 1807–13, Amita Das, edited and updated by Aditya Das

Provincial Society and Empire: The Cumbrian Counties and the East Indies, 1680–1829, K. J. Saville-Smith

British Houses in Late Mughal Delhi, Sylvia Shorto

The English East India Company's Silk Enterprise in Bengal, 1750–1850: Economy, Empire and Business, Karolina Hutková

Singapore, Chinese Migration and the Making of the British Empire, 1819–67, Stan Neal

British Art and the East India Company, Geoff Quilley

British Traders in the East Indies, 1770–1820: 'At Home in the Eastern Seas', W. G. Miller

An Innovative Physician and Scientist Britain in British India: The Life and Times of Sir William Brooke O'Shaughnessy, 1808–1889, Neil MacGillivray

Printed and bound by CPI Group (UK) Ltd, Croydon, CR0 4YY

16/09/2026

14963057-0002